Introduction to COMPUTER NETWORKS

Step-by-Step Guide to Computer Networks

THE AUTHOR

Dr. Sunita is a distinguished academician and researcher with a Ph.D. in the area of Speech Recognition. As a JRF/NET-qualified scholar, she brings an exceptional level of expertise and dedication to her work. With 16 years of extensive teaching and research experience, she has made significant contributions to the field of computer science, particularly in computer networks, Artificial intelligence, Machine learning & software engineering etc.Dr. Sunita has an impressive portfolio of research publications, showcasing her depth of knowledge and commitment to advancing her discipline. Her active involvement in academic communities includes serving as a Session Chair in various prestigious conferences, where she has facilitated discussions on emerging trends and innovative technologies.

Introduction to COMPUTER NETWORKS

Step-by-Step Guide to Computer Networks

Dr. Sunita

ACADEMIC ENCLAVE

First Edition, 2025

ISBN: 978-93-48642-41-7

Published by
ACADEMIC ENCLAVE™
House No. 10/15, Ground Floor,
Block-A, Street No. 14/3, Kamal Vihar,
Kamal Pur, Burari, Delhi-110084
Email: info@academicenclave.com
Mobile: +91-7042423166
Website: www.academicenclave.com

PREFACE

This book, Introduction to Computer Networks, is designed to provide a comprehensive and structured understanding of how modern computer networks function—from foundational concepts to advanced application-layer services. In today's hyper-connected world, networking knowledge is essential for anyone entering the fields of computer science, information technology, or communications. This book covers both the theoretical underpinnings and practical applications of networking concepts, ensuring that students and professionals alike gain a robust grasp of the subject. Beginning with introductory concepts, the book explores the goals, applications, and categories of networks, the structure and organization of the Internet, and essential models such as the OSI reference model and the TCP/IP protocol suite. Readers will also become familiar with critical networking components and devices. The subsequent chapters delve into the Physical Layer, examining transmission media, topologies, encoding techniques, and performance factors—setting the stage for deeper explorations into higher layers. The Link Layer and Medium Access Control (MAC) topics are covered in detail, including framing, error handling, flow control, channel allocation, and LAN standards. Real-world technologies such as Ethernet, Wi-Fi, switches, and bridges are explored through the lens of IEEE standards and protocols. The book then progresses to the Network Layer, providing insights into addressing schemes, routing protocols, and IPv6, followed by an in-depth study of the Transport Layer, focusing on reliable communication, congestion control, and protocol mechanisms like TCP and UDP. Finally, the Application Layer introduces key Internet services such as DNS, HTTP, email, FTP, and network management, along with foundational concepts in data compression and cryptography. With a clear pedagogical approach, illustrative diagrams, tables, and practical examples, this book is an essential resource for students, educators, and networking professionals seeking to master the principles and practices of computer networks.

Dr. Sunita

CONTENTS

CHAPTER

1

INTRODUCTORY CONCEPTS

Chapter 1 serves as the foundational framework for understanding computer networks, beginning with their core goals and wide-ranging applications across various sectors including communication, business, education, and entertainment. The chapter introduces key network types—ranging from local to wide area networks—and explains how their distinct characteristics cater to specific organizational needs. It also explores the evolution and structure of the Internet, including the role of Internet Service Providers (ISPs) in ensuring global connectivity. Furthermore, the chapter delves into the layered structure of network architecture, explaining the significance of services, protocols, and standards that enable interoperability between heterogeneous systems. Core conceptual models like the OSI reference model and the TCP/IP protocol suite are introduced to help learners understand how data is transmitted across networks in a structured manner. The section concludes by familiarizing readers with essential network devices and components, laying a solid technical groundwork for the subsequent chapters on physical, link, and higher network layers.

Goals and Applications of Networks

Computer networks are essential infrastructure in today's digital world, providing the framework that connects devices, systems, and people. The primary goal of a network is to enable communication and resource sharing across different locations and platforms. Whether it's a small office setup or the vast Internet, networks ensure seamless interaction between devices and applications.

One of the most fundamental goals of networking is resource sharing. This allows multiple users to access common resources like printers, storage devices, scanners, and internet connections. By centralizing hardware and software resources, organizations can significantly reduce operational costs and improve efficiency. Modern networks support a wide array of communication tools, including emails, messaging platforms, video conferencing, and Voice over Internet Protocol (VoIP). These tools foster better collaboration between individuals and teams regardless of their physical location, enabling businesses and institutions to operate across geographic boundaries. Networks facilitate access to data and systems from remote locations. Centralized databases and cloud platforms allow users to log in and retrieve or update data anytime, from anywhere. This is especially crucial in remote work scenarios and global business operations where timely access to data is critical (Figure 1.1).

Figure 1.1: Computer Network Goals.

One of the most fundamental goals of networking is resource sharing. This allows multiple users to access common resources like printers, storage devices, scanners, and internet connections. By centralizing hardware and software resources, organizations can significantly reduce operational costs and improve efficiency. Modern networks support a wide array of communication tools, including emails, messaging platforms, video conferencing, and Voice over Internet Protocol (VoIP). These tools foster better collaboration between individuals and teams regardless of their physical location, enabling businesses and institutions to operate across geographic boundaries. Networks facilitate access to data and systems from remote locations. Centralized databases and cloud platforms allow users to log in and retrieve or update data anytime, from anywhere. This is especially crucial in remote work scenarios and global business operations where timely access to data is critical (Figure 1.1).

A well-designed network should be scalable to accommodate growth in users, devices, and data. Scalability ensures that as organizations expand, the network infrastructure can be upgraded or extended with minimal disruption. Technologies like modular switches and virtual LANs help maintain this scalability efficiently. Modern networks are expected to adapt to changing demands quickly. Software-defined networking (SDN) and virtualization technologies make networks more flexible, allowing administrators to allocate resources dynamically based on current needs, such as bandwidth for video calls or processing power for cloud applications.

Network reliability is achieved by designing systems with redundancy and failover capabilities. This includes backup servers, redundant links, and load balancers that ensure continuous service even if one component fails. Redundancy minimizes downtime and enhances trust in the network's availability. Networks significantly reduce costs by consolidating IT infrastructure. Instead of multiple standalone systems, shared resources are used more effectively. This also reduces maintenance expenses, as centralized updates and remote troubleshooting can be performed without physically visiting each device. Security is a critical goal in networking. Secure networks implement encryption, firewalls, intrusion detection systems (IDS), and strong access control mechanisms. These measures protect data from unauthorized access, breaches, and cyber-attacks, ensuring that sensitive information remains confidential and intact.

Centralized management allows administrators to monitor, configure, and maintain the network from a single point. This improves control over network traffic, device configuration, and software deployment, making it easier to enforce policies and respond to issues quickly. Networks enable distributed computing by connecting multiple systems to work together on complex problems. Tasks such as scientific research simulations, data mining, and blockchain processing benefit from distributed network environments where resources are pooled together for maximum computational power. A key application of networks is the integration of various digital services. Networks enable the convergence of voice, video, and data into a unified platform, supporting applications like multimedia streaming, e-learning platforms, and integrated IoT ecosystems such as smart homes and healthcare monitoring systems.

In academic environments, networks provide students and researchers with access to digital libraries, learning management systems (LMS), and collaborative platforms. Research institutions rely heavily on networks to share datasets, access computational clusters, and publish findings globally. Businesses leverage networks for enterprise applications like customer relationship management

(CRM), enterprise resource planning (ERP), and automated industrial control systems. Industries implement IoT networks to monitor production lines, detect anomalies, and ensure efficient operations.

Table 1.1: Applications of Networks by Domain

Domain	Applications	Network Goal Fulfilled
Business	Email, ERP, CRM, File Sharing	Communication, Resource Sharing
Education	Online Classes, LMS, Virtual Labs	Collaboration, Data Access
Healthcare	Telemedicine, Electronic Health Records (EHR)	Remote Access, Security
Finance	Online Banking, ATM Networks, Payment Gateways	Centralized Control, Reliability
Entertainment	Video Streaming, Online Gaming, Social Media	Integration, High Bandwidth
Manufacturing	Industrial Automation, IoT-enabled Production Monitoring	Distributed Computing, Flexibility
Government	E-Governance Portals, Surveillance Networks	Centralization, Security

The goals and applications of networks are broad and vital to modern living. From basic resource sharing to enabling global communication and intelligent systems integration, networks underpin nearly every aspect of contemporary digital infrastructure (Table 1.1). As technologies evolve, networks will continue to adapt and expand their capabilities to meet future challenges.

Categories of Networks

Computer networks are broadly categorized based on factors such as geographical coverage, ownership, hardware architecture, and functional usage. These classifications help define the scope, scale, and purpose of different network types. Among the most commonly recognized categories are Personal Area Networks (PAN), Local Area Networks (LAN), Campus Area Networks (CAN), Metropolitan Area Networks (MAN), and Wide Area Networks (WAN). Each type is designed to serve specific operational needs, ranging from personal device connectivity to global communications infrastructure. Personal Area Networks (PANs) are limited to a few meters and typically support personal devices, while LANs connect computers within a building or office, enabling high-speed data exchange and resource sharing. CANs extend LAN capabilities across multiple buildings, as seen in university or corporate campuses. MANs are larger, linking networks across cities, often managed by telecom companies. WANs, the broadest in scope, span across countries or continents and form the backbone of global communication, with the Internet being the most prominent example. These classifications help in designing networks that align with specific organizational and operational goals.

1. Personal Area Network (PAN)

A Personal Area Network (PAN) is the smallest and most limited type of computer network, designed to interconnect devices in close proximity to an individual user. The primary purpose of a PAN is to enable communication among personal computing devices such as smartphones, tablets, laptops, and wearable devices. It is often set up in a home, office desk, or while traveling, allowing users to connect their gadgets wirelessly or via cable within a short distance. PANs typically operate within a range of 1 to 10 meters, making them ideal for personal use. They support various technologies, including Bluetooth, Infrared, Near Field Communication (NFC), and USB connections. Bluetooth is the most commonly used PAN technology due to its ease of pairing and widespread compatibility across consumer devices. For instance, users can listen to music on wireless earbuds while simultaneously receiving notifications from a connected smartwatch.

One of the core advantages of a PAN is portability and flexibility. Because most PANs are wireless, they enable hassle-free mobility for users without the limitations of physical cabling. A user can walk around while remaining connected to their smartphone via a smartwatch or health tracker, making PANs particularly useful for mobile and wearable computing. These networks are also simple to configure and require minimal infrastructure, making them highly user-friendly. Security is an essential consideration in PANs. Since devices are typically linked wirelessly and used in public or semi-public spaces, encryption protocols such as Secure Simple Pairing (SSP) in Bluetooth help protect data exchange. However, due to their limited range and localized nature, PANs are generally considered less vulnerable to external threats than larger networks. Use cases of PANs are growing with the rise of the Internet of Things (IoT). From syncing fitness data from a wearable to a mobile app, to transferring files between a laptop and smartphone, PANs provide the foundation for seamless personal device integration. They are increasingly used in smart homes, healthcare wearables, and proximity-based services like contactless payments and device unlocking.

The Figure 1.2 shows a user at the center surrounded by various interconnected personal devices. A smartphone, laptop, Bluetooth headphones, smartwatch, fitness tracker, and printer are shown within a circular zone representing the 10-meter range. Arrows between the devices indicate wireless connections using Bluetooth and USB. Each device is labeled with its function, and a Bluetooth symbol denotes the communication protocol.

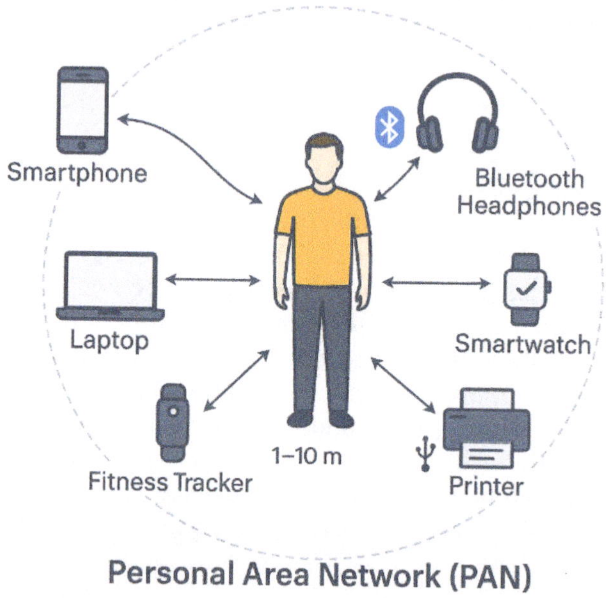

Figure 1.2: Personal Area Network (PAN)

2. Local Area Network (LAN)

A Local Area Network (LAN) is a computer network that connects multiple devices—such as computers, printers, and servers—within a limited geographical area like a home, office, school, or single building. It is one of the most commonly used types of networks and forms the backbone of most organizational IT infrastructures. LANs are essential for facilitating fast and secure communication between connected devices in close physical proximity. The defining characteristic of a LAN is its high data transfer speed, typically ranging from 100 Mbps to several Gbps. These speeds are made possible by modern networking technologies such as Ethernet and Wi-Fi. Ethernet provides wired connectivity using switches and routers, offering greater stability and bandwidth, while Wi-Fi supports wireless connections that enhance mobility and convenience within the network area.

LANs support resource sharing, allowing multiple users to access printers, storage devices, and applications from different computers without the need for direct connections. This centralized resource access improves efficiency and reduces the cost of redundant hardware. Additionally, file sharing and collaborative software applications are easier to implement within a LAN environment.Another important advantage of LANs is centralized management. Network administrators can monitor and control the entire network from a single location, configure devices, manage security policies, and deploy updates. This makes LANs more manageable, scalable, and secure compared to ad hoc peer-to-peer networks.LANs are predominantly used in homes, educational institutions, and corporate offices to support internal communication, data exchange, and collaborative tasks. Whether it's students accessing online resources from a school network or employees sharing documents in a corporate intranet, LANs provide the speed and reliability required for daily digital operations. While the typical range of a LAN is confined to a single building or a group of nearby structures (such as on a campus), its architecture can be expanded using routers and switches to create sub-networks or VLANs. This flexibility makes LANs highly adaptable for various organizational needs.

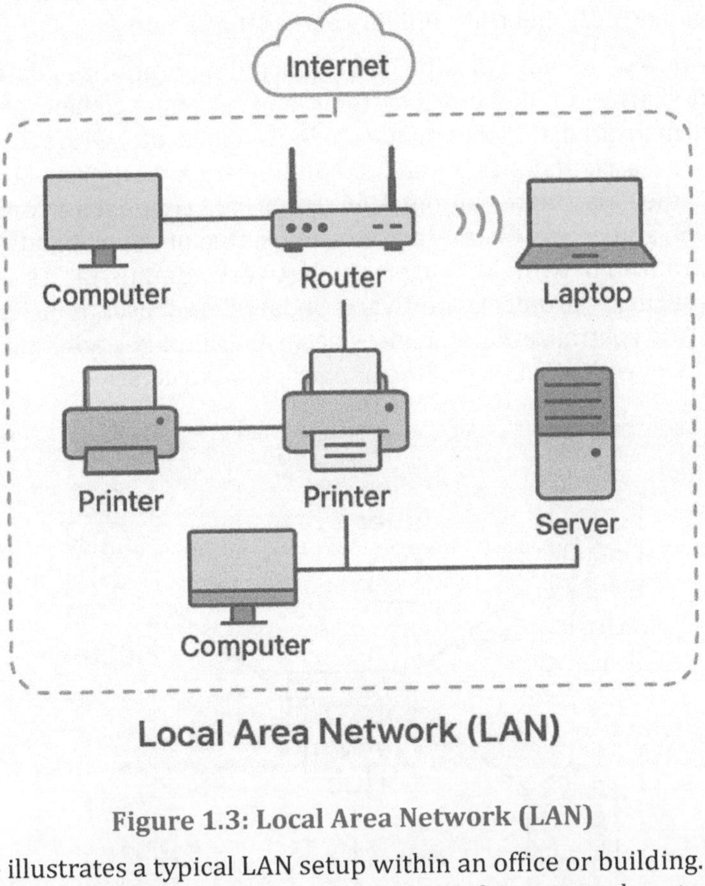

Figure 1.3: Local Area Network (LAN)

The Figure illustrates a typical LAN setup within an office or building. It includes several computers, laptops, and printers connected to a central router or switch, which in turn is connected to a server. Some devices connect via Ethernet cables, while others are linked through Wi-Fi. Arrows indicate the flow of data, and a cloud-shaped icon labeled "Internet" shows external access. The range is marked within the boundary of a building, with each device labeled accordingly.

3. Campus Area Network (CAN)

A Campus Area Network (CAN) is a specialized type of network that spans across multiple buildings within a limited geographical area, such as a university, business park, or military base. It is larger than a Local Area Network (LAN) but smaller than a Metropolitan Area Network (MAN). The key purpose of a CAN is to interconnect several LANs within a campus-like setting to facilitate seamless communication and data sharing among departments or buildings. Unlike LANs, which are typically confined to a single building, CANs are built to connect buildings such as libraries, laboratories, administrative offices, and dormitories. This interconnection is achieved through high-speed backbone links, often implemented using optical fiber cables to ensure high bandwidth and minimal latency. CANs may also integrate Ethernet and wireless technologies to support a wide range of devices and user mobility across the campus.

CANs support a wide range of applications, including centralized data access, file and printer sharing, unified email systems, and real-time collaboration tools. In educational institutions, CANs provide students and faculty with access to course materials, research databases, and communication platforms. In industrial campuses, they facilitate automation, internal communication, inventory management, and access to enterprise systems. One of the main advantages of a CAN is centralized network management. Network administrators can maintain consistent security protocols, software updates, and user policies across all buildings. This centralization enhances security, simplifies administration, and improves the overall efficiency of the network infrastructure.

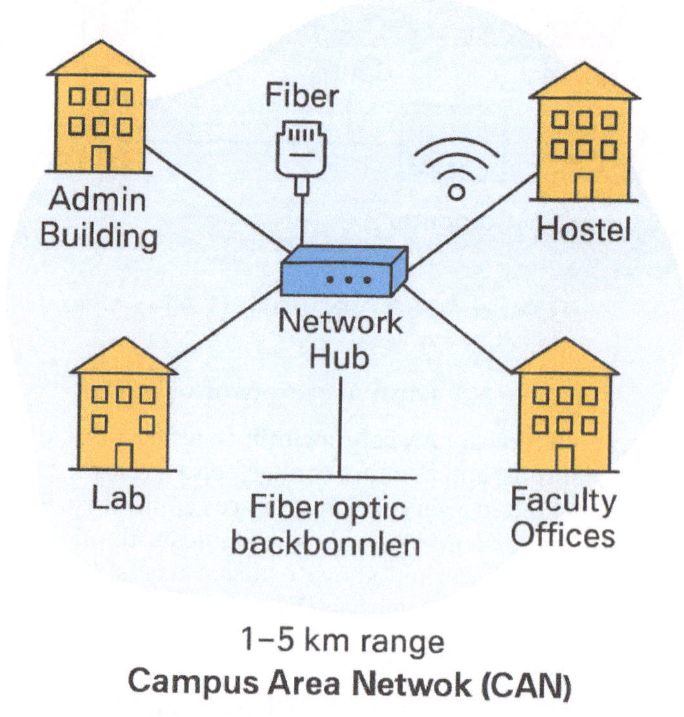

Figure 1.4: Campus Area Network (CAN)

The typical range of a Campus Area Network spans 1 to 5 kilometers, making it ideal for medium-sized organizations that operate across several closely located buildings. This range ensures connectivity while maintaining manageable infrastructure costs. CANs often serve as a private network that ensures high performance and reliability for an institution's internal operations. With the increasing demand for real-time collaboration, cloud access, and IoT integration, CANs have become a vital part of modern educational and industrial infrastructure. They provide a scalable, secure, and efficient networking environment that supports the diverse digital needs of campus-based organizations.

The figure illustrates a university campus with multiple buildings such as an Admin Block, Library, Lab, Hostel, and Faculty Offices, each containing its own LAN. These LANs are connected via fiber-optic backbone lines to a central network hub. Both wired Ethernet and wireless Wi-Fi icons show connectivity across buildings. The overall area is marked within a boundary labeled "1–5 km range"

4. Metropolitan Area Network (MAN)

A Metropolitan Area Network (MAN) is a large-scale network designed to cover a geographic area the size of a city or a large campus. It connects multiple Local Area Networks (LANs) within a metropolitan region to enable fast and reliable communication across organizations, government bodies, academic institutions, and commercial hubs. MANs serve as a middle layer between LANs and Wide Area Networks (WANs), offering greater coverage than LANs but with more localized control and speed than WANs. MANs are commonly built and managed by telecommunication companies, Internet service providers (ISPs), or large enterprises. These networks use high-speed infrastructure, such as fiber optic cables, DSL (Digital Subscriber Line), and wireless broadband technologies to ensure robust and efficient data transmission over long distances—ranging between 5 to 50 kilometers. MANs often act as backbones that interconnect multiple LANs within a city and serve as gateways to WANs like the Internet.

One of the key advantages of a MAN is its ability to offer high bandwidth connections across different organizational sites within a city. For example, a city government may use a MAN to connect municipal buildings such as city hall, fire departments, libraries, and public schools, enabling seamless communication, data sharing, and service integration. Educational institutions and healthcare systems can also leverage MANs to synchronize administrative data and provide centralized services. MANs are typically optimized for urban infrastructure, and can support real-time applications such as video conferencing, IP telephony, traffic monitoring, and emergency response coordination. They are also instrumental in building smart cities, where data from sensors and IoT devices across various urban systems—transportation, utilities, waste management—is transmitted and processed in real time.

Security and quality of service are important considerations in MANs. These networks often employ Virtual Private Network (VPN) tunneling, encryption, traffic prioritization, and redundancy mechanisms to ensure secure and uninterrupted services. Telecom providers offering MAN services usually implement Service Level Agreements (SLAs) to guarantee performance levels. As urban digital infrastructure evolves, the importance of MANs continues to grow. They form the digital nervous system of modern cities, supporting critical public services, enterprise operations, and high-speed broadband for densely populated regions.

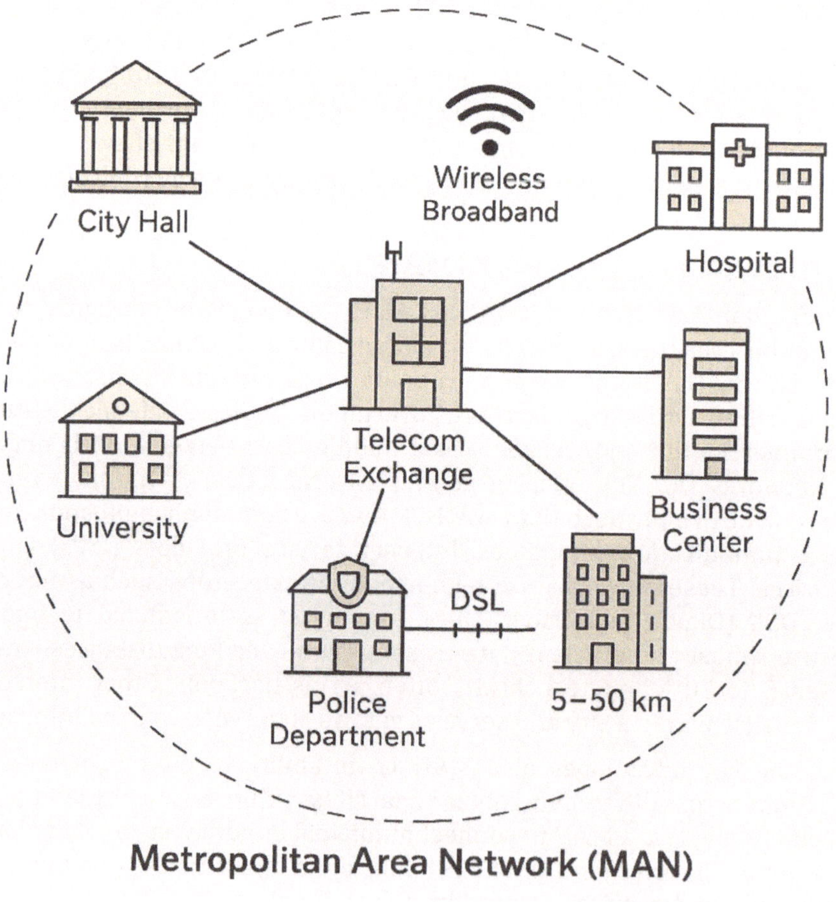

Figure 1.5: Metropolitan Area Network (MAN)

The diagram illustrates a city map showing various LAN-connected buildings—like a City Hall, Hospital, University, Police Department, and Business Center—interconnected through fiber optic lines. All buildings link back to a central telecom exchange hub, representing the MAN backbone. The coverage area is shown spanning 5–50 km, with icons for fiber, DSL, and wireless broadband.

5. Wide Area Network (WAN)

A Wide Area Network (WAN) is a type of network that spans a very large geographic area—ranging from cities and countries to continents and the entire globe. WANs are designed to facilitate long-distance communication and data transfer between distributed computer systems, branch offices, or regional facilities. Unlike smaller networks such as LANs or MANs, a WAN can connect multiple remote sites, regardless of their location, to form a single unified network. The most prominent example of a WAN is the Internet, which interconnects billions of devices across the world. WANs are essential for organizations with geographically dispersed operations, such as multinational corporations, government agencies, financial institutions, and research organizations. They provide a robust platform for applications such as email, cloud services, enterprise resource planning (ERP), and video conferencing on a global scale.

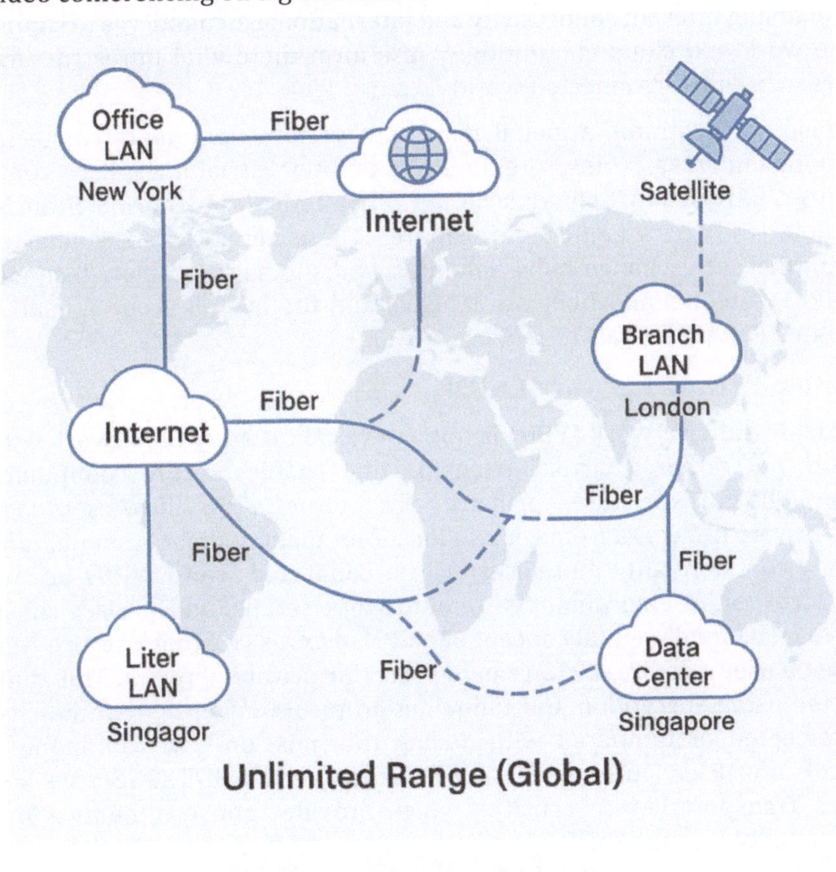

Figure 1.6: Global Map

WANs utilize a wide array of transmission technologies to maintain connectivity over long distances. Common technologies include MPLS (Multiprotocol Label Switching) for efficient routing, satellite communication for remote areas, and fiber optic cables, including undersea links, for high-speed, high-bandwidth data transmission. These networks are often built and maintained through partnerships between telecommunications providers, who lease the physical infrastructure and bandwidth. One of the distinguishing features of WANs is their decentralized management. Because WANs often span multiple service providers and international boundaries, they are governed by shared protocols, global standards, and service level agreements (SLAs). This collaboration ensures interoperability, uptime, and data integrity across diverse network systems and physical infrastructures.

WANs are also optimized for resilience and scalability. They incorporate redundancy and backup routes to avoid downtime in the event of hardware failures or cable breaks. Technologies like VPN (Virtual Private Network) and encryption are used to secure data during transmission across public or shared networks. In summary, WANs play a foundational role in global communications. From enabling Internet connectivity and international e-commerce to supporting remote work and cloud computing, WANs form the digital infrastructure that powers today's interconnected world.

The diagram illustrates a global map with various continents connected by fiber optic undersea cables, satellite links, and terrestrial lines. Each continent contains a LAN or MAN cloud, such as "Office LAN – New York," "Branch LAN – London," and "Data Center – Singapore." These networks are connected via lines to Internet exchange hubs, satellites, and submarine cables. Technologies like MPLS, satellite, and fiber are labeled, and the overall scope is marked as "Unlimited Range (Global)."

6. Virtual Private Network (VPN)

A Virtual Private Network (VPN) is not a physical category of network like LAN or WAN, but rather a virtual extension that enables secure communication over a public infrastructure—primarily the Internet. VPNs allow users to safely access private networks from remote locations, making them essential tools for ensuring confidentiality and security in a connected world. VPNs are widely used in corporate environments, remote work setups, and privacy-conscious browsing. The fundamental concept of a VPN involves creating a secure "tunnel" between a user's device and a remote server or private network. This tunnel is protected using encryption and tunneling protocols, ensuring that data cannot be intercepted or tampered with during transmission. Two commonly used protocols are IPsec (Internet Protocol Security) and SSL/TLS (Secure Sockets Layer / Transport Layer Security), which provide robust authentication and confidentiality mechanisms.

VPNs are especially important for organizations that have remote employees, satellite offices, or contractors who need access to internal resources like databases, file servers, or intranet applications. By connecting through a VPN, users gain access to their company's network as if they were physically present in the office, all while maintaining the integrity and confidentiality of data exchanged.

In addition to corporate use, VPNs are increasingly adopted by individual users seeking privacy and anonymity online. A VPN can mask the user's IP address, hide browsing activity from ISPs, and allow access to geo-restricted content. This makes them valuable for users accessing the Internet from unsecured networks, such as public Wi-Fi in cafes, airports, or hotels.

While the range of a VPN is technically unlimited, its effectiveness depends on Internet connectivity. As long as users have access to the Internet, they can establish a secure VPN connection from any location worldwide. VPNs may slightly reduce connection speed due to the overhead introduced by encryption, but this is typically acceptable given the trade-off for enhanced security. In summary, VPNs offer a practical and essential solution for both businesses and individuals aiming to protect their data, ensure secure remote access, and maintain privacy in an increasingly digital and mobile world.

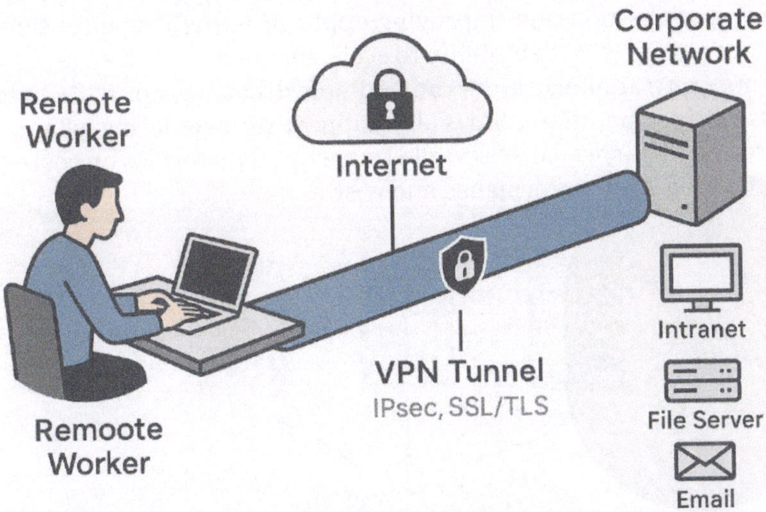

Figure 1.7: Remote Worker at Home Connected via a VPN Tunnel

The diagram shows a remote worker at home connected via a VPN tunnel to a corporate network (head office). A laptop sends data through a secure tunnel over the Internet, encrypted using IPsec or SSL/TLS, shown with a lock icon. The VPN server is connected to the office LAN, including services like an intranet, file server, and email. The public Internet cloud is labeled with an unlocked icon, and the VPN tunnel with a lock and shield icon.

7. Storage Area Network (SAN)

A Storage Area Network (SAN) is a high-speed, specialized network designed to provide block-level access to consolidated data storage. Unlike traditional networks where storage devices are attached directly to individual servers, a SAN separates storage from the computing environment, allowing multiple servers to access shared storage resources simultaneously. This architectural model is particularly beneficial in environments where data integrity, speed, and availability are mission-critical. SANs are widely used in enterprise data centers and server rooms, where large volumes of data must be stored, retrieved, backed up, and managed efficiently. A SAN architecture supports features such as centralized storage management, fast backup and recovery, data replication, and high-performance I/O operations, making it ideal for applications such as databases, ERP systems, and virtualized workloads.

Technologies that enable SAN functionality include Fibre Channel (FC) and iSCSI (Internet Small Computer Systems Interface). Fibre Channel provides ultra-fast connectivity over optical fiber, supporting high throughput and low latency, while iSCSI allows data transmission over standard IP networks. These technologies ensure that storage traffic is handled separately from the main LAN, reducing congestion and improving application performance. One of the key advantages of SANs is their ability to scale and virtualize storage. As storage requirements grow, administrators can add new disk arrays or SSDs to the SAN without disrupting operations. SANs also support storage tiering, where critical data is stored on high-speed drives while less active data resides on cost-effective disks—optimizing both performance and cost.

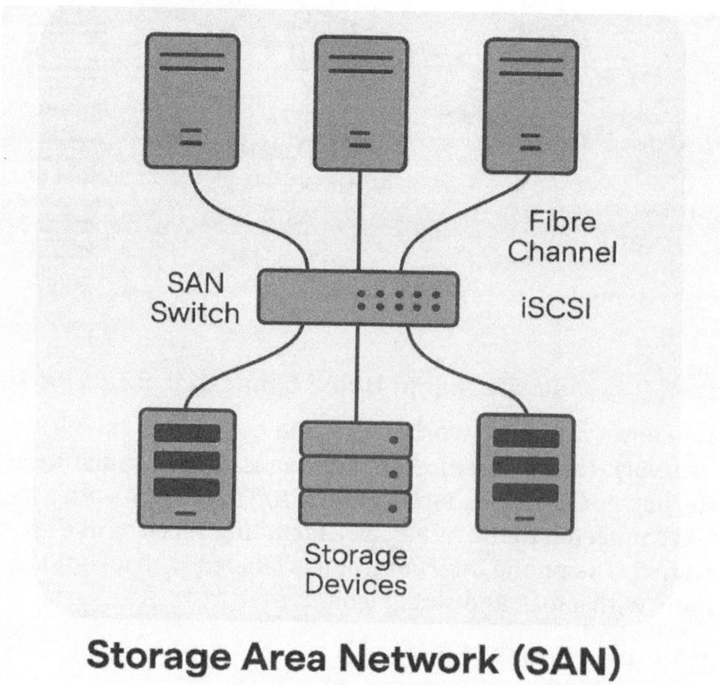

Figure 1.8: Storage Area Network (SAN)

SANs enhance data availability and fault tolerance through features like redundant paths, RAID configurations, and automated failover systems. In the event of hardware failure, data remains accessible, ensuring business continuity. SANs also integrate with disaster recovery strategies by replicating data across remote sites. In summary, SANs provide a robust, scalable, and centralized solution for enterprise-level data storage, improving performance, reliability, and manageability across complex IT infrastructures.

The Figure shows a SAN architecture within a data center. Multiple servers are connected to a SAN switch, which routes traffic to a centralized pool of storage devices (RAID arrays). The storage systems are labeled with technologies like Fibre Channel and iSCSI, and the setup is marked as operating in a data center/ server room. Arrows indicate block-level data transfer between the servers and storage units, with icons showing redundancy and backup paths (Table 1.2).

Table1.2: Categories of Networks

Network Type	Coverage Area	Speed	Ownership	Examples
PAN	1–10 meters	Low	Individual	Bluetooth headset, personal hotspot
LAN	Up to 1 km	High	Private	Office network, Wi-Fi at home
CAN	1–5 km	Very High	Institutional	University campuses
MAN	Up to 50 km	High	Government/ ISP	City-wide fiber network
WAN	Unlimited	Variable	Shared/ Private	Internet, multinational companies
VPN	Virtual	Depends on host	Private over public	Remote access to corporate resources
SAN	Internal (Data Center)	Very High	Private	Enterprise storage access

Organization of the Internet

The Internet is a vast, complex, and decentralized global network that connects millions of private, public, academic, business, and government networks. Its organization is not governed by a single central authority but rather by a collaborative framework of interconnected systems, protocols, and administrative bodies. This distributed design allows it to scale efficiently and support billions of devices worldwide.

Hierarchical Structure

The Internet is organized in a hierarchical, multi-layered structure that includes:

- Tier 1 Networks: These are the backbone providers (like AT&T, NTT, and Tata Communications) with global coverage and no need to purchase IP transit. They exchange traffic freely via peering agreements.
- Tier 2 Networks: These networks purchase transit from Tier 1 networks but also peer with other Tier 2s. They serve large regional ISPs and enterprises.
- Tier 3 Networks: These are typically local ISPs or smaller networks that purchase internet access from Tier 2 providers and deliver it to end users.
- This hierarchy forms the physical infrastructure of the Internet, ensuring data can be routed from any source to any destination across the globe.

Internet Service Providers (ISPs)

Internet Service Providers (ISPs) are fundamental to the structure and functioning of the Internet, acting as intermediaries that connect individuals, businesses, and institutions to the global network. ISPs operate at different hierarchical levels, each serving a unique role. Backbone ISPs (Tier 1) provide the core infrastructure of the Internet; they own and maintain high-speed, high-capacity international networks and interconnect with each other through peering agreements without purchasing Internet access. Regional ISPs (Tier 2) rely on Tier 1 providers for connectivity and serve as distributors, extending services to broader geographic areas such as states or regions. At the lowest tier, Local ISPs (Tier 3) purchase bandwidth from Tier 2 providers and deliver Internet services directly to end-users, including homes, schools, and small businesses. Each ISP manages a range of IP addresses allocated by a Regional Internet Registry (RIR) and maintains its own routing infrastructure to direct data efficiently. These routing tables, often dynamically updated through protocols like BGP (Border Gateway Protocol), enable ISPs to forward packets across networks and ensure that data reaches its correct destination, thus playing a critical role in global Internet accessibility and traffic management.

Domain Name System (DNS)

The Domain Name System (DNS) plays a crucial role in making the Internet more accessible and user-friendly by translating human-readable domain names (such as www.example.com) into numeric IP addresses (like 192.0.2.1) that computers use to locate and communicate with each other. Without DNS, users would have to remember complex numerical addresses for every website they want to visit. Acting like a phonebook for the Internet, DNS allows users to enter easily memorable domain names while the system resolves them into machine-understandable IP addresses. DNS is structured hierarchically to ensure scalability and manageability across the globe. At the top of this hierarchy are the Root DNS servers, which handle requests for top-level domains (TLDs). Beneath them are the Top-Level Domains (TLDs) such as .com, .org, .net, and country-specific domains like .in (India) or .uk (United Kingdom). Further down the hierarchy are Second-Level Domains (e.g., google.com), which are registered and managed by individuals, organizations, or companies. This globally distributed system is replicated across thousands of servers to ensure high availability, redundancy, and performance, making it a critical component for locating services and routing traffic across the Internet.

Internet Protocol (IP) and Routing

The Internet uses the Internet Protocol (IP) to identify and locate devices across the network. The two versions in use are IPv4 and IPv6. IP routing ensures that packets take the best possible path to reach their destination, guided by routing protocols like:

- BGP (Border Gateway Protocol) – used to exchange routing information between autonomous systems (AS).
- OSPF, IS-IS – used within large organizational networks for internal routing.

The global routing infrastructure is based on Autonomous Systems (ASes), which are large networks or groups of networks under a common administration.

Internet Governance

While the Internet is decentralized, several international organizations and governing bodies coordinate its resources and standards:

- ICANN (Internet Corporation for Assigned Names and Numbers) – manages domain names, IP addresses, and DNS root.
- IANA (Internet Assigned Numbers Authority) – oversees IP allocations and protocol assignments.
- IETF (Internet Engineering Task Force) – develops Internet standards (like TCP/IP).
- RIRs (Regional Internet Registries) – allocate IP addresses in five global regions (e.g., ARIN, RIPE NCC, APNIC).

These bodies ensure that the Internet remains open, secure, and interoperable.

Content Delivery and Services

To efficiently distribute content across the Internet, especially multimedia and large data, Content Delivery Networks (CDNs) like Akamai, Cloudflare, and Amazon CloudFront use edge servers strategically placed across the globe. These reduce latency and improve load times by serving content from the nearest geographical location. Additionally, cloud service providers like AWS, Microsoft Azure, and Google Cloud play a central role by hosting applications, storage, and compute services used by millions of users and enterprises.

The organization of the Internet is a multi-layered system involving hardware (routers, switches, cables), protocols (IP, BGP, DNS), and administrative frameworks (ISPs, ICANN, IETF). Its decentralized and hierarchical nature allows for scalability, resilience, and global accessibility. Despite its complexity, the collaborative coordination between organizations and technologies enables the seamless delivery of information across the world.

ISP

An Internet Service Provider (ISP) is an organization that offers services for accessing, using, and participating in the Internet. ISPs serve as the gateway between users and the vast infrastructure of the Internet, enabling individuals, businesses, and institutions to connect to online services, websites, applications, and communication platforms. They provide essential services such as broadband Internet access, email hosting, domain name registration, and web hosting. ISPs are typically categorized into three hierarchical tiers based on their infrastructure and connectivity scope. Tier 1 ISPs, also known as backbone providers, own and operate large-scale international networks with direct access to every part of the Internet. They interconnect with other Tier 1 providers through peering agreements and do not need to purchase bandwidth from anyone else. These ISPs form the core infrastructure of the Internet, handling high-capacity, global data traffic.

Tier 2 ISPs connect to Tier 1 providers and often peer with other Tier 2 ISPs. They purchase Internet transit to reach parts of the Internet not covered by their peers. Tier 2 providers typically operate within national or regional boundaries and resell bandwidth to smaller ISPs or large organizations. Tier 3 ISPs are the local providers that purchase bandwidth from Tier 2 ISPs and deliver Internet services directly to residential and small business users. They often include cable companies, telephone providers, and wireless Internet providers. Each ISP is assigned blocks of IP addresses by Regional Internet Registries (RIRs) such as ARIN, RIPE NCC, or APNIC. They are responsible for managing these addresses and maintaining routing tables to efficiently direct incoming and outgoing Internet traffic. To ensure effective routing across the global Internet, ISPs rely on protocols like BGP (Border Gateway Protocol), which helps determine the best paths for data transmission. In addition to providing connectivity, ISPs are also involved in network security, traffic shaping, customer support, and adherence to regulations set by national telecommunications authorities. They may offer value-added services like Virtual Private Networks (VPNs), anti-virus protections, or parental controls. With the increasing demand for high-speed and reliable Internet, ISPs play a central role in expanding digital infrastructure, reducing the digital divide, and supporting the growing dependence on online services in both personal and professional settings.

Network Structure and Architecture (layering principles, services, protocols and standards)

The structure and architecture of computer networks are designed to support reliable, scalable, and interoperable communication between devices and systems. A key design principle that governs this architecture is layering, which divides the complex process of networking into manageable, well-defined functional layers. This layered architecture enables modularity, simplifies troubleshooting, and ensures compatibility between various technologies and vendors.The most widely used models that describe network architecture are the OSI (Open Systems Interconnection) model and the TCP/IP (Transmission Control Protocol/Internet Protocol) suite. Both models are structured into layers, each responsible for specific networking functions. The OSI model has seven layers—Physical, Data Link, Network, Transport, Session, Presentation, and Application—while TCP/IP consolidates these into four or five layers: Link, Internet, Transport, and Application.

Each layer provides services to the layer above it and uses services from the layer below. For example, the Transport layer provides reliable data transmission services to the Application layer, while using the Network layer for routing data across networks. This service abstraction allows each layer to evolve independently and improves the flexibility of network design. Protocols are the rules and conventions that govern communication within and between layers. Examples include HTTP at the application layer, TCP/UDP at the transport layer, IP at the network layer, and Ethernet at the link layer. Protocols ensure that data is formatted, transmitted, and interpreted correctly by all participating systems. Multiple protocols can operate at the same layer to support different requirements—for instance, TCP is used for reliable transmission, while UDP is used for faster, connectionless communication.

To ensure interoperability across systems and vendors, global organizations define networking standards. These standards, issued by bodies like the IEEE (Institute of Electrical and Electronics Engineers), IETF (Internet Engineering Task Force), and ISO (International Organization for Standardization), provide specifications for physical cabling (e.g., IEEE 802.3 for Ethernet), wireless communication (e.g., IEEE 802.11 for Wi-Fi), and data exchange protocols (e.g., IPv4, IPv6).Encapsulation is another important concept in layered architecture. As data moves down the protocol stack from the application to the physical layer, each layer adds its own header (and sometimes a trailer), forming a protocol data unit (PDU). At the receiving end, these headers are stripped away in reverse order during decapsulation, allowing the original data to be delivered to the appropriate application.

The advantages of layering include simplification of network design, modular implementation, and ease of debugging. It also allows hardware and software vendors to develop components that fit into the larger network ecosystem without requiring access to the full system. The OSI model, although not used in practical implementation as much as the TCP/IP model, is essential for educational and conceptual understanding. It provides a comprehensive framework to understand the flow of data and the role of each layer in tasks like error handling, flow control, and session management. Modern network architectures also support additional services like QoS (Quality of Service), NAT (Network Address Translation), and VPNs, which operate across or within multiple layers. These services enhance network efficiency, security, and reliability in today's complex and dynamic digital environments. In summary, the network structure and layered architecture are fundamental to how data is transmitted, managed, and understood across heterogeneous systems. Through well-defined layers, services, protocols, and international standards, computer networks have become robust, scalable, and interoperable systems that support billions of devices and diverse applications worldwide.

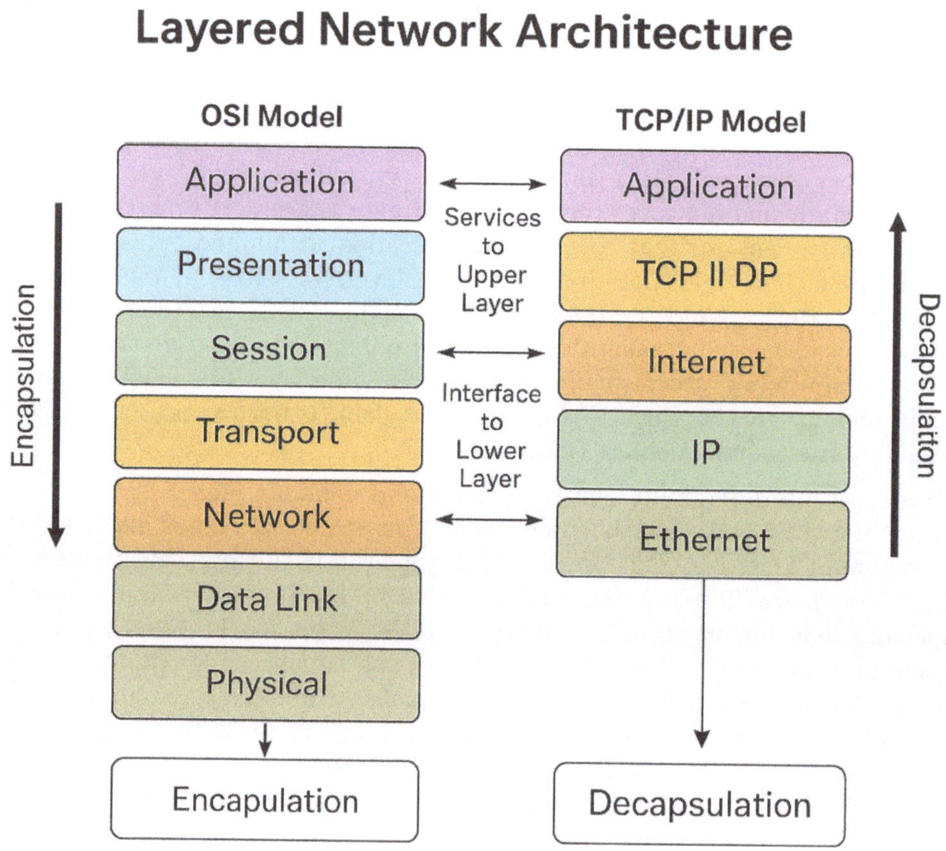

Figure 1.9: Layer Network Architecture.

The Figure will depict the OSI Model's 7 layers side by side with the TCP/IP 4-layer model. Each layer is shown with its typical protocols and responsibilities. Arrows demonstrate encapsulation (from top to bottom) and decapsulation (bottom to top). Common protocols like HTTP, TCP, IP, and Ethernet are visually mapped to their respective layers. There's also a label for "Services to Upper Layer" and "Interface to Lower Layer" between each block.

The OSI Reference Model

The OSI (Open Systems Interconnection) Reference Model is a conceptual framework developed by the International Organization for Standardization (ISO) to standardize the functions of a telecommunication or computing system into seven distinct layers. This model enables different systems to communicate using standard protocols and interfaces, regardless of their underlying architecture. Each layer in the OSI model performs a specific role in the process of transmitting data over a network, and interacts only with the layers directly above and below it, promoting modularity and easier troubleshooting. The seven layers of the OSI model, from bottom to top, are: Physical, Data Link, Network, Transport, Session, Presentation, and Application. The lower layers (1–4) handle physical transmission, addressing, routing, and reliable delivery, while the upper layers (5–7) manage data representation, session control, and user interface. For example, the Transport layer ensures reliable data delivery using protocols like TCP, while the Application layer provides services like email or web browsing. Though modern networks primarily use the TCP/IP model, the OSI model remains an essential educational and conceptual tool for understanding how network communication functions in a layered and standardized manner.

TCP/IP Protocol Suite

The TCP/IP Protocol Suite is the foundational framework of the modern Internet and most private networks. Developed by the U.S. Department of Defense, TCP/IP (Transmission Control Protocol/Internet Protocol) defines a set of standardized protocols that allow diverse computer systems to communicate over interconnected networks. Unlike the OSI model's seven-layer structure, the TCP/IP model is typically represented with four layers: Application, Transport, Internet, and Network Access (or Link Layer).The Application layer encompasses protocols used by end-user applications to interact with the network. These include HTTP (web browsing), FTP (file transfer), SMTP (email), and DNS (domain resolution). The Transport layer provides end-to-end communication between devices, using protocols like TCP for reliable, connection-oriented transmission and UDP for faster, connectionless communication.

The Internet layer is responsible for logical addressing and routing of packets across networks. The key protocol at this layer is IP (Internet Protocol), which ensures that data is sent to the correct destination using IP addresses. Supporting protocols include ICMP (for diagnostics) and ARP (for address resolution). Below this, the Network Access layer deals with the physical transmission of data over network media, interfacing with technologies like Ethernet, Wi-Fi, or DSL.TCP/IP's layered design allows for flexibility, interoperability, and scalability, making it well-suited for real-world networking environments. It has become the de facto standard for Internet communication due to its robust architecture, support for heterogeneous systems, and adaptability to both local and global networking needs.

Network Devices and Components

Computer networks rely on various devices and components to facilitate communication, manage traffic, ensure security, and enable connectivity across systems. These devices operate at different layers of the network and play unique roles in data transmission, routing, switching, and filtering (Table 1.3).

Router: A router connects multiple networks together and directs data packets between them based on IP addresses. Operating primarily at the network layer (Layer 3) of the OSI model, routers determine the best path for forwarding packets. In home or enterprise environments, routers also act as gateways to the Internet.

Switch: A network switch operates at the data link layer (Layer 2) and connects devices within the same network, such as computers, printers, or servers. Switches use MAC addresses to forward data only to the intended recipient device, making them more efficient than older hubs.

Hub: A hub is a basic device that connects multiple Ethernet devices in a LAN. Unlike a switch, it broadcasts incoming data to all connected devices regardless of the destination, leading to more traffic and potential collisions. It operates at the physical layer (Layer 1).

Modem: A modem (modulator-demodulator) is used to connect a local network to the Internet by converting digital signals from a computer into analog signals suitable for transmission over telephone or cable lines and vice versa. It typically interfaces with an ISP.

Access Point (AP): A wireless access point enables Wi-Fi-capable devices to connect to a wired network. It extends the range and capacity of a network and works in conjunction with routers and switches. APs are essential in wireless LANs and support multiple devices over radio waves.

Network Interface Card (NIC): Every device on a network uses a NIC to connect to the network. It may be wired (Ethernet) or wireless (Wi-Fi). NICs operate at Layer 1 and Layer 2, providing the physical interface and MAC address necessary for communication.

Firewall: A firewall is a security device or software that monitors and controls incoming and outgoing network traffic. Positioned between internal networks and external threats, firewalls apply rules to allow or block traffic based on IP addresses, port numbers, and protocols.

Repeater: A repeater amplifies and retransmits network signals to extend the range of a network. It is used in large networks or areas where signal degradation occurs due to distance. Repeaters operate at the physical layer.

Bridge: A bridge connects two separate LAN segments, allowing them to function as a single network. It filters traffic based on MAC addresses and reduces collisions. Bridges work at the data link layer.

Table1.3 : Summary of Network Devices and Functions

Device	OSI Layer	Primary Function	Key Use Case
Router	Layer 3 (Network)	Routes data between networks	Internet access, inter-network routing
Switch	Layer 2 (Data Link)	Forwards data based on MAC addresses	LAN communication
Hub	Layer 1 (Physical)	Broadcasts data to all connected devices	Basic LAN connectivity (legacy)
Modem	Layer 1/2	Converts digital and analog signals	Internet connectivity via ISP
Access Point	Layer 2	Connects wireless clients to wired networks	Wireless LANs
NIC	Layer 1/2	Provides network interface for a device	Device-level connectivity
Firewall	Layer 3–7	Monitors and controls traffic for security	Network protection and access control
Repeater	Layer 1	Boosts signal to extend network range	Large buildings or remote areas
Bridge	Layer 2	Connects and filters traffic between LAN segments	Extending LANs

Conclusion

In conclusion, this chapter has laid a strong foundation for understanding the fundamental concepts of computer networks. It began by exploring the goals and applications of networks, emphasizing how connectivity supports communication, resource sharing, and data management across various sectors. The chapter then categorized different types of networks—such as PAN, LAN, CAN, MAN, and WAN—highlighting their range, technologies, and typical use cases. A detailed overview of the Internet's organization, including the role of ISPs, the DNS hierarchy, and layered protocol structures like the OSI and TCP/IP models, has also been provided to illustrate the complexity and scalability of global networking systems. Moreover, the chapter explained network architecture, layering principles, services, and the standardized protocols that ensure seamless data transmission. It introduced key network devices and components—routers, switches, firewalls, access points, and more—detailing their functions and significance within both small-scale and enterprise networks. Together, these insights offer a comprehensive introduction to how computer networks are designed, structured, and utilized, forming the basis for more advanced topics in networking.

Exercise Questions

- Define a computer network. What are the primary goals of networking?
- Differentiate between PAN, LAN, CAN, MAN, and WAN based on range and use cases.
- Explain the hierarchical structure of the Internet and the role of ISPs.
- What is the Domain Name System (DNS)? How does it resolve domain names to IP addresses?
- Describe the OSI reference model. List and explain the function of each of its seven layers.
- Compare and contrast the OSI model with the TCP/IP protocol suite.
- What is encapsulation in the context of network communication?
- List and describe the functions of at least five common networking devices.
- How do routers differ from switches in terms of functionality and OSI layer operation?
- Why are protocols and standards necessary in network communication?

CHAPTER

2

PHYSICAL LAYER

Chapter 2 delves into the Physical Layer of the network architecture, which serves as the foundational layer in the OSI model. This layer is primarily concerned with the transmission of raw bits over a communication medium and is responsible for the physical connection between devices. It governs the hardware components, electrical signaling, transmission techniques, and media that enable data to travel from one point to another. The chapter provides essential insights into the design and functioning of the physical aspects of networking systems. Key topics covered include network topology design, which outlines the structural layout of network elements and how devices are interconnected. It also explores types of connections (point-to-point and multipoint), various transmission media (such as copper cables, fiber optics, and wireless), and the mechanisms of signal transmission and encoding. Additionally, the chapter discusses factors affecting network performance and the transmission impairments that can degrade data signals. Concepts like switching techniques and multiplexing are introduced to explain how data is efficiently managed and transferred in high-traffic environments. Overall, this chapter lays the technical groundwork for understanding how digital data physically travels through networks.

Network Topology Design

Network topology design refers to the structured layout of network devices and their interconnections, both physically (how they are wired) and logically (how data flows). A well-planned topology is crucial for ensuring efficient communication, minimizing costs, reducing latency, and enabling scalability and fault tolerance (Figure 2.1). The design of a network's topology is influenced by various factors such as the number of users, geographic distribution, budget, performance requirements, and the types of services required (e.g., voice, data, video).

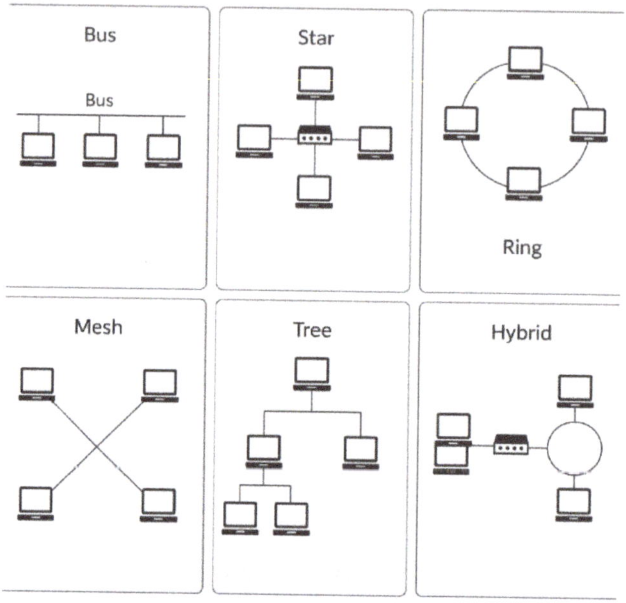

Figure 2.1: Network Topology Design

Bus Topology

In a bus topology, all network devices are connected to a single central cable, called the bus or backbone, which carries the data. When a device sends data, it travels along the bus in both directions until it reaches its destination. Devices communicate in a linear fashion, and only one device can transmit at a time to avoid data collisions. Bus topologies use terminators at each end of the cable to prevent signal reflection and maintain data integrity. Although simple and inexpensive to install, bus topology has several limitations. As more devices are added, performance degrades due to increased traffic and collisions. A failure in the central bus can bring down the entire network. This topology is mostly obsolete today but was common in early Ethernet networks and is still occasionally used in temporary or small-scale setups.

Star Topology

The star topology connects each device to a central hub or switch, forming a layout that resembles a star. Data sent from any device passes through the central node before reaching its destination. This allows for centralized management, easier troubleshooting, and better performance since data collisions are minimized in switched star networks. This topology is widely used in modern LANs due to its simplicity, scalability, and fault isolation. If one cable or device fails, it does not affect the rest of the network. However, the central hub/switch is a critical point of failure—if it goes down, the entire network becomes inoperable. Nonetheless, its manageability and performance benefits make it ideal for schools, offices, and home networks.

Ring Topology

In a ring topology, each device is connected to exactly two others, forming a closed loop or circle. Data travels in one direction (unidirectional) or in both directions (bidirectional in dual-ring systems). Each device has a repeater that receives data, checks if it's addressed to it, and passes it along to the next device if not. Ring topology provides orderly data transfer and predictable performance, especially with token-passing protocols that reduce collisions. However, a single break in the ring can disrupt the entire network unless a secondary ring is used. Troubleshooting can also be difficult. While rarely used today in LANs, ring topology is still employed in some fiber-optic metro networks and industrial systems.

Mesh Topology

In a mesh topology, every device is connected to every other device directly. This creates a full mesh where the number of links equals n(n-1)/2, or a partial mesh, where some devices have multiple connections but not all. Mesh networks provide multiple paths for data to travel, ensuring high availability and reliability. Mesh topology is extremely fault-tolerant—if one connection fails, data can take an alternate route. It is ideal for critical applications where uptime is essential, such as military systems, financial networks, and data centers. However, it is expensive and complex to implement, requiring more cabling and configuration, especially as the number of devices increases.

Tree Topology

Tree topology is a hierarchical structure that combines features of bus and star topologies. It organizes devices in a layered fashion, starting with a root node (usually a central hub or switch) and branching out in a parent-child manner. Each branch can include multiple star networks. Tree topology is highly scalable and manageable, making it suitable for large networks, such as those used in university campuses, corporate offices, and data centers. However, if the root or backbone connection fails, large portions of the network can go down. Proper planning and redundancy are crucial to maintaining tree topology reliability.

Hybrid Topology

A hybrid topology combines two or more different topologies—like star-ring, star-bus, or mesh-tree—to leverage the benefits of each and address specific organizational needs. For example, a corporate network might use star topology in departments while connecting them through a ring backbone. Hybrid topologies are highly flexible and scalable, allowing designers to tailor the network architecture for performance, cost, and fault tolerance. However, the complexity of design, installation, and maintenance increases. These topologies are ideal for enterprises with complex structures, where different areas require different communication patterns and levels of reliability.

Table 2.1: Comparison of Network Topologies

Topology	Structure	Cost	Scalability	Reliability	Fault Isolation	Use Case
Bus	Single backbone cable	Low	Poor	Low	Difficult	Small offices, legacy systems
Star	Devices connected to a hub	Medium	High	Medium	Easy	Modern LANs, schools, offices
Ring	Circular loop	Medium	Medium	Medium	Difficult	Industrial networks, older systems
Mesh	Fully connected nodes	High	Low	Very High	Excellent	Military, mission-critical systems
Tree	Hierarchical star-bus hybrid	Medium-High	High	Medium	Medium	Large campuses, enterprises
Hybrid	Combination of two or more	Variable	Very High	High	Depends on design	Complex enterprise networks

The comparison Table 2.1 summarizes key characteristics of common network topologies—Bus, Star, Ring, Mesh, Tree, and Hybrid—based on factors such as structure, cost, scalability, reliability, fault isolation, and typical use cases. Bus topology, with a single backbone cable, is cost-effective but lacks scalability and fault tolerance. Star topology, widely used today, offers easy management and fault isolation but relies heavily on a central device. Ring topology ensures orderly communication but is vulnerable to cable failures. Mesh topology excels in reliability and fault tolerance due to multiple redundant paths, though it is expensive and complex. Tree topology is scalable and suited for large hierarchical networks, while hybrid topology combines the strengths of various designs for maximum flexibility, making it ideal for complex enterprise environments.

Types of Connections

In computer networking, types of connections refer to the ways in which devices (nodes) are linked for communication and data transmission. These connections can be classified based on physical configuration, communication direction, and transmission techniques. Understanding these connection types is fundamental to designing an efficient and reliable network infrastructure. Below are the major types of connections used in network environments (Figure 2.2):

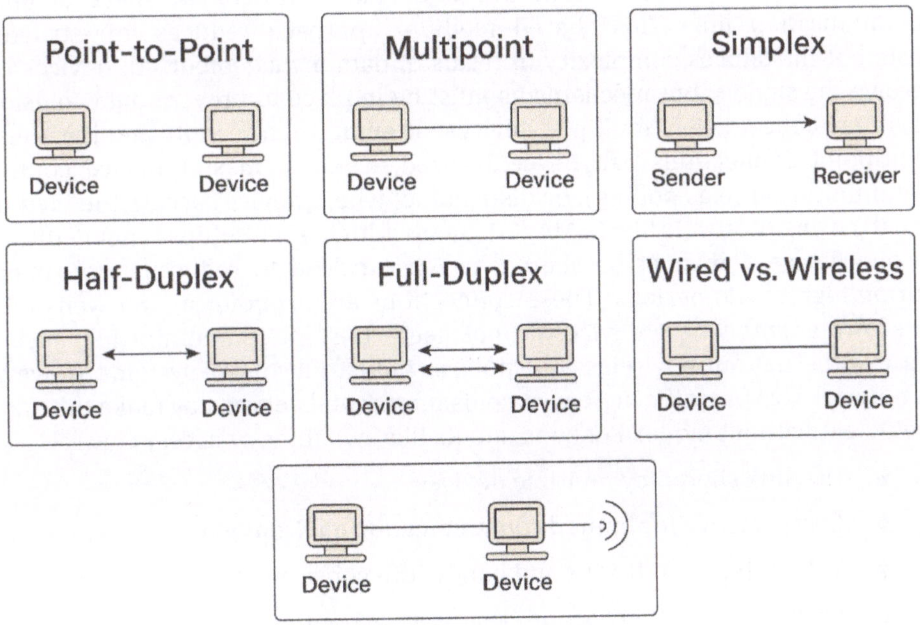

Figure 2.2: Types of Connections

Point-to-Point Connection

A Point-to-Point (P2P) connection establishes a direct communication link between two devices, with no intermediaries involved. This dedicated pathway ensures that all bandwidth is available exclusively to the connected devices, resulting in high performance and minimal latency. Point-to-point links can be either wired (e.g., Ethernet cable, fiber optic) or wireless (e.g., microwave, laser links).In such a configuration, data travels uninterrupted between sender and receiver, making it highly efficient and reliable. Because there is no competition for bandwidth, performance remains consistent and predictable. This setup also makes troubleshooting and security management easier, as there are no shared nodes or pathways. Point-to-point connections are commonly used in scenarios that demand stable and secure communication, such as leased lines in enterprise networks, backbone links between routers in WANs, or even USB connections between a computer and peripherals like printers. The absence of shared traffic minimizes interference and ensures data integrity.

- Direct link between two devices
- Full bandwidth usage
- High performance and security
- Common in leased lines, USB, and WAN links

Multipoint (Multidrop) Connection

A Multipoint connection allows three or more devices to share a single communication link. This shared medium approach reduces infrastructure costs but introduces complexity in terms of data management. All devices can receive the signals, but mechanisms must be in place to prevent data collisions or interference when multiple devices attempt to transmit simultaneously. Multipoint connections can be centralized, where a master device controls communication (e.g., polling), or distributed, where devices access the medium equally using protocols like CSMA/CD. Bandwidth in such setups is not dedicated to one device and must be shared, which can lead to reduced performance during high traffic periods. These connections are economical and well-suited to environments where devices do not need constant communication, such as legacy Ethernet hubs, wireless hotspots, or industrial control systems. However, as network size or traffic increases, collision risk and delays may make this setup inefficient without modern enhancements like switching or access control.

- One link shared by multiple devices
- Cost-effective for limited communication environments
- Vulnerable to collisions and bandwidth constraints
- Seen in older Ethernet and basic wireless networks

Simplex Communication

In Simplex communication, data flows strictly in one direction—from the sender to the receiver—with no return channel. This unidirectional mode is the simplest form of communication, ideal for systems where feedback isn't necessary or practical. A common analogy is a one-way street, where vehicles (data) only move forward. Simplex systems are easy to implement and cost-effective due to their simplicity. They are typically found in applications where a continuous or one-sided data flow is required, such as television broadcasts, digital signage, or keyboards transmitting keystrokes to a CPU. In these cases, the receiving device simply accepts input without sending anything back. However, the major limitation of simplex systems is their lack of interactivity. There's no way to confirm receipt, request retransmission, or signal errors, which makes them unsuitable for many real-time or critical communication systems. Their utility is limited to applications where monitoring or feedback is unnecessary.

- One-way communication
- No acknowledgment or error correction
- Useful in TV broadcasts, keyboards
- Simple but limited in functionality

Half-Duplex Communication

Half-duplex communication allows data transmission in both directions, but only one direction at a time. When one device is sending, the other must wait until the transmission is complete before responding. This sequential communication pattern is managed by protocols or hardware logic to avoid collision. Half-duplex systems are more advanced than simplex, as they enable two-way interaction while conserving bandwidth. However, because only one device can transmit at a time, they are subject to delays and interruptions, especially in systems where both parties try to communicate frequently or simultaneously. This type of communication is common in systems like walkie-talkies, older Ethernet using hubs, and some wireless intercoms, where a "push-to-talk" mechanism controls the transmission direction. While not ideal for real-time applications, half-duplex setups are still useful where simultaneous interaction is not critical.

- Two-way, but one direction at a time
- More flexible than simplex
- Causes delay under high usage
- Examples: Walkie-talkies, early Ethernet

Full-Duplex Communication

Full-duplex communication supports simultaneous two-way communication, allowing both devices to send and receive data at the same time. This is similar to a two-lane road, where vehicles (data) can move in both directions without interference. It significantly increases communication efficiency and reduces latency. This mode is used in modern Ethernet networks, phone systems, and video conferencing, where real-time, uninterrupted communication is essential. Full-duplex transmission typically uses either separate transmission channels (in wired systems) or advanced channel division techniques (in wireless systems). While full-duplex systems require more complex and costly hardware, their advantages in speed, reliability, and user experience outweigh the drawbacks in most modern applications. As bandwidth demand grows, full-duplex systems have become the standard for network communication.

- Simultaneous two-way data transfer
- High speed and efficient communication
- Ideal for real-time systems like VoIP
- Requires sophisticated hardware

Wired vs. Wireless Connections

Connections can also be classified based on physical medium:

Wired connections use tangible cables—twisted pair, coaxial, or fiber optic—to link network devices. These connections offer higher speed, better stability, and security, making them ideal for critical infrastructure, offices, and data centers. Fiber optics, in particular, offer extremely high bandwidth and immunity to electromagnetic interference. Wireless connections, on the other hand, use radio frequency (RF), microwave, or infrared signals to transmit data without physical cables. These offer mobility, flexibility, and ease of installation, but are generally more vulnerable to interference, signal loss, and security threats. Wi-Fi, Bluetooth, and cellular networks fall under this category. In modern networks, hybrid environments combining both wired and wireless connections are common. Wireless connections serve mobile users, while wired connections handle high-bandwidth, latency-sensitive applications like servers and storage.

- Wired: Stable, secure, high-speed; limited mobility
- Wireless: Flexible, mobile, but prone to interference
- Commonly used together in hybrid network designs

Transmission Media

Transmission media refers to the physical or logical pathways used to transmit data between devices in a computer network. These media serve as the carrier of signals, either in the form of electrical impulses, light pulses, or electromagnetic waves. Transmission media are generally classified into two broad categories: guided (wired) and unguided (wireless) media. Each type of media has distinct characteristics that affect data rate, transmission distance, interference, security, and cost (Figure 2.3).

1. Twisted Pair Cable

Twisted pair cables are one of the most widely used guided transmission media, especially in Local Area Networks (LANs) and telecommunication systems. These cables consist of pairs of copper wires twisted around each other to minimize electromagnetic interference from external sources and adjacent pairs. The twisting helps cancel out noise and crosstalk.

There are two main types:

1. Unshielded Twisted Pair (UTP): Commonly used in Ethernet networks, telephone systems, and home wiring. It is economical and easy to install.
2. Shielded Twisted Pair (STP): Includes an additional shielding layer around the wire pairs to protect against more severe EMI, making it suitable for environments with heavy machinery or industrial noise.

Twisted pair cables support speeds ranging from 10 Mbps (Cat3) to 10 Gbps (Cat6a/Cat7) over distances of up to 100 meters. However, they are more susceptible to signal degradation compared to fiber optics, and performance drops over longer distances. Despite this, their low cost and ease of use make them ideal for short-distance applications like office networking. In conclusion, twisted pair cables strike a good balance between cost, flexibility, and performance in structured cabling environments, particularly where ultra-high bandwidth or long-distance transmission is not required.

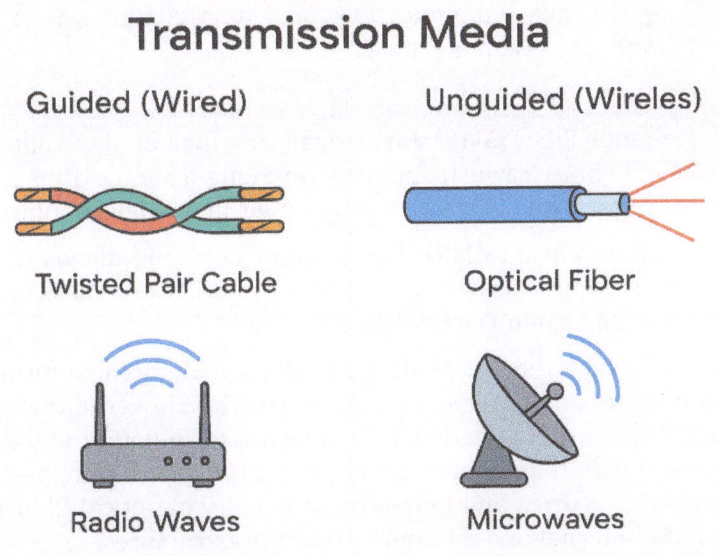

Figure 2.3: Transmission Media

2. Coaxial Cable

Coaxial cables are constructed with a central copper conductor surrounded by an insulating layer, a metallic shield (braid or foil), and a protective outer jacket. This configuration provides better resistance to electromagnetic interference (EMI) than twisted pair cables, allowing coaxial to carry signals over longer distances without significant loss. Historically, coaxial cables were widely used in early Ethernet networks (10Base2, 10Base5) and are still extensively deployed in cable television (CATV) systems, CCTV surveillance, and broadband Internet connections. Coaxial cable supports data rates higher than those of basic UTP cables and can maintain signal quality over distances of up to 500 meters without amplification.

There are different grades of coaxial cables depending on the impedance (typically 50 or 75 ohms). RG-6 and RG-59 are common standards, used respectively in broadband Internet and television. Coaxial cables use connectors like BNC, F-type, and N-type, depending on the application. Although newer Ethernet installations now favor twisted pair and fiber optics, coaxial cables remain relevant due to their ruggedness, shielding, and effectiveness in transmitting high-frequency signals in media and broadcast applications.

3. Optical Fiber Cable

Fiber optic cables use light pulses to transmit data through strands of glass or plastic, offering very high bandwidth, low signal loss, and immunity to electromagnetic interference. They are the preferred medium for backbone networks, long-haul telecommunications, and data centers where high-speed and secure data transmission is critical.

There are two main types:

1. Single-Mode Fiber (SMF): Has a small core diameter and allows only one mode of light to travel. It supports very long-distance transmission (tens of kilometers) and is ideal for long-range, high-speed applications.
2. Multi-Mode Fiber (MMF): Has a larger core and allows multiple light modes. It supports shorter distances (up to 2 km) and is more suitable for LANs and campus networks.

Fiber optics offer data rates exceeding 100 Gbps, making them future-proof for high-speed Internet and enterprise-grade networks. However, they are costlier to install and require specialized tools for splicing, termination, and testing. They are also more fragile than copper-based media. Despite the higher initial cost, the performance, security, and long-term scalability of optical fiber make it the backbone of the Internet and mission-critical infrastructures.

4. Radio Waves

Radio waves are a type of unguided (wireless) transmission medium used for long-range, omnidirectional communication. They travel through the air and can pass through walls, making them suitable for broadcasting and mobile communication. Frequencies range from 3 kHz to 1 GHz, depending on the application. They are commonly used in Wi-Fi networks, AM/FM radio broadcasting, television, Bluetooth, and mobile communication. Because of their omnidirectional nature, a single transmitter can cover a wide area, making deployment economical in urban and rural regions alike.

One of the main advantages of radio waves is their ability to cover large geographic areas, even without line-of-sight in some frequencies. However, they are highly susceptible to interference from electronic devices, weather, and physical obstructions. Additionally, since radio frequencies are publicly accessible, they are more vulnerable to eavesdropping and unauthorized access. In summary, radio waves offer unmatched convenience and coverage in wireless networking but require strong encryption, careful channel selection, and interference management to ensure reliability and security.

5. Microwaves

Microwaves operate at higher frequencies (typically 1 GHz to 30 GHz) and require line-of-sight transmission, meaning that the sending and receiving antennas must be aligned directly without obstacles. They are used in point-to-point links, satellite communication, cellular base stations, and microwave relay networks. Microwave signals are capable of transmitting large amounts of data over long distances, especially when using relay stations or satellites. Terrestrial microwave systems can span distances of 30–50 kilometers between relay towers. They are popular in locations where physical cabling is impractical due to terrain, cost, or mobility. Despite their high data rate and coverage, microwave signals are affected by environmental conditions like rain, fog, and storms (a phenomenon known as rain fade). They also require precise alignment of antennas and suffer from interference from other microwave systems. Microwave communication remains essential in telecommunication backbones, rural connectivity, and mobile network towers, offering a high-bandwidth, scalable alternative to fiber optics in difficult terrains.

6. Infrared

Infrared transmission uses infrared light waves (300 GHz to 430 THz) for short-range, line-of-sight communication. Infrared is commonly used in remote controls, infrared ports in older laptops, and some wireless mouse/keyboard setups. Infrared signals do not penetrate walls and are restricted to a very short range (typically up to a few meters). This makes them ideal for secure, room-based communication, as signals cannot leak to neighboring spaces. They also experience minimal interference and are suitable for controlled environments. However, infrared is easily blocked by obstacles, including walls and even people moving between devices. It also requires precise alignment between sender and receiver, limiting its flexibility and scalability.

While infrared has largely been replaced by Bluetooth and Wi-Fi in personal devices, it still finds use in specific applications like biometric scanners, temperature sensors, and consumer electronics due to its low cost and energy efficiency (Table 2.2).

Table 2.2: Transmission Media

Media Type	Category	Bandwidth	Interference	Distance	Cost	Typical Use
UTP	Wired	Low to Moderate	High	Up to 100 meters	Low	LANs, telephone systems
Coaxial Cable	Wired	Moderate	Moderate	Up to 500 meters	Medium	TV, legacy networks
Fiber Optic Cable	Wired	Very High	None	Several kilometers	High	Backbone networks, ISPs
Radio Waves	Wireless	Moderate	High	Several kilometers	Low/Medium	Wi-Fi, cellular, broadcast
Microwaves	Wireless	High	Medium	Long (line-of-sight)	Medium/High	Satellite, WAN links
Infrared	Wireless	Low	Low	Up to a few meters	Low	Remote controls, IR ports

The choice of transmission media significantly affects the performance, cost, and reliability of a network. Wired media like fiber optics are preferred for high-speed and secure connections, while wireless media offer flexibility and mobility in modern networks. A combination of both—known as a hybrid approach—is commonly implemented to balance performance with scalability and convenience.

Signal Transmission and Encoding

Signal transmission is the process by which data is sent from one point to another in a network using either analog or digital signals. The raw binary data generated by devices cannot travel directly across a medium, so it must be converted into a form suitable for transmission. This is where encoding comes in—it transforms digital data into signals that can traverse a medium such as copper wire, fiber optic cable, or air (wireless).

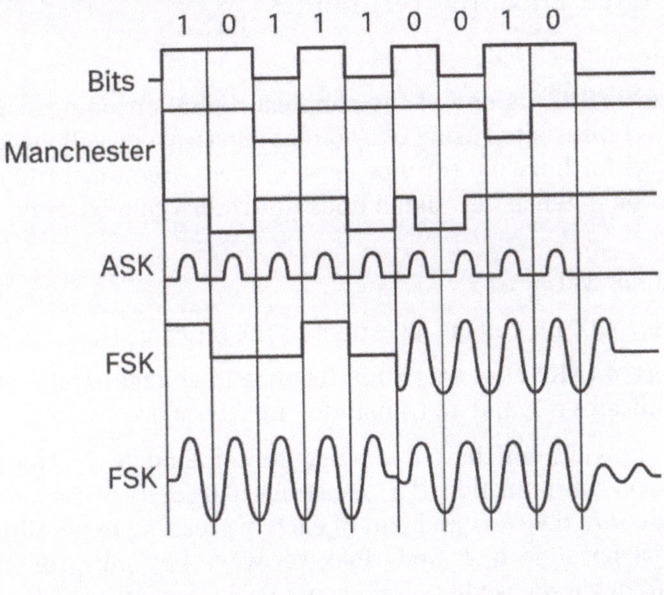

Figure 2.4: Common Signal Encoding Schemes

The Figure 2.4illustrates four common signal encoding schemes, each representing how binary data is transmitted over a medium using variations in voltage, amplitude, frequency, or phase:

- NRZ (Non-Return to Zero) – This waveform shows binary 1s and 0s as constant voltage levels without returning to zero between bits. It clearly demonstrates how long sequences of identical bits result in a flat signal, which can cause synchronization problems.
- Manchester Encoding – The waveform displays a mid-bit transition for each bit. A binary 0 is represented by a high-to-low transition, and a

binary 1 by a low-to-high transition. These transitions help with clock recovery at the receiver end.

- ASK (Amplitude Shift Keying) – In this representation, binary data is encoded by varying the amplitude of the carrier wave. A higher amplitude represents a binary 1, while a lower or zero amplitude represents a binary 0.
- PSK (Phase Shift Keying) – This part of the figure shows phase changes to represent binary values. For instance, a phase shift from 0° to 180° might indicate a change from 0 to 1. The waveform illustrates how the phase of the signal changes with the data.

Together, these visuals compare how different encoding methods translate binary data into signal formats suitable for reliable transmission over various physical media.

1. Digital-to-Digital Encoding Techniques

a. Non-Return to Zero (NRZ)

Non-Return to Zero (NRZ) is one of the simplest digital encoding schemes. In NRZ, binary data is represented using two voltage levels: a high voltage for binary 1 and a low voltage for binary 0 (or vice versa). There are no neutral or "zero" voltages between bits; hence, the signal does not return to a baseline between pulses.

NRZ has two common variants:

- NRZ-Level (NRZ-L): Voltage level defines the bit value (high = 1, low = 0).
- NRZ-Inverted (NRZ-I): A transition (change in voltage) at the beginning of a bit indicates a 1, and no transition indicates a 0.

While NRZ is bandwidth-efficient and easy to implement, it has a major drawback—lack of synchronization. If a long series of 0s or 1s is transmitted, the receiver cannot identify the start and end of each bit, leading to possible errors. Additionally, signal baseline drift and clock recovery become problematic in such scenarios.NRZ is rarely used in modern networking standards due to these limitations but remains important for understanding the fundamentals of digital signaling.

b. Manchester Encoding

Manchester encoding solves the synchronization issue seen in NRZ by combining clock and data into a single self-synchronizing signal. Each bit period is split into two halves: a transition from high to low represents a 0, and a transition from low to high represents a 1 (or vice versa, depending on the convention). Because every bit has a guaranteed transition in the middle, it's easier for the receiver to stay synchronized with the sender. This makes Manchester encoding ideal for environments where signal synchronization is critical, such as Ethernet

(10BASE-T).The trade-off is that Manchester encoding requires twice the bandwidth of NRZ for the same data rate, due to the increased number of signal changes. However, the added reliability often justifies this overhead in critical applications. Manchester encoding is still used in RFID systems, magnetic stripe cards, and some infrared remote controls where self-clocking and data integrity are priorities.

c. Differential Manchester Encoding

Differential Manchester encoding is a variation of Manchester encoding that improves upon its robustness by encoding data based on signal transitions rather than absolute voltage levels. A transition occurs at the midpoint of every bit to maintain synchronization. The presence or absence of a transition at the start of the bit indicates the bit value: no transition for a 1 and a transition for a 0.This scheme is less sensitive to polarity errors than standard Manchester because it relies on changes rather than fixed voltages, making it suitable for systems where signal inversion might occur. Differential Manchester is used in Token Ring networks and some industrial communication systems. While it offers improved noise immunity and reliable clock recovery, the encoding also increases bandwidth usage due to multiple transitions per bit. Nevertheless, its reliability in noisy environments makes it useful in electrically harsh settings. In summary, Differential Manchester is ideal when signal integrity must be preserved under challenging physical layer conditions.

2. Digital-to-Analog Encoding Techniques

a. Amplitude Shift Keying (ASK)

Amplitude Shift Keying (ASK) is a modulation technique in which the amplitude of a carrier signal is varied in accordance with the digital data being transmitted. A high amplitude might represent a binary 1, and zero amplitude (or lower amplitude) might represent a binary 0.ASK is conceptually simple and is used in low-bandwidth applications like early modems and RFID systems. However, its main limitation is that it is highly susceptible to noise. Since amplitude is easily affected by external interference (e.g., from power lines or other signals), ASK's reliability suffers in noisy environments. Despite its simplicity, ASK is not widely used in modern high-speed systems. However, it remains a foundational concept in digital modulation and serves as the basis for more complex modulation techniques like Quadrature Amplitude Modulation (QAM).In systems where noise is minimal and simplicity is valued over speed, ASK can still provide an effective means of transmitting binary data over analog channels.

b. Frequency Shift Keying (FSK)

Frequency Shift Keying (FSK) represents binary data through two distinct frequencies. For example, a binary 1 might be transmitted using a 1200 Hz tone, and a binary 0 with a 2200 Hz tone. Because frequency is less affected by noise than amplitude, FSK is more reliable in noisy environments than ASK.FSK is used in modem communication, two-way radios, and caller ID systems. It's particularly useful in environments with potential amplitude distortion, such as wireless radio links or telephone lines. One of the trade-offs of FSK is its larger bandwidth requirement compared to ASK. However, the increased reliability often justifies this bandwidth cost in applications where data integrity is more important than efficiency. Advanced forms like Multiple-FSK (M-FSK) use more than two frequencies to transmit more bits per symbol, increasing throughput.

c. Phase Shift Keying (PSK)

Phase Shift Keying (PSK) encodes data by changing the phase of the carrier wave. For example, in Binary PSK (BPSK), a 0 might be represented by a 0-degree phase shift, and a 1 by a 180-degree shift. PSK provides better bandwidth efficiency and is more robust against certain types of noise compared to ASK and FSK. More advanced versions like Quadrature PSK (QPSK) and 8-PSK allow multiple bits per symbol by using more phase shifts. QPSK, for instance, uses 0°, 90°, 180°, and 270° phase shifts to represent two bits per symbol, effectively doubling the data rate.

PSK is widely used in modern communication systems such as Wi-Fi (IEEE 802.11), satellite communication, and 4G/5G mobile networks. It offers a good balance between speed, reliability, and spectral efficiency. Although more complex to implement, PSK's high efficiency makes it a preferred choice for high-speed and bandwidth-sensitive applications.

Table 2.3: Common Signal Encoding Techniques

Encoding Type	Technique	Description	Used In
Digital-to-Digital	NRZ	High for 1, low for 0 (or vice versa); no mid-bit transitions	Early serial protocols
Digital-to-Digital	Manchester	Mid-bit transition for each bit; self-synchronizing	Ethernet (10BASE-T)
Digital-to-Digital	Differential Manchester	Transition = 0, no transition = 1 (start of bit)	Token Ring networks
Digital-to-Analog	ASK	Bit values change signal amplitude	Modem transmissions
Digital-to-Analog	FSK	Bit values change signal frequency	Radio communication, old modems
Digital-to-Analog	PSK	Bit values change signal phase	DSL, Wi-Fi

Encoding Type	Technique	Description	Used In
Analog-to-Digital	PCM	Samples analog signal and encodes it digitally	Voice over IP
Analog-to-Analog	AM	Modulates amplitude of carrier signal	AM radio
Analog-to-Analog	FM	Modulates frequency of carrier signal	FM radio
Analog-to-Analog	PM	Modulates phase of carrier signal	Some analog radio systems

The Table 2.3 summarizes key signal encoding techniques across digital and analog domains, highlighting how data is converted for transmission using voltage levels, amplitude, frequency, or phase changes. It outlines their respective use cases, such as Ethernet for Manchester encoding and modems or wireless systems for ASK, FSK, and PSK.

Network Performance and Transmission Impairments

Network Performance

Network performance refers to how efficiently a network transmits data, and it is evaluated using several measurable parameters. These metrics help determine the quality, reliability, and effectiveness of data communication in a network.

a. Bandwidth

Bandwidth is the maximum amount of data that can be transmitted over a network connection in a given amount of time. It is typically measured in bits per second (bps), kilobits per second (Kbps), megabits per second (Mbps), or gigabits per second (Gbps). A higher bandwidth means the network can carry more data simultaneously, which improves the speed and responsiveness of data transmission. Bandwidth is often considered the capacity of the communication link, much like the width of a highway determines how many vehicles can travel side by side. It plays a crucial role in applications that require high data rates such as HD video streaming, online gaming, cloud computing, and large file transfers. However, having high bandwidth alone doesn't guarantee performance—other factors like latency and packet loss must also be optimal.

b. Throughput

Throughput is the actual rate at which data is successfully transmitted over a network connection. It is often lower than bandwidth due to various real-world inefficiencies such as protocol overhead, retransmissions, congestion, or hardware limitations. While bandwidth is the theoretical maximum, throughput is what users truly experience in practice. Measuring throughput helps in assessing the efficiency and health of a network, especially under load. High throughput is essential for maintaining performance in environments with many simultaneous users or high traffic, such as enterprise networks, data centers, and content delivery networks. Continuous monitoring of throughput helps identify bottlenecks and optimize network usage.

c. Latency (Delay)

Latency refers to the time it takes for a data packet to travel from the source to the destination. It consists of several components: processing delay (time taken to process headers), transmission delay (time to push the packet onto the link), propagation delay (time for the signal to travel through the medium), and queuing delay (time spent in routing queues).Low latency is essential for real-time applications such as VoIP, online gaming, and video conferencing, where even slight delays can affect performance and user experience. High latency can lead to sluggish response times, voice echoes, and difficulty in live interaction. Therefore, minimizing latency is a key goal in performance-sensitive networks.

d. Jitter

Jitter refers to the variation in packet arrival times during data transmission. Even if latency is low, inconsistent arrival intervals (caused by jitter) can result in choppy audio, video freezing, or buffering issues in real-time applications. It is typically measured in milliseconds (ms) and is especially problematic for streaming media and voice applications.

To handle jitter, networks often use jitter buffers—temporary storage that holds packets for reordering before playback. While jitter is a natural consequence of routing variations and congestion, excessive jitter indicates instability in the network and needs to be addressed through QoS (Quality of Service) mechanisms and network design improvements.

e. Error Rate

Error rate measures the number of corrupted or lost bits or packets in a transmission compared to the total sent. It is a key indicator of signal quality and transmission integrity. Errors may result from electrical interference, faulty hardware, poor cabling, or signal degradation over distance, especially in analog or wireless links. A high error rate leads to packet retransmissions, increasing network traffic, reducing throughput, and causing delays. It affects applications that rely on data accuracy such as file transfers, database synchronization, and secure communications. Error correction techniques such as checksums, CRC, and FEC (Forward Error Correction) are often implemented to mitigate its impact.

2. Transmission Impairments

Transmission impairments are physical phenomena that degrade the quality and reliability of signals as they travel through the communication medium. These impairments can lead to errors, signal loss, or distortion, ultimately affecting network performance.

a. Attenuation

Attenuation refers to the gradual loss of signal strength as it travels through a transmission medium, such as copper cables, fiber optics, or even air (in wireless networks). As the distance between the sender and receiver increases, the signal becomes weaker and may eventually become too faint to be properly interpreted. Attenuation is measured in decibels (dB) and depends on factors like the type of medium, the signal frequency, and the presence of interference. To counteract attenuation, especially in long-distance communication, repeaters or amplifiers are used. These devices regenerate or boost the signal to restore its original strength before it is passed on to the next segment. Without these corrective measures, attenuation can result in loss of data, reduced throughput, and communication errors. Fiber optic cables generally have lower attenuation than copper, making them ideal for high-speed, long-distance networking.

b. Noise

Noise refers to unwanted electrical or electromagnetic interference that corrupts a transmitted signal. It can be introduced from both internal and external sources, including power lines, electronic devices, and natural environmental conditions. Noise can alter the original signal, leading to bit errors or complete data loss, especially in analog transmissions or poorly shielded media.

There are several common types of noise:

- Thermal noise arises from the random motion of electrons due to heat and is present in all electronic systems.
- Crosstalk occurs when signals in adjacent cables interfere with each other.
- Impulse noise results from sudden, high-energy disturbances such as power surges or lightning.
- Effective shielding, grounding, and error correction mechanisms are critical for minimizing noise-related issues in network communication.

c. Distortion

Distortion occurs when a signal's shape is altered during transmission, making it difficult for the receiver to correctly interpret the original data. This usually happens when different frequency components of a signal travel at different speeds, a phenomenon known as delay distortion. The result is that parts of the signal may arrive at different times, causing overlapping or spreading of signal bits. Distortion is especially problematic in high-speed digital communications and over long distances, where synchronization between sender and receiver is crucial. It can lead to data corruption and reduced performance if not properly managed. Solutions include using equalizers to adjust signal timing and filtering techniques to minimize the impact of frequency-dependent delays.

d. Latency-Related Impairments

Latency-related impairments stem from various delays introduced along the network path. These delays are not necessarily harmful in isolation, but they become problematic when they accumulate or vary unpredictably. Key contributors include propagation delay (time taken for the signal to travel through the medium), transmission delay (time to push bits onto the link), processing delay (time for devices to inspect and forward data), and queuing delay (time spent waiting in buffers due to congestion).These impairments are particularly impactful in real-time applications like VoIP, online gaming, and video conferencing, where even small delays can disrupt communication. Reducing latency requires optimizing routing, upgrading hardware, implementing Quality of Service (QoS), and managing traffic flow to prevent congestion. Efficient network design and resource allocation are essential to minimize the impact of these delays.

The figure visually summarizes the key factors affecting network performance, including bandwidth, throughput, latency, jitter, and error rate. It contrasts the ideal data flow (maximum bandwidth) with actual throughput, illustrating how real-world conditions reduce performance. Latency is shown as the time delay across the network path, while jitter appears as variations in packet arrival times (Figure 2.5). Error rate is depicted through corrupted or dropped packets caused by transmission impairments like noise, attenuation, and distortion. Overall, the figure highlights how these impairments directly impact the efficiency and reliability of data transmission, making it clear that both physical and logical factors must be optimized to ensure smooth network operation.

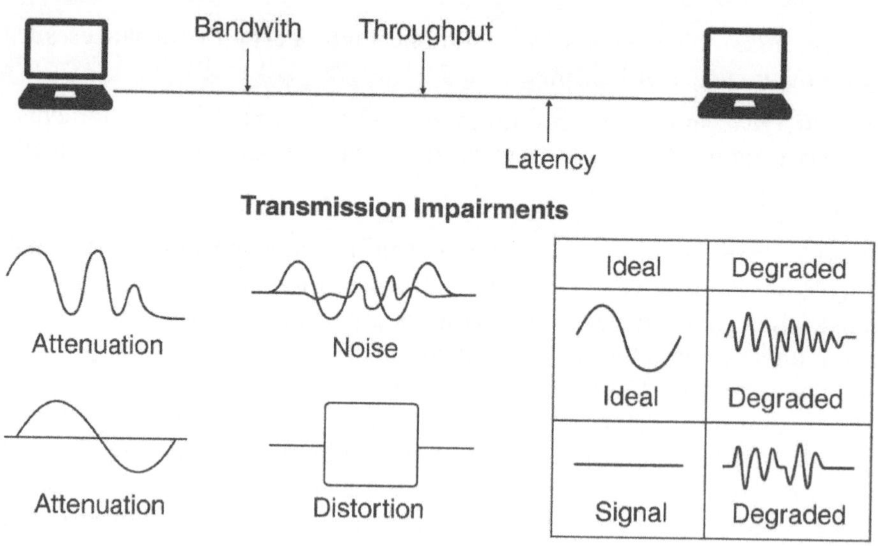

Figure 2.5: Latency-Related Impairments

Switching Techniques and Multiplexing

The figure provides a side-by-side visual comparison of switching techniques and multiplexing methods used in computer networks. On the switching side, it illustrates how circuit switching establishes a fixed path between sender and receiver, guaranteeing consistent communication. In contrast, packet switching shows packets taking different paths to the destination and reassembling at the end, emphasizing flexibility and efficiency. Message switching is also depicted, highlighting its store-and-forward nature where entire messages are buffered at each node before proceeding to the next hop. On the multiplexing side, the diagram shows four types: FDM displays multiple signals using separate frequency bands on a shared medium, while TDM uses time slots to alternate data from different users on the same channel (Figure 2.6). WDM is visualized with different colored light signals traveling through a single optical fiber, representing data channels at different wavelengths. CDM is represented by overlapping coded signals that can be separated and decoded using unique keys. Together, these visuals help explain how data sharing and routing are optimized in network communication.

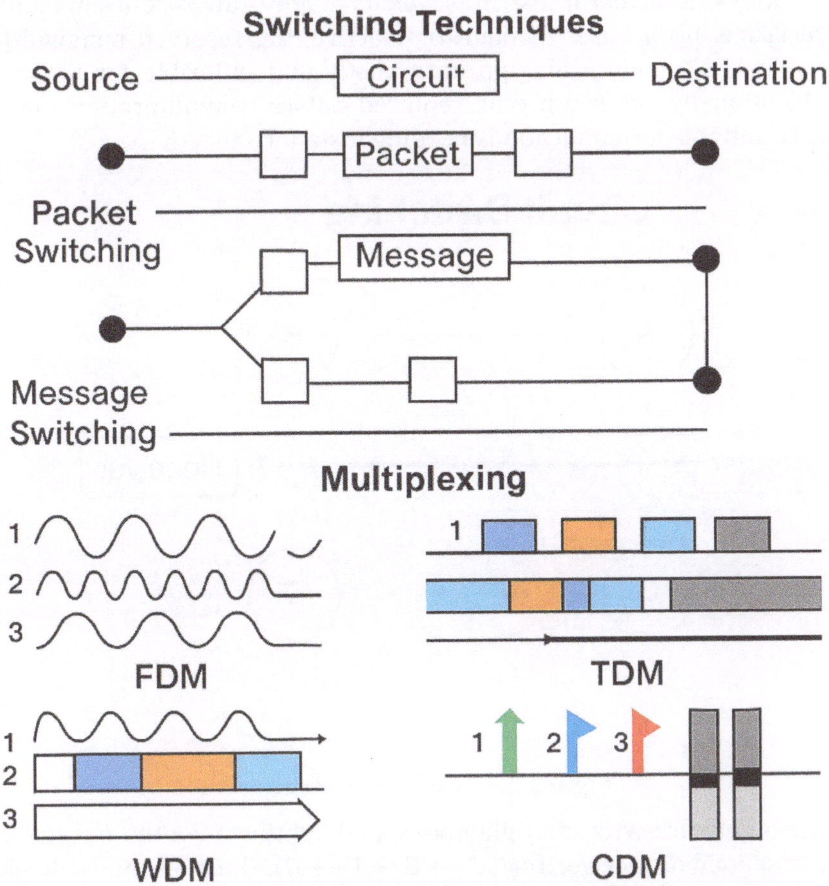

Figure 2.6: Switching Technique.

1. Switching Techniques

Switching in networking refers to the process of directing data from a source to its destination through intermediate nodes (switches or routers). It enables efficient use of network resources, especially in large and complex networks. There are three primary types of switching techniques:

a. Circuit Switching

Circuit switching is a method where a dedicated communication path is established between two devices before any data is transmitted. This path remains reserved exclusively for that communication session until it ends. The entire communication uses the same route, ensuring that the connection is reliable, constant, and predictable in terms of data flow and delay. It mimics the working of traditional telephone systems, where a physical line between two phones is kept open for the entire duration of the call. One of the primary advantages of circuit switching is that it offers guaranteed bandwidth and consistent performance, making it ideal for real-time communication such as voice or video calls, where delays or jitter can be disruptive. However, its major drawback lies in inefficient resource usage. If one user is silent or inactive, the reserved bandwidth still remains blocked, making this approach costly and inflexible for bursty data traffic. Additionally, the setup time required before communication can begin may not be suitable for applications needing instant connectivity.

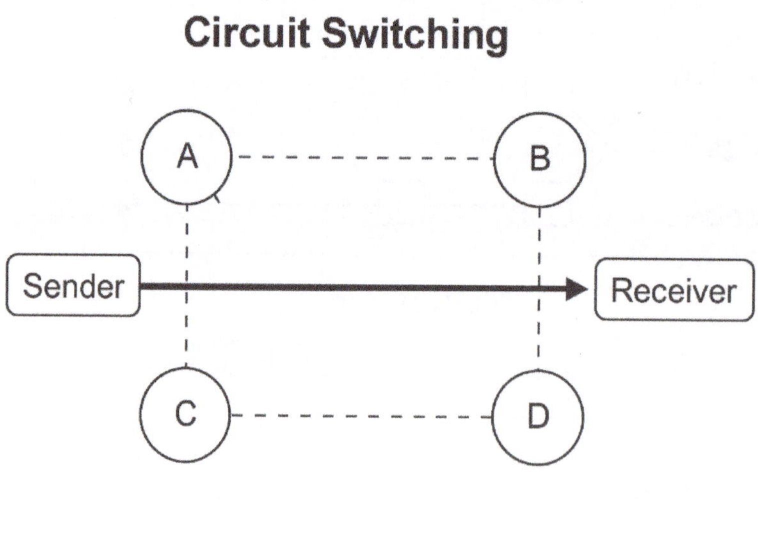

Figure 2.7: Circuit Switching

Figure 2.7 a network with multiple nodes, highlighting a continuous dedicated path from sender to receiver (e.g., A → B → C → D). Once established, all data (represented as a stream) flows along this path. It will visually demonstrate that other users cannot access these links during the session, even when idle.

b. Packet Switching

Packet switching divides data into small, manageable packets, each of which can travel independently across the network. Unlike circuit switching, packet switching does not reserve a dedicated path. Each packet contains source and destination information and can take the most efficient route available at any moment. On reaching the destination, the packets are reassembled into the original message.

There are two variations:

- Datagram packet switching, where packets are routed independently and may arrive out of order.
- Virtual circuit packet switching, which sets a logical path before sending packets, giving a middle ground between circuit and datagram switching.

Packet switching makes highly efficient use of network bandwidth and allows better fault tolerance and load balancing. If one route fails, packets can be rerouted dynamically. However, since packets can arrive in a disordered or delayed manner, applications must handle sequencing and error checking, which adds complexity.

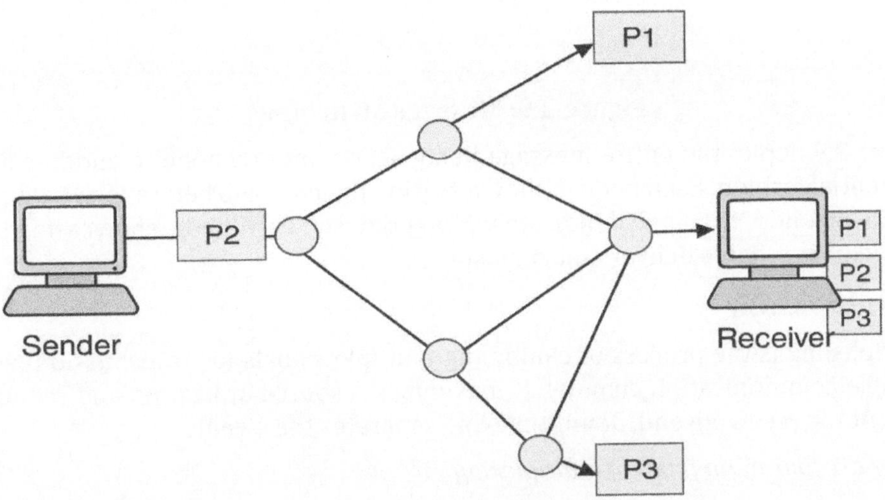

Figure 2.8: Packet Switching

The Figure 2.8will show multiple packets (P1, P2, P3...) from a sender taking different paths through various network nodes to the receiver. It will illustrate asynchronous arrival and out-of-order delivery, followed by reassembly at the destination. This highlights flexibility and efficient use of network paths.

c. Message Switching

In message switching, the complete message is sent from source to destination as a single unit without dividing it into packets. The message is temporarily stored at each intermediate node and forwarded when the next link becomes available. This method is also known as store-and-forward switching. One key advantage is that message switching does not require a dedicated path and can hold the message if the receiver or next node is busy. It is useful in asynchronous communication, like email systems or messaging queues. However, this approach introduces significant delays, especially for long messages, and requires large buffer memory at intermediate nodes to hold entire messages before forwarding.

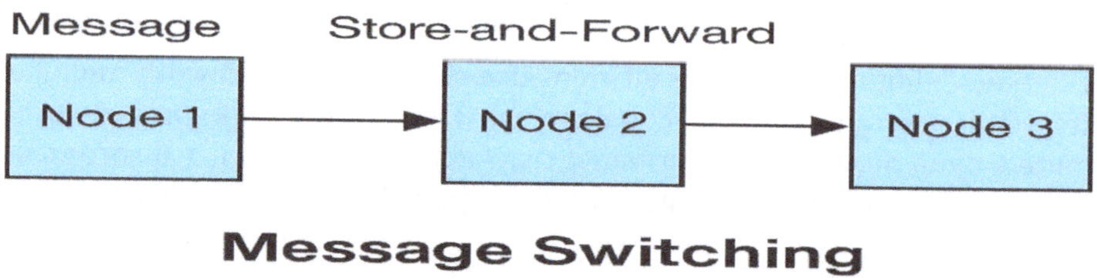

Figure 2.9: Message Switching

Figure 2.9 depict the entire message being sent from one node to another in a sequential fashion. Each node is shown storing the message before forwarding it to the next hop. Labels will indicate waiting times at each node, showcasing the delayed but reliable delivery mechanism.

2. Multiplexing

Multiplexing is the process of combining multiple signals for transmission over a single communication channel. It maximizes resource utilization and reduces cost. At the receiving end, demultiplexing separates the signals.

There are four main types of multiplexing:

a. Frequency Division Multiplexing (FDM)

Frequency Division Multiplexing (FDM) divides the available bandwidth of a communication channel into multiple non-overlapping frequency bands, each assigned to a different signal or user. Each signal modulates a unique carrier frequency, and all modulated signals are transmitted simultaneously over the same physical medium. At the receiving end, the signals are separated using bandpass filters tuned to specific frequencies, a process called demultiplexing. FDM is widely used in radio and television broadcasting, cable TV systems, and analog telephone networks, where multiple channels must coexist on a single medium. One of its strengths is that it allows simultaneous transmission of data streams, maximizing channel utilization when each user transmits continuously. However, it requires precise frequency allocation to avoid overlap and is susceptible to interference and cross-talk, especially in noisy environments.

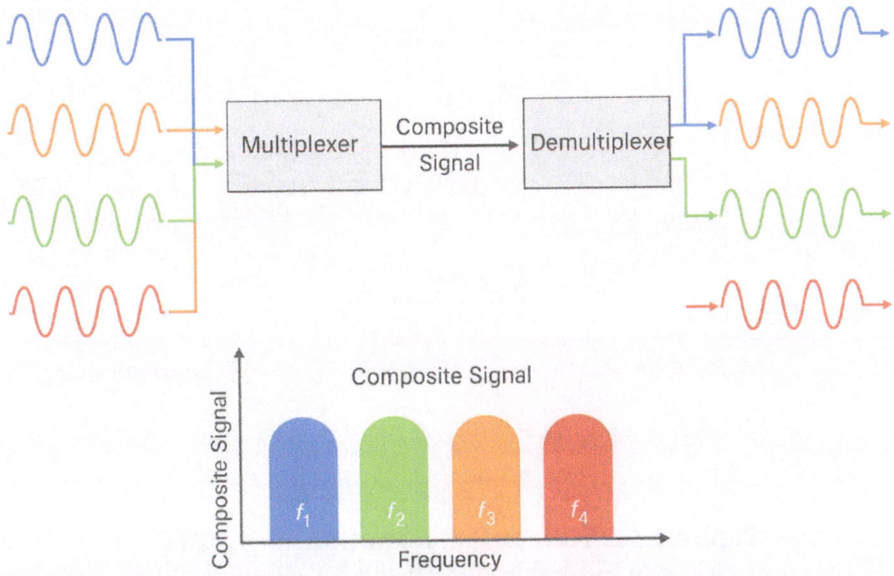

Figure 2.10: Frequency Division Multiplexing (FDM)

The Figure 2.10 visually explains Frequency Division Multiplexing (FDM) by showing multiple signals—each occupying a unique frequency band—being combined through a multiplexer into a single composite signal for transmission over a shared medium. At the receiving end, a demultiplexer separates the signals based on their assigned frequencies. This illustrates how FDM enables simultaneous transmission of multiple signals without interference, making efficient use of bandwidth in applications like cable TV and radio broadcasting.

b. Time Division Multiplexing (TDM)

Time Division Multiplexing (TDM) shares a single communication channel among multiple users by dividing time into equal slots. Each user is allocated a unique time slot for transmission in a round-robin fashion. During its time slot, a user sends data, and the next user transmits in the subsequent slot. This continues cyclically and rapidly enough that users perceive continuous service.

There are two types:

- Synchronous TDM assigns fixed time slots regardless of whether the user has data to send, which can lead to wastage if slots are unused.
- Asynchronous (or Statistical) TDM dynamically assigns slots based on demand, improving efficiency under variable traffic loads.

TDM is commonly used in digital telephony (e.g., T1, E1 lines) and SONET (Synchronous Optical Network) systems. It's effective in environments with predictable, regular traffic, but may underutilize bandwidth when demand is inconsistent.

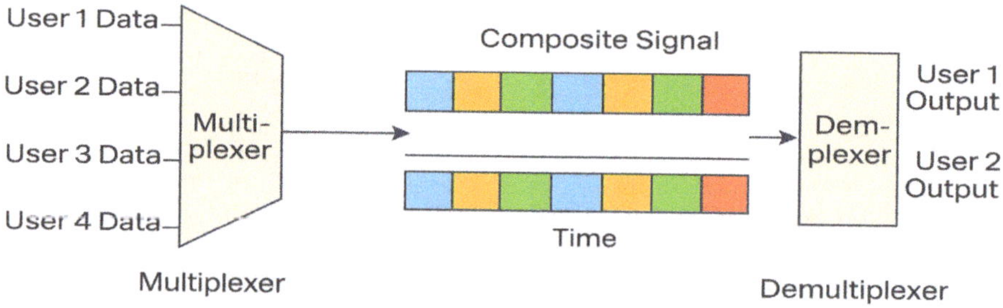

Figure 2.11: Time Division Multiplexing (TDM)

The Figure 2.11 illustrates TDM by showing how multiple data streams (User 1–4) are combined sequentially into time slots through a multiplexer, creating a composite signal. The time slots are transmitted in a repeating cycle, ensuring each user's data is sent in its assigned slot. At the destination, a demultiplexer splits the signal back into the original user data streams. This clearly shows how TDM shares a single channel efficiently by dividing time, enabling multiple users to transmit over one medium in an organized sequence.

c. Wavelength Division Multiplexing (WDM)

Wavelength Division Multiplexing (WDM) is a technique used in fiber optic communication, where multiple data streams are transmitted simultaneously over the same fiber using different wavelengths (colors) of light. Each wavelength acts as an independent communication channel, allowing extremely high data throughput without additional fibers.

WDM systems come in two forms:

- CWDM (Coarse WDM) uses wider spacing between wavelengths (fewer channels, lower cost).
- DWDM (Dense WDM) uses tighter spacing (more channels, higher capacity).

WDM is extensively used in optical backbone networks to support the exploding demand for Internet bandwidth. It supports data rates in the hundreds of gigabits per second, making it ideal for long-distance communication. However, it requires highly precise and expensive optical components, including lasers and multiplexers/demultiplexers.

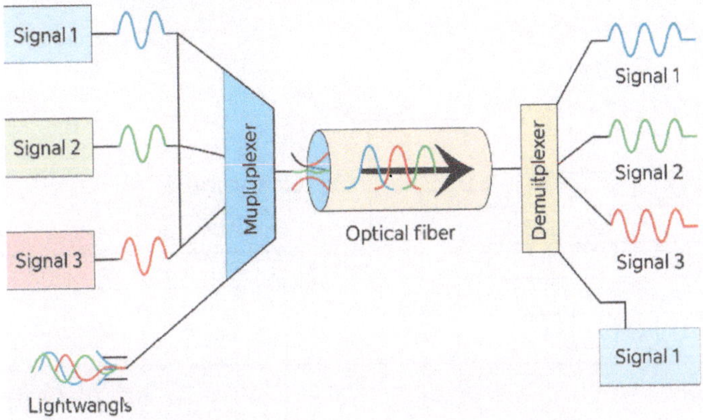

Figure 2.12: Wavelength Division Multiplexing (WDM)

The Figure 2.12illustrates how WDM combines multiple signals, each modulated on a unique wavelength (or color of light), into a single optical fiber using a multiplexer. Inside the fiber, all wavelengths travel simultaneously without interfering with each other. At the destination, a demultiplexer separates them back into their individual signals. This demonstrates how WDM maximizes bandwidth and supports high-capacity, long-distance transmission in fiber-optic networks.

d. Code Division Multiplexing (CDM)

Code Division Multiplexing (CDM), or Code Division Multiple Access (CDMA), allows multiple signals to share the same transmission channel by assigning each user a unique code. All users transmit simultaneously over the entire bandwidth, but the receiver uses the code to extract the intended signal while treating other signals as noise. CDM is robust against interference, supports secure transmission, and provides graceful degradation in performance under high traffic loads. It is used in mobile cellular networks (CDMA 2000, 3G), GPS, and satellite communication systems. The primary challenge with CDM lies in the complex signal processing required for encoding, decoding, and managing synchronization. Nevertheless, its ability to support many simultaneous users with good spectral efficiency makes it a powerful multiplexing strategy in wireless and spread-spectrum systems.

The Figure 2.13illustrates how CDM allows multiple users to transmit data over a shared channel simultaneously by assigning each user a unique spreading code. Each user's data is multiplied with their code sequence, and all encoded signals are added together to form a composite signal. At the receiver end, the signal is decoded using the intended user's code, allowing the correct data to be extracted while treating other users' signals as noise. This diagram demonstrates CDM's ability to support secure, robust, and concurrent communication across shared bandwidth.

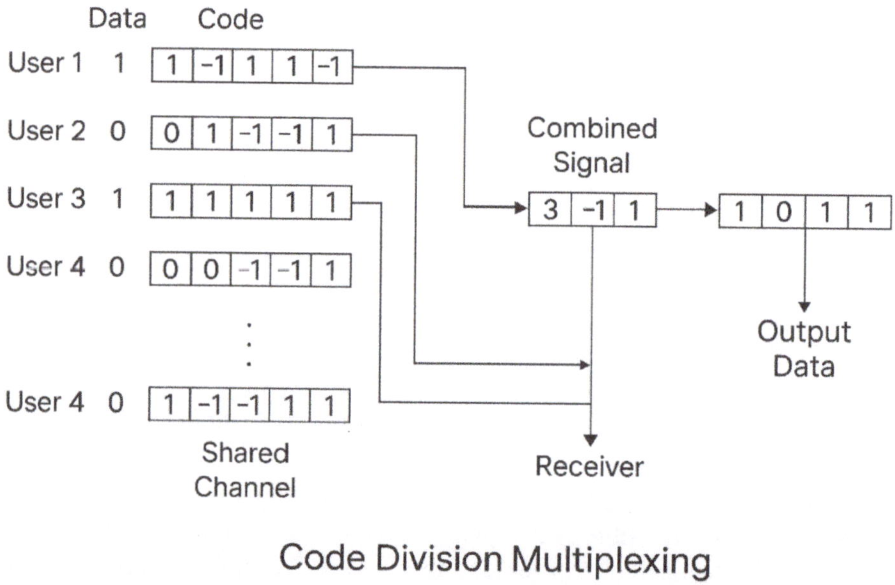

Figure 2.13: Code Division Multiplexing (CDM)

Conclusion

In this chapter, we explored the foundational aspects of the Physical Layer in computer networks, which is responsible for the transmission of raw bits over physical media. Starting with network topology design, we understood how the arrangement of devices—such as in bus, star, ring, mesh, tree, and hybrid topologies—affects performance, fault tolerance, and scalability. We also examined types of connections, including point-to-point and multipoint links, and communication modes like simplex, half-duplex, and full-duplex. Furthermore, the chapter detailed the transmission media, including guided (twisted pair, coaxial, fiber optic) and unguided (radio, microwave, infrared) types, highlighting their characteristics, applications, and limitations. We then delved into signal transmission and encoding, explaining how binary data is transformed into transmittable signals using various encoding techniques. The chapter also addressed critical aspects of network performance—such as bandwidth, throughput, latency, jitter, and error rate—as well as transmission impairments like attenuation, noise, and distortion. Lastly, we explored switching techniques (circuit, packet, and message switching) and multiplexing methods

(FDM, TDM, WDM, CDM), which enable efficient data transfer and channel sharing. Together, these topics provide a comprehensive understanding of how the physical infrastructure and signal mechanics underpin the operation of modern digital communication systems.

Exercise Questions

- Define the Physical Layer and explain its primary functions in the OSI model.
- Compare and contrast bus, star, and mesh topologies with suitable diagrams.
- Differentiate between point-to-point and multipoint connections with examples.
- Explain the differences between simplex, half-duplex, and full-duplex transmission modes.
- Describe the types of guided and unguided transmission media, along with their advantages.
- What is attenuation? How can it be mitigated in long-distance networks?
- Compare NRZ and Manchester encoding with diagrams. What are their key differences?
- Explain the differences between circuit switching, packet switching, and message switching.
- Discuss the advantages and disadvantages of FDM, TDM, and CDM.
- What are the major transmission impairments in a network? How do they affect performance?

CHAPTER

3

LINK LAYER

Chapter 3 delves into the Link Layer, the second layer in the OSI model, which plays a vital role in enabling reliable communication between directly connected nodes. This layer is responsible for framing data, detecting and correcting errors, and managing flow control between devices on the same local network. It acts as a bridge between the physical transmission of bits and the higher-layer protocols, ensuring that data is structured correctly and transmitted reliably over the physical medium. The chapter begins by explaining framing techniques that delineate where data frames start and end, followed by methods of error detection and correction, such as parity checks, checksums, and cyclic redundancy checks (CRC). It also covers flow control protocols like the Elementary Data Link Protocols and the Sliding Window Protocol, which regulate data transmission rates to prevent overflow. The latter part of the chapter focuses on Medium Access Control (MAC) in Local Area Networks (LANs), including channel allocation, multiple access protocols (like ALOHA and CSMA), and widely adopted LAN standards such as Ethernet and Wi-Fi. Finally, the chapter introduces link layer switches and bridges, explaining how devices use learning algorithms and spanning tree protocols to manage traffic and prevent loops within a network. Together, these topics provide a comprehensive understanding of how the link layer ensures efficient, organized, and reliable communication at the local network level.

Framing

Framing is a crucial function of the Link Layer in the OSI model that involves dividing the stream of bits received from the Network Layer into manageable data units called frames. These frames are the basic units of data transmission at the link level, and they encapsulate both data and control information (such as addressing, error detection, and synchronization bits) needed for proper delivery.

Framing serves several essential purposes:

- Data segmentation: It enables the segmentation of data into structured blocks so that the receiving end can process, verify, and acknowledge them effectively.

- Synchronization: Frames allow the receiver to identify the start and end of each data unit, which is especially important in serial communication where data flows continuously.
- Error control: Frames include mechanisms (like checksums or CRC) to detect errors during transmission.
- Addressing: Each frame may contain source and destination MAC addresses to identify communicating devices on the network.

Framing Techniques

There are several techniques for marking frame boundaries:

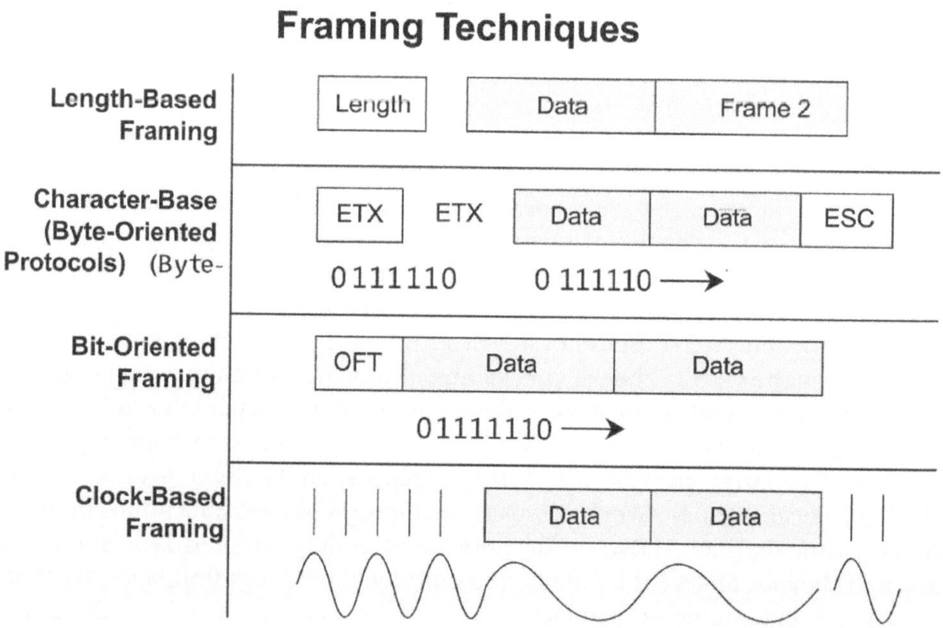

Figure 3.1: Comparative View of Four Framing Techniques

The Figure 3.1 presents a comparative view of four key framing techniques: length-based, character-based, bit-oriented, and clock-based. It shows how each method marks frame boundaries—using a length field, special control characters (STX/ETX), a unique bit pattern (01111110), or timing synchronization, respectively. It also illustrates associated mechanisms like character stuffing and bit stuffing to handle control data appearing within the payload. This visual helps clarify how different approaches ensure reliable and distinct separation of frames in data transmission across networks.

1. Length-Based Framing

Length-based framing uses a header field to specify the exact length of the frame. This allows the receiver to know how many bytes to expect, thus enabling it to correctly identify the end of the frame without needing special delimiter characters. This approach is efficient and straightforward, as it minimizes framing overhead and works well in structured data environments. The primary advantage of length-based framing is its simplicity and low overhead. By including just a length field in the header, it avoids the need for character or bit-level stuffing and allows high data throughput. It's commonly used in high-speed network protocols where overhead minimization is essential. However, the method is highly vulnerable to errors. If the length field itself becomes corrupted during transmission, the receiver might misinterpret the frame's boundary, leading to frame misalignment or data corruption. This can cause synchronization issues or cascading errors in subsequent frames. Therefore, it's often combined with error detection mechanisms like checksums or CRCs to ensure reliability. Due to its limitations, length-based framing is typically used in controlled environments where data integrity is highly reliable or additional error-checking layers are present—such as in fiber-optic networks or internal bus systems.

2. Character-Based Framing (Byte-Oriented Protocols)

Character-based framing, also known as byte-oriented framing, marks the start and end of frames using special characters. For example, protocols may use STX (Start of Text) to indicate the beginning of a frame and ETX (End of Text) to indicate its conclusion. This method is easy to implement and human-readable, making it popular in early communication protocols like RS-232 and ASCII-based systems. A challenge arises when the data itself contains these special control characters. For instance, if the data includes an ETX byte, the receiver might mistakenly interpret it as the end of the frame. To solve this, an escape character (ESC) is introduced. Whenever a control character appears in the data, it is "escaped" by preceding it with an ESC byte, a process known as character stuffing. While effective in many scenarios, character-based framing introduces processing overhead, particularly when control characters frequently appear in data. Each escape character adds an extra byte, increasing transmission time and reducing efficiency. Moreover, it's limited to 8-bit character systems, making it less suitable for binary or multimedia data streams that don't align with character boundaries. Despite its limitations, this technique remains useful in serial communication, modem protocols, and simple embedded systems where human-readable framing and straightforward implementation are more valuable than speed or efficiency.

3. Bit-Oriented Framing

Bit-oriented framing represents data frames using a specific bit pattern, often called a flag sequence. A common example is the High-Level Data Link Control (HDLC) protocol, which uses the 8-bit flag 01111110 to mark both the beginning and end of a frame. This technique allows the transmission of binary data without relying on character interpretation, making it highly flexible. To avoid misinterpreting a flag within the payload, bit stuffing is used. During transmission, if five consecutive 1s appear in the data, a 0 is automatically inserted after them. The receiver, knowing this rule, removes the extra 0s to reconstruct the original data correctly. This ensures the flag sequence only appears where intended and prevents false frame boundaries.

Bit-oriented framing is more efficient and robust than character-based framing, especially in environments dealing with binary or multimedia data. It enables seamless data encapsulation and is adaptable to any bitstream, regardless of byte alignment or character sets. This makes it suitable for protocols requiring high data integrity and flexibility, such as PPP, HDLC, and ISDN. However, the method requires more complex logic for bit insertion and removal and may slightly increase bandwidth usage due to bit stuffing. Still, its ability to support diverse data formats and prevent ambiguity in frame delimitation makes it a preferred choice in modern digital communication systems.

4. Clock-Based Framing

Clock-based framing, also known as synchronous framing, does not use explicit frame delimiters. Instead, it relies on timing synchronization between the sender and receiver. Frames are identified by a fixed, periodic timing signal that aligns both ends of the communication, allowing them to recognize when a new frame begins. This method is most often found in synchronous transmission systems like SONET (Synchronous Optical Network) or T1 lines.The core benefit of clock-based framing is its low overhead—since it doesn't require special flags or length fields within the data stream, it maximizes bandwidth usage. It is particularly effective in environments where high-speed, continuous data transmission is critical, such as in fiber-optic backbone systems and carrier-grade telecommunications. However, the system is highly dependent on precise synchronization. Any drift between the sender and receiver clocks can cause frame misalignment, leading to data loss or corruption. To mitigate this, clock recovery circuits and synchronization protocols are used to keep devices aligned. Clock-based framing is best suited for fixed-length frames and real-time systems where the timing consistency of data transmission is more critical than flexibility. It excels in deterministic, high-throughput environments where frame boundaries can be predicted based on time rather than markers.

Framing Process

The framing process involves encapsulating data from the Network Layer into a structured unit called a frame, which can be reliably transmitted over the physical medium. A frame typically consists of three main parts: a header, a payload, and a trailer. This structure ensures that the receiving device can interpret the beginning and end of the frame, process its contents, and verify its integrity. The header is the first part of the frame and contains critical control information, including source and destination MAC addresses, frame type, and possibly sequence numbers or priority flags. This information is essential for routing the frame to the correct device on the local network and managing communication protocols. The header may also include information related to flow control or QoS (Quality of Service), depending on the protocol used.

The payload is the central portion of the frame and carries the actual data segment passed down from the Network Layer. It may contain application data, a segment of an IP packet, or other protocol information. The size of the payload is often limited by the maximum transmission unit (MTU) of the link layer technology (e.g., 1500 bytes for Ethernet).Finally, the trailer is appended to the end of the frame and typically includes error-detection codes, such as a Cyclic Redundancy Check (CRC). The receiver uses this to verify the integrity of the received frame. If the CRC value does not match, the frame is considered corrupted and is discarded or a retransmission is requested.

Error Detection and Correction

In data communication, errors can occur due to noise, signal distortion, interference, or hardware malfunctions. These errors can result in bit-level corruption—where a 0 becomes a 1 or vice versa—during transmission. To ensure data integrity, networks employ error detection and correction techniques at the Data Link Layer. These techniques are essential for detecting corrupted frames and, in some cases, correcting them without retransmission.

The Figure 3.2 illustrates various error detection and correction techniques in data communication. It shows how a data frame is transmitted with added redundancy bits, such as a parity bit, checksum, or CRC, and highlights how these methods help the receiver detect errors during transmission. For error correction, the diagram visualizes how techniques like Hamming Code and Forward Error Correction (FEC) can not only detect but also correct corrupted bits without the need for retransmission. The figure also contrasts ARQ protocols, where errors are detected using CRC or checksums, prompting the receiver to request a retransmission (depicted via ACK/NAK signals). By visually mapping how each method processes or recovers from transmission errors, the figure clearly differentiates between error detection-only methods and those capable of both detection and correction, aiding in the understanding of their respective roles in reliable communication.

1. Parity Checking

Parity checking is one of the simplest error detection methods. It involves adding a parity bit to a data unit (such as a byte) to make the total number of 1s either even (even parity) or odd (odd parity). This bit is recalculated and verified at the receiver's end. If the parity doesn't match the expected value, an error is assumed. While easy to implement and requiring minimal processing, parity checking can only detect single-bit errors. It is not capable of detecting errors where an even number of bits are flipped, nor can it correct errors. This method is mostly used in low-complexity systems like serial communication and some memory modules.

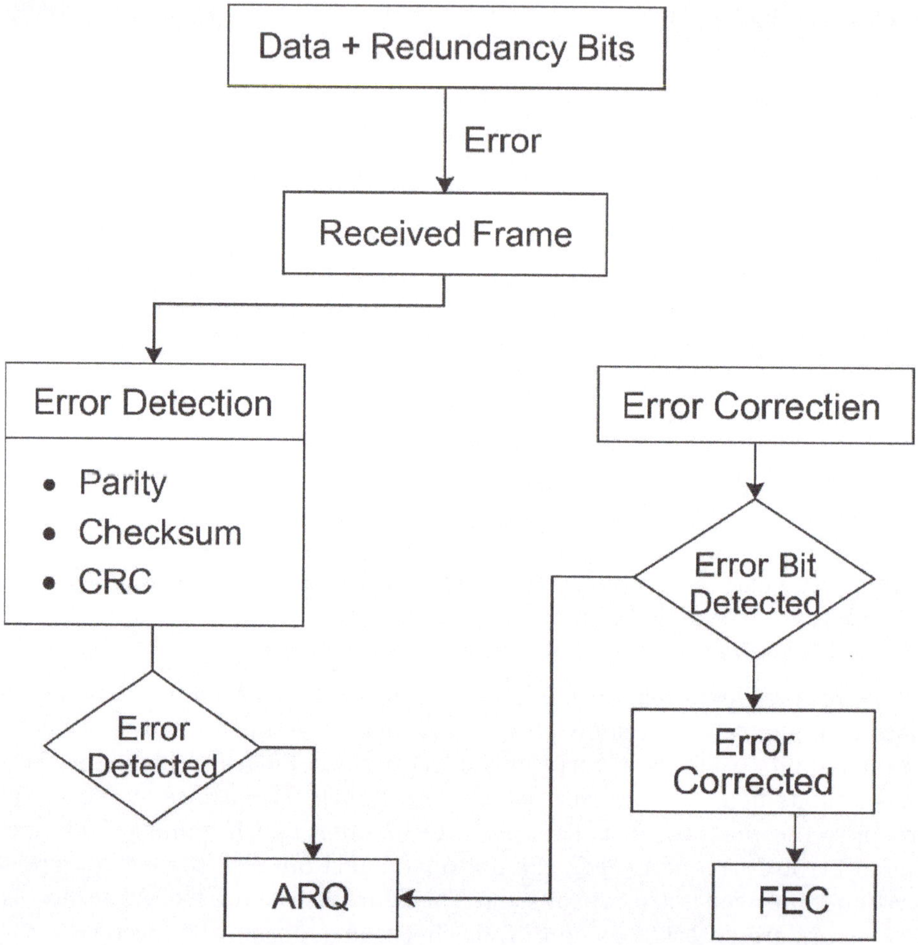

Figure 3.2: Error Detection and Correction Techniques

2. Checksum

A checksum is a simple method used to detect errors in a data block. It involves dividing the message into equal-sized segments, summing the values using binary addition, and transmitting the sum (checksum) alongside the data. At the receiving end, the data is again summed and compared with the received checksum. This technique is effective in detecting common transmission errors, especially accidental alterations such as those due to noise or hardware glitches. Checksum is used in many Internet protocols including IP, UDP, and TCP, where it provides a balance of performance and reasonable reliability. However, it is less powerful than CRC in detecting complex error patterns.

3. Cyclic Redundancy Check (CRC)

CRC is a robust error detection method based on polynomial division. The sender performs a modulo-2 division of the data by a predetermined generator polynomial, and appends the remainder (called the CRC bits) to the message. The receiver performs the same division and checks whether the result is zero to confirm integrity. CRC is highly effective at detecting burst errors and multiple bit errors. It is widely adopted in Ethernet, HDLC, storage devices, and digital networks. Though it does not correct errors, its high detection accuracy ensures that corrupted data is not accepted by the receiver. The efficiency of CRC depends on the generator polynomial used.

4. Hamming Code

Hamming Code is a forward error correction technique that adds multiple parity bits to a data word. These bits are positioned at power-of-two locations and calculated based on a set of data bits. Upon receiving the message, the receiver uses these parity bits to calculate a syndrome, which identifies the exact bit position of any single-bit error. The receiver can then flip the erroneous bit to correct the message. Hamming codes are efficient for detecting and correcting single-bit errors, and can detect but not correct two-bit errors. They are commonly used in RAM, communication satellites, and microcontrollers, where immediate correction without retransmission is needed.

5. Forward Error Correction (FEC)

FEC techniques allow the receiver to correct errors without retransmission. This is done by adding redundant data in a mathematically structured way (using codes like Reed-Solomon, Convolutional codes, or Turbo codes). These methods allow for correction of multiple bit errors based on statistical models and coding theory. FEC is particularly useful in real-time communication systems where retransmissions introduce unacceptable delay—such as satellite links, video streaming, and VoIP. While FEC increases processing overhead and bandwidth usage, it ensures continuous data delivery in challenging or latency-sensitive environments.

6. Automatic Repeat Request (ARQ)

ARQ is an error control protocol that relies on error detection and retransmission. The sender keeps a copy of the sent frame and waits for an acknowledgment (ACK). If the frame is received correctly, an ACK is returned. If a negative acknowledgment (NAK) or timeout occurs, the sender retransmits the frame.

Variants of ARQ include:

- Stop-and-Wait ARQ
- Go-Back-N ARQ
- Selective Repeat ARQ

ARQ is widely used in TCP/IP networks and wireless communication. Though it doesn't correct errors directly, it ensures reliable delivery through retransmission and is effective in environments where bandwidth is not highly constrained.

Flow control (Elementary Data Link Protocols, Sliding Window protocols)

Flow control is a technique used at the Data Link Layer to regulate the rate of data transmission between a sender and a receiver. It ensures that the sender does not overwhelm the receiver by sending data faster than it can process. Without flow control, high-speed senders might cause buffer overflow at slower receivers, resulting in data loss or corruption.

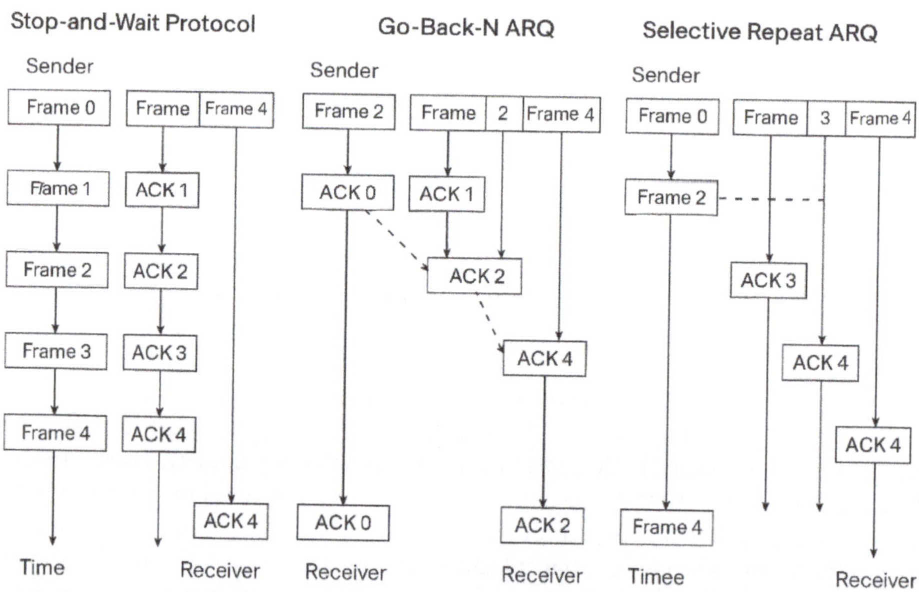

Figure 3.3: Flow Control Techniques

The Figure 3.3 illustrates three flow control techniques: Stop-and-Wait, Go-Back-N, and Selective Repeat. In Stop-and-Wait, the sender transmits one frame and waits for an acknowledgment before proceeding, leading to idle time between frames. In Go-Back-N, multiple frames are sent before waiting for an acknowledgment, but if a frame is lost, the sender retransmits that frame and all subsequent ones. Selective Repeat improves efficiency by allowing the receiver to accept out-of-order frames and only requests retransmission of the specific erroneous frame, reducing redundancy and optimizing bandwidth usage.

1. Elementary Data Link Protocols

a. Stop-and-Wait Protocol

The Stop-and-Wait protocol is the simplest flow control method used in data communication. In this approach, the sender transmits one frame and then waits for an acknowledgment (ACK) from the receiver before sending the next frame. This ensures that data is transmitted reliably and at a rate the receiver can handle. This protocol is easy to implement and guarantees no data loss in ideal, error-free environments. It works effectively in low-latency and low-bandwidth scenarios, such as simple serial communication, where overhead is minimal and traffic volume is low. However, it is inherently inefficient in high-latency or high-bandwidth networks. Because the sender must wait after every transmission, the communication channel remains idle during acknowledgment delays. This reduces overall throughput, especially in long-distance links like satellite communication. Moreover, if the acknowledgment is delayed or lost, the sender remains idle for longer than necessary, further degrading performance. To resolve this limitation, enhanced protocols with timeout and retransmission mechanisms (like ARQ) are used in real-world scenarios.

b. Stop-and-Wait with Error Control (ARQ)

Stop-and-Wait ARQ (Automatic Repeat reQuest) builds on the basic Stop-and-Wait protocol by introducing error detection (e.g., using checksums or CRC) and timeout-based retransmission. After sending a frame, the sender starts a timer and waits for an ACK. If an acknowledgment is not received before the timer expires, the frame is retransmitted. This enhancement allows the protocol to function in unreliable or noisy communication environments, where frames or ACKs may be lost or corrupted. It improves reliability by ensuring that every frame is either acknowledged or resent. However, this protocol still suffers from low efficiency due to the idle wait time between transmissions, especially over links with high propagation delays. Additionally, retransmitting entire frames can waste bandwidth if only ACKs are lost or delayed. Stop-and-Wait ARQ is primarily used in simple or low-bandwidth systems, such as early dial-up modems, where simplicity outweighs throughput requirements.

2. Sliding Window Protocols

a. Go-Back-N ARQ

The Go-Back-N protocol allows the sender to transmit multiple frames (up to N) consecutively without waiting for individual acknowledgments. These frames are stored in a buffer called the sending window, which slides forward as ACKs are received. If a frame is found to be lost or corrupted, the receiver discards it and all subsequent frames, regardless of their correctness. The sender, upon timeout or receiving a NAK, must retransmit the lost frame and all that followed, hence the name "go back N."This protocol improves utilization of the communication channel compared to Stop-and-Wait, especially over long-delay networks. However, its primary drawback is inefficiency during error conditions. If a single frame is lost, retransmitting all subsequent frames—even if they were received correctly—can waste bandwidth. Despite this limitation, Go-Back-N is widely used in protocols like HDLC and early versions of TCP, where moderate efficiency and low complexity are desired.

b. Selective Repeat ARQ

Selective Repeat ARQ enhances the Go-Back-N model by allowing the receiver to accept and buffer out-of-order frames. It sends individual acknowledgments for each frame, and if a frame is found to be missing or corrupt, only that specific frame is retransmitted. The sender maintains a window of sent but unacknowledged frames, and the receiver maintains a window of expected frames, including the ability to store those received out-of-sequence. This reduces the number of retransmissions and significantly improves bandwidth efficiency, especially in high-error or long-delay environments. Selective Repeat is more complex to implement because it requires both sender and receiver to manage buffers for out-of-order frames, track sequence numbers, and handle individual acknowledgments. However, this complexity is justified in environments where link bandwidth is precious or latency is high, such as wireless networks and satellite communication. Its precision in error handling makes Selective Repeat suitable for modern, high-throughput systems, and it forms the foundation of advanced protocols like TCP with selective acknowledgment (SACK).

Medium Access Control and Local Area Networks

In computer networks, particularly Local Area Networks (LANs), the Medium Access Control (MAC) sublayer of the Data Link Layer governs how multiple devices share a common transmission medium without collisions or data loss. Since LANs are often built over broadcast channels (such as Ethernet or wireless), it's crucial to manage who gets to transmit, when, and how—which is the primary function of MAC.

1. Channel Allocation Problem

In a shared medium, such as Ethernet or Wi-Fi, channel allocation determines how multiple devices access the medium fairly and efficiently. There are two main approaches:

- Static Allocation: Pre-assigns time slots or frequency bands (like in TDM or FDM). It's efficient when traffic is predictable but leads to wasted resources if devices are idle.
- Dynamic Allocation: Devices contend for the medium as needed. This is more flexible and responsive to varying network loads, commonly used in LANs.

2. Multiple Access Protocols

Multiple access protocols define the rules that devices follow when trying to transmit data on a shared channel. They are typically classified as follows:

a. Random Access Protocols

ALOHA: Devices transmit at will; if a collision occurs, they retransmit after a random delay. Variants include Pure ALOHA and Slotted ALOHA.

- Carrier Sense Multiple Access (CSMA): Devices listen (sense) before transmitting.
- CSMA/CD (Collision Detection): Used in wired Ethernet. Devices stop transmitting when a collision is detected and retry later.
- CSMA/CA (Collision Avoidance): Used in Wi-Fi. Devices avoid collisions by using random backoff and acknowledgments.

b. Controlled Access Protocols

- Polling: A central controller asks each device in turn whether it wants to transmit.
- Token Passing: A special token circulates; only the device holding the token may transmit. Used in Token Ring networks.

c. Channelization Protocols

Based on dividing the channel into time slots (TDM), frequency bands (FDM), or codes (CDM), allowing multiple users to transmit simultaneously.

3. LAN Standards

The most common LAN technologies include:

- Ethernet (IEEE 802.3): Based on CSMA/CD. Supports data rates from 10 Mbps to 400 Gbps. Operates in star topology using switches.
- Wi-Fi (IEEE 802.11): Based on CSMA/CA. Used in wireless LANs. Includes standards like 802.11n/ac/ax.
- Token Ring (IEEE 802.5): Uses a token-passing protocol. Rare today but important historically.
- Bluetooth (IEEE 802.15): Used for personal area networks (PANs), with a form of polling access.

4. Link Layer Switches and Bridges

Switches and bridges are hardware devices operating at the Data Link Layer that forward frames based on MAC addresses (Table 3.1). They reduce collision domains and improve LAN performance.

- Learning Bridge: Automatically builds a MAC address table by observing traffic, then forwards frames only to the appropriate segment.
- Spanning Tree Protocol (STP): Prevents loops in bridged networks by selectively disabling redundant links, ensuring a loop-free topology.

The table compares various MAC protocols used in LANs based on their access type, usage environment, collision handling method, and efficiency. It highlights how random access methods like CSMA/CD are used in Ethernet, while controlled access and channelization offer better collision avoidance in structured or wireless networks.

Table 3.1: Comparison of MAC Protocols in LANs

Protocol	Type	Used In	Collision Handling	Efficiency
ALOHA	Random Access	Satellite networks	Retransmit after delay	Low (18–36%)
CSMA/CD	Random Access	Ethernet (wired)	Detect and abort	Moderate
CSMA/CA	Random Access	Wi-Fi (wireless)	Avoid before transmit	High in wireless
Polling	Controlled Access	Bluetooth, legacy LANs	No collision	High (centralized)
Token Passing	Controlled Access	Token Ring	No collision	Efficient, reliable
TDM/FDM/CDM	Channelization	Wired/ Wireless LANs	No collision	Depends on usage

Channel Allocation

Channel allocation is the process of determining how multiple users or devices in a network share access to a common communication medium. In environments like LANs, wireless networks, or satellite links, where bandwidth is shared among many users, efficient channel allocation is essential to prevent collisions, delays, and bandwidth wastage. It forms the backbone of Medium Access Control (MAC) in the Data Link Layer.

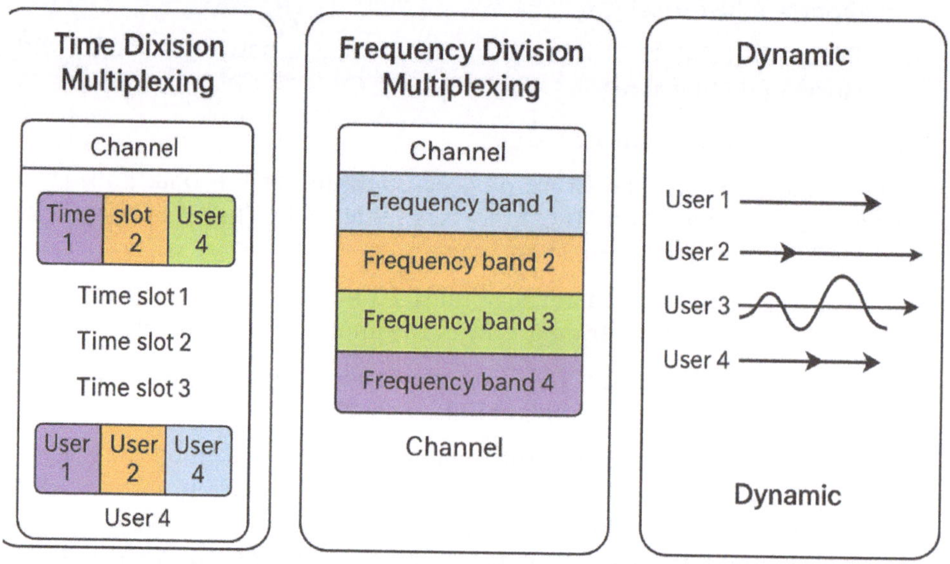

Figure 3.4: Three Primary Channel Allocation Techniques

The Figure 3.4illustrates three primary channel allocation techniques: Time Division Multiplexing (TDM), Frequency Division Multiplexing (FDM), and Dynamic Access (e.g., CSMA). In TDM, the shared channel is divided into sequential time slots, each assigned to a specific user. This ensures orderly, collision-free communication but can lead to wasted slots if a user has no data to send. In contrast, FDM allocates unique frequency bands to each user, allowing simultaneous transmissions across different frequencies—commonly seen in radio and cable systems. The dynamic access section shows multiple users contending for a shared channel using protocols like CSMA, where devices sense the medium before transmitting. If the channel is busy, they wait and retry, helping avoid collisions. Unlike fixed allocation, this method adapts to real-time traffic but introduces the possibility of delays and retransmissions under high load. Together, the diagram contrasts the efficiency, coordination method, and collision handling of each approach in shared network environments.

1. Fixed Allocation Methods

In fixed channel allocation, each user is assigned a dedicated portion of the channel—whether in time, frequency, or code. This technique ensures that users do not interfere with each other since the allocation is predetermined. It is ideal for systems with predictable, uniform traffic where resource requirements are constant. Examples include traditional TDM in telephone networks and FDM in cable TV systems. Time Division Multiplexing (TDM) divides the channel into time slots, and each device transmits only during its slot. This avoids collisions but can lead to inefficiency if a user has no data to send during their turn. Frequency Division Multiplexing (FDM) assigns each user a specific frequency range; this is common in radio broadcasting. Code Division Multiplexing (CDM), used in some wireless systems, gives each user a unique spreading code to share the same frequency band simultaneously.

Fixed methods offer low complexity, predictability, and no contention. However, the major drawback is waste of bandwidth—when assigned users are idle, their portions of the channel remain unused. This rigidness makes fixed allocation less suitable for modern data networks, where traffic is often bursty or varies over time. Thus, fixed allocation methods are best suited to environments with constant communication demands, such as synchronous digital circuits or structured telecommunication links.

2. Dynamic Allocation Methods

Unlike fixed allocation, dynamic channel allocation assigns channel resources as needed, allowing devices to contend for the medium. This approach is more adaptive and efficient, especially in systems where traffic is irregular or sporadic, such as computer LANs and wireless networks. It forms the basis for many random access protocols like ALOHA, CSMA, and token-based methods. In ALOHA, devices transmit freely and wait for acknowledgments. If a collision occurs, they wait a random amount of time before retransmitting. Slotted ALOHA improves on this by dividing time into slots and allowing transmissions only at slot boundaries, reducing collision probability. CSMA (Carrier Sense Multiple Access) introduces a "listen-before-talk" strategy, where a device checks if the medium is free before transmitting. Dynamic allocation ensures better resource utilization and scalability, as idle users don't waste bandwidth. However, under high load, contention-based methods can result in collisions, delays, and retransmissions, decreasing overall performance. Therefore, dynamic methods often include backoff algorithms, priority scheduling, or acknowledgments to manage contention. Such methods are extensively used in Ethernet (CSMA/CD) and Wi-Fi (CSMA/CA), where devices operate independently and share the same communication channel based on demand.

3. Centralized vs. Distributed Allocation

In centralized channel allocation, a single controller (like a server or master node) manages which device can use the channel and when. This approach is efficient and fair, ensuring that no device monopolizes resources. It works well in small networks or systems where a central authority (e.g., a Wi-Fi access point or Bluetooth master) can monitor and schedule usage. The benefits include predictable performance, easy management, and simplified synchronization. However, centralized systems suffer from scalability issues and are prone to single points of failure. If the controller crashes or is overloaded, the entire network may halt.

In contrast, distributed allocation allows devices to make independent decisions about channel access, often using contention-based protocols like CSMA or token passing. These systems are more scalable and resilient, especially in decentralized networks like ad hoc wireless systems or mesh networks. The trade-off with distributed allocation is complex coordination, as devices must detect collisions, manage timing, and handle retransmissions independently. Despite this, distributed models are favored in large, dynamic networks where devices frequently join or leave.

4. Channel Allocation in Wired vs. Wireless LANs

Wired LANs, such as Ethernet, rely on physical cabling where all connected devices share the same medium. To manage access, they use CSMA/CD (Collision Detection)—devices check if the cable is in use, transmit if it's free, and listen for collisions during transmission. If a collision occurs, devices stop and retry after a random delay. In contrast, wireless LANs face more complexity due to the inability to detect collisions easily. Hence, Wi-Fi (IEEE 802.11) uses CSMA/CA (Collision Avoidance). Devices use techniques like Request-to-Send/Clear-to-Send (RTS/CTS), acknowledgment packets, and random backoff times to reduce collision likelihood. Additionally, wireless networks can use multiple channels (frequencies) to reduce interference and increase overall throughput. Access points may switch clients to less congested channels, or use frequency hopping techniques. These differences highlight how the physical characteristics of the medium influence the choice of allocation strategies. While Ethernet can rely on clear collision signals, Wi-Fi must use proactive avoidance to maintain performance.

5. Trade-offs and Performance

Choosing a channel allocation method involves balancing efficiency, complexity, fairness, and delay. Fixed allocation offers high predictability and low collision but suffers from poor bandwidth usage when traffic is variable. Dynamic allocation is more flexible but may introduce collisions and overhead due to retransmission or contention handling. Centralized systems simplify control and guarantee fair access but don't scale well. Distributed systems scale effectively and handle dynamic changes gracefully but require robust coordination mechanisms. In practice, modern networks often employ hybrid approaches. For example, Wi-Fi uses distributed CSMA/CA with optional centralized coordination via access points. Cellular systems use frequency reuse with dynamic scheduling to combine the best of both worlds. Performance tuning involves adjusting parameters like slot size, backoff intervals, or channel width, based on the specific network environment and application demands.

Multiple Access Protocols

Multiple Access Protocols are crucial in networks where multiple devices share the same communication medium, such as in Ethernet or wireless LANs. These protocols define rules for how devices access the medium and coordinate transmissions to avoid data collisions and ensure fair usage. They are primarily categorized into three classes: Random Access, Controlled Access, and Channelization Protocols.

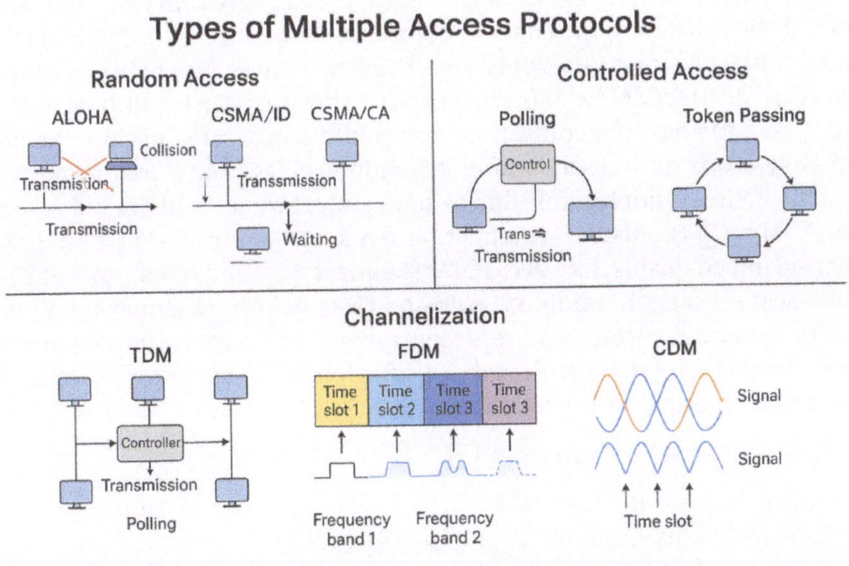

Figure 3.4: Multiple Access Protocols

The Figure 3.4visually categorizes multiple access protocols into three main types: Random Access, Controlled Access, and Channelization. In the Random Access section, it illustrates how devices transmit freely (e.g., in ALOHA or CSMA), with collisions and backoff depicted. The Controlled Access part shows structured methods like polling, where a central controller grants permission, and token passing, where a circulating token controls access. The Channelization section highlights how users share the medium using TDM (time slots), FDM (separate frequencies), and CDM (unique codes)—enabling simultaneous, collision-free communication. The diagram effectively contrasts their mechanisms and medium-sharing strategies.

1. Random Access Protocols

Random access protocols are designed for networks where multiple devices share the same communication medium without a central authority. In this approach, devices transmit data whenever they are ready, without prior coordination. While this simplicity allows for flexible and fast communication during light traffic, it also introduces the risk of collisions when two or more devices attempt to send data simultaneously. One of the earliest and simplest random access protocols is ALOHA, which allows devices to transmit data immediately. If a collision occurs, the affected devices wait for a random amount of time before retransmitting. The protocol exists in two forms: Pure ALOHA, which transmits at any time, and Slotted ALOHA, which improves efficiency by restricting transmissions to discrete time slots. Despite these improvements, the maximum efficiency remains relatively low—18% for Pure ALOHA and 36% for Slotted ALOHA—making it unsuitable for high-traffic environments.

To enhance performance, Carrier Sense Multiple Access (CSMA) was introduced. In CSMA, devices listen to the channel before transmitting. If the channel is busy, they wait until it becomes idle, which significantly reduces the chance of collisions compared to ALOHA. CSMA/CD (Collision Detection), used in traditional Ethernet, takes it a step further: if a collision is detected during transmission, the device immediately stops and resends after a random delay. For wireless networks, collision detection is not feasible due to signal interference and limited feedback. Instead, CSMA/CA (Collision Avoidance) is used, as seen in Wi-Fi (IEEE 802.11). It relies on mechanisms like RTS/CTS (Request to Send/Clear to Send) and random backoff timers to minimize collision risks before transmission. While all these random access protocols are decentralized and easy to implement, their efficiency tends to decrease with higher traffic loads due to increased chances of collisions and resulting retransmissions.

2. Controlled Access Protocols

In controlled access, devices take turns or require permission to transmit, ensuring no collisions. Common techniques include:

- Polling: A central controller asks each node in turn if it wants to transmit. It's efficient but centralized, often used in Bluetooth and legacy systems.

- Token Passing: A special frame (token) circulates in the network. A device can transmit only if it holds the token. Used in Token Ring networks and FDDI.

These protocols offer better determinism and fairness than random access but require more overhead and management, and are vulnerable to failure if the poller or token is lost.

3. Channelization Protocols

Channelization protocols enable multiple users to share a communication medium simultaneously and without collisions by dividing the channel based on time, frequency, or code. In Time Division Multiplexing (TDM), users are assigned fixed time slots in a repeating schedule, ensuring that only one user transmits at any given time. Frequency Division Multiplexing (FDM) allocates distinct frequency bands to each user, allowing them to transmit at the same time on separate frequencies. Code Division Multiplexing (CDM) assigns each user a unique spreading code that allows all users to transmit over the same channel simultaneously, with minimal interference, as used in CDMA mobile networks. These methods are inherently collision-free and provide predictable performance when the channel is fully utilized. However, their main drawback is inefficiency under low or bursty traffic conditions. If a user is idle, their allocated time slot or frequency remains unused, leading to wasted bandwidth. Channelization protocols are best suited for environments with consistent traffic demands, such as cellular networks, satellite communication, and fiber-optic systems, where maximizing throughput and maintaining separation between users is critical.

Random access protocols are best for low to moderate traffic and offer simple decentralized control, whereas controlled access protocols work better in deterministic or high-traffic networks where fairness is critical. Channelization protocols shine in environments where users have consistent and predictable usage patterns. In practical networks like Ethernet (CSMA/CD) and Wi-Fi (CSMA/CA), random access dominates due to its flexibility and scalability. However, features like collision avoidance and dynamic backoff are added to mitigate high-traffic inefficiencies.

LAN Standards

Local Area Networks (LANs) are designed to connect computers and devices within a limited geographical area such as homes, offices, campuses, or data centers. To ensure seamless communication and interoperability among devices from different manufacturers, LAN standards are established and maintained by various organizations like the IEEE (Institute of Electrical and Electronics Engineers). These standards define both physical and data link layer specifications, including data rates, media types, access methods, and addressing mechanisms.

1. IEEE 802.3 – Ethernet

Ethernet, defined under the IEEE 802.3 standard, is the most widely used LAN technology. It supports various physical media including twisted pair cables, fiber optics, and coaxial cable. Ethernet operates using CSMA/CD (Carrier Sense Multiple Access with Collision Detection) in its traditional form, although modern switched Ethernet eliminates collisions by creating point-to-point links.

Key Ethernet standards include:

- 10BASE-T: 10 Mbps over twisted pair
- 100BASE-TX (Fast Ethernet): 100 Mbps
- 1000BASE-T (Gigabit Ethernet): 1 Gbps
- 10GBASE-T / 40GBASE-T / 100GBASE-T: 10 to 100 Gbps for high-performance networks

Ethernet is favored for its simplicity, scalability, and cost-effectiveness, and is widely deployed in both small and large-scale enterprise networks.

2. IEEE 802.11 – Wireless LAN (Wi-Fi)

IEEE 802.11 defines standards for wireless LANs, commonly referred to as Wi-Fi. It enables wireless communication between devices using radio frequencies, allowing mobility and flexibility in networking.

Notable 802.11 variants include:

- 802.11b/g: Operate in the 2.4 GHz band, offering up to 54 Mbps.
- 802.11n: Introduced MIMO (multiple-input, multiple-output) and supports up to 600 Mbps.
- 802.11ac (Wi-Fi 5): Operates in 5 GHz band, supports Gbps speeds.
- 802.11ax (Wi-Fi 6): Enhances efficiency, speed, and capacity, ideal for dense environments.

Wi-Fi uses CSMA/CA (Collision Avoidance) instead of CSMA/CD due to the inability to detect collisions effectively over wireless media. It supports security protocols like WPA2 and WPA3 to ensure safe communication.

3. IEEE 802.5 – Token Ring (Obsolete)

Token Ring, defined in IEEE 802.5, was once a popular LAN standard, particularly in IBM environments. In this protocol, a token circulates around the network. A device must hold the token to transmit data, preventing collisions. Though Token Ring offered predictable access and better performance under heavy load, it has largely been replaced by Ethernet due to Ethernet's cost efficiency, higher speeds, and flexibility.

4. IEEE 802.15 – Bluetooth (PANs)

Though not traditionally classified as a LAN, Bluetooth, governed by IEEE 802.15, provides short-range wireless communication typically within 10 meters.

It is used in Personal Area Networks (PANs) for connecting peripherals like headphones, keyboards, and smartphones. Bluetooth uses a master-slave polling mechanism and frequency hopping to avoid interference. While not ideal for high-bandwidth applications, it is extremely effective for low-power, short-range communication.

5. Other Emerging LAN Standards

- IEEE 802.1Q: Defines VLAN tagging to allow logical segmentation within a LAN.
- IEEE 802.3bt (PoE++): Supports Power over Ethernet, enabling devices like IP cameras and access points to receive power and data over the same cable.
- IEEE 802.3bz: Supports 2.5GBASE-T and 5GBASE-T Ethernet over existing Cat5e/Cat6 cabling.

LAN standards ensure consistent, reliable, and interoperable communication across a variety of wired and wireless environments. IEEE 802.3 (Ethernet) remains the backbone of wired LANs, while IEEE 802.11 (Wi-Fi) dominates wireless networking. Though older standards like Token Ring are obsolete, modern LANs continue to evolve through higher speeds, wireless advancements, and intelligent power and VLAN management. These standards collectively support the scalability, mobility, and flexibility required in today's data-driven environments (Table 3.2).

Table 3.2: Summarizing the Major LAN Standards

Standard	Name/ Technology	Medium	Speed	Access Method	Typical Use
IEEE 802.3	Ethernet	Twisted pair, fiber	10 Mbps – 400 Gbps	CSMA/ CD (now switched)	Most common wired LAN
IEEE 802.11	Wi-Fi	Wireless (2.4/5 GHz)	Up to 10 Gbps (Wi-Fi 6)	CSMA/CA	Wireless LANs (homes, offices, public)
IEEE 802.5	Token Ring (obsolete)	Twisted pair	4 or 16 Mbps	Token Passing	Legacy IBM networks
IEEE 802.15	Bluetooth (PAN)	Wireless (2.4 GHz)	Up to 3 Mbps (Classic)	Polling (Master-Slave)	Short-range device communication
IEEE 802.1Q	VLAN Tagging	Any Ethernet medium	N/A	VLAN-based switching	Logical segmentation in networks
IEEE 802.3bt	Power over Ethernet (PoE)	Twisted pair	Up to 90W power + data	Ethernet (Layer 2)	Powering IP cameras, VoIP, APs
IEEE 802.3bz	Multi-Gig Ethernet	Twisted pair	2.5/5 Gbps	Ethernet	Upgrading networks on existing cables

Link Layer Switches & Bridges (learning bridge and spanning tree algorithms)

Switches and Bridges

Switches and bridges are fundamental devices that operate at the Data Link Layer (Layer 2) of the OSI model. Both are used to connect different parts of a LAN and manage the flow of data based on MAC addresses. A bridge typically connects two network segments and forwards frames intelligently to reduce traffic. A switch, by contrast, is a multi-port bridge capable of connecting many devices in a more scalable manner. Switches differ from hubs in that they do not flood all traffic to every port. Instead, they read the MAC address of each incoming frame and forward it only to the appropriate destination port. This significantly improves performance, especially in busy networks. They create separate collision domains, allowing simultaneous transmissions across different ports without interference. Both devices help minimize network congestion and allow segmentation of traffic within the LAN. Switches have largely replaced bridges in modern networks due to their scalability, better performance, and support for features like VLANs and QoS (Quality of Service).While bridges were originally introduced to extend networks across segments, switches have evolved to support higher speeds (e.g., Gigabit and 10-Gigabit Ethernet), integrate with routers (Layer 3 switches), and deliver advanced packet handling capabilities.

Learning Bridge Algorithm

A key feature of bridges and switches is the learning bridge algorithm. When a frame arrives at a switch port, the device examines the source MAC address and maps it to the incoming port. This information is stored in the MAC address table, allowing the switch to know which devices are connected to which ports. If the destination MAC address is known (i.e., exists in the table), the switch forwards the frame directly to the correct port. If it's unknown, the switch floods the frame to all ports except the source port. As communication continues, the MAC table becomes more accurate and complete, reducing unnecessary traffic over time.

This mechanism allows switches to "learn" the network topology dynamically and respond efficiently to changing device locations. It eliminates the need for static configurations and enables plug-and-play functionality. However, since MAC tables have limited memory, entries are periodically aged out (removed after inactivity), ensuring that obsolete addresses do not linger and cause misrouting of frames.

Spanning Tree Algorithm (STA)

In a network with redundant paths, loops can form—resulting in broadcast storms, duplicate frames, and MAC table instability. To avoid this, switches implement the Spanning Tree Protocol (STP), which creates a loop-free logical topology. STP works by electing a root bridge, then calculating the shortest paths to the root from all other switches. Any link not part of this shortest path tree is placed in a blocked state, effectively removing loops without physically disconnecting devices. If a primary link fails, STP can re-enable blocked links, ensuring fault tolerance and high availability. Modern versions like Rapid STP (RSTP) reduce the time required for network convergence, which is crucial in large, dynamic environments. This loop-avoidance feature is especially important in enterprise networks and data centers, where redundancy is critical for uptime, but loops can have disastrous effects.

Benefits and Practical Applications

Switches offer a range of benefits including efficiency, security, and scalability. By forwarding frames only to the required destination, they reduce traffic and increase effective bandwidth. They support advanced features like VLANs, which allow logical segmentation of networks regardless of physical layout. Port security features in switches enable control over which MAC addresses can send or receive data on a given port, helping protect against spoofing or unauthorized access. QoS mechanisms prioritize certain types of traffic (e.g., VoIP or video conferencing) to maintain performance. In real-world usage, switches are ubiquitous—from small office setups to enterprise networks and industrial IoT systems. They form the backbone of most LANs and are often stacked or deployed in hierarchical layers (access, distribution, and core).The principles of learning bridges and spanning trees are still embedded in how modern switches operate, even as Layer 3 (routing-capable) switches and SDN (software-defined networking) add intelligence and automation to network infrastructures.

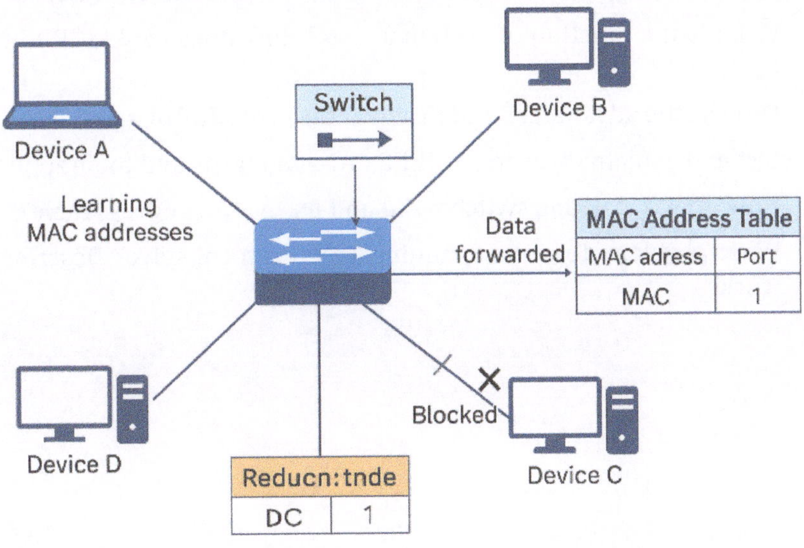

Figure 3.5: Switch Operation with MAC Table and Spanning Tree

The Link Layer plays a vital role in ensuring reliable and efficient communication within local networks by managing how data frames are transmitted over physical links (Figure 3.5). Through mechanisms like framing, error detection and correction, and flow control, the link layer ensures that data is packaged properly, errors are identified or corrected, and transmission rates between sender and receiver are synchronized. It also includes crucial methods for medium access control (MAC), which coordinate how multiple devices share the same communication channel to avoid collisions and ensure fairness. Additionally, link layer components such as switches and bridges optimize traffic flow and improve network performance by dynamically learning MAC addresses and managing redundant paths through the Spanning Tree Protocol (STP). Standards like Ethernet (IEEE 802.3) and Wi-Fi (IEEE 802.11) define the physical and logical characteristics of LANs, ensuring interoperability across devices. Together, these elements form the foundation for building secure, scalable, and high-performance local area networks.

Exercise Questions

- What is framing in the context of the data link layer? Explain its purpose and structure.
- Describe any three framing techniques and explain how they mark frame boundaries.
- How does CRC help in error detection? Illustrate with an example.
- Compare Stop-and-Wait ARQ and Sliding Window Protocols.
- Explain the differences between Go-Back-N and Selective Repeat ARQ.
- What is the function of MAC in a LAN? How does CSMA/CD differ from CSMA/CA?
- Discuss the advantages and disadvantages of ALOHA and CSMA.
- List and explain three major IEEE LAN standards and their applications.
- How does a learning switch build and use a MAC address table?
- What problem does the Spanning Tree Protocol solve? Describe how it works.

CHAPTER

4

NETWORK LAYER

The Network Layer is the third layer in the OSI (Open Systems Interconnection) model and plays a pivotal role in the functioning of computer networks. It is primarily responsible for the logical transmission of data packets between devices across different networks. Unlike the Data Link Layer, which deals with node-to-node communication within the same network segment, the Network Layer handles end-to-end communication and ensures that data can travel across diverse and interconnected networks. This layer provides the mechanism for addressing, routing, and forwarding, enabling data to find the most efficient path from source to destination. One of the key responsibilities of the Network Layer is logical addressing, which is typically implemented using IP (Internet Protocol) addresses. Each device on a network is assigned a unique IP address that identifies it on the network. This is essential because it allows data packets to be routed across different networks, even when the physical addressing (such as MAC addresses) changes from one network to another. IP addresses are hierarchical, which allows for efficient and scalable routing mechanisms in large networks. IPv4 and IPv6 are the two most common versions of IP addressing used today, with IPv6 being developed to address the limitations of the IPv4 address space. Another fundamental function of the Network Layer is routing, the process of determining the best path for a data packet to travel from the source to the destination. Routers operate at this layer, examining the destination IP address in each packet and forwarding it based on routing tables and algorithms. Routing can be static, where paths are manually configured, or dynamic, where protocols like RIP, OSPF, and BGP automatically update routing tables based on changing network conditions. The dynamic nature of routing helps networks maintain efficiency and reliability even in the face of congestion or link failures. The packet forwarding mechanism is also governed by the Network Layer. Forwarding refers to the actual movement of packets from the input of a router to the appropriate output interface based on the destination address. To do this effectively, routers use a combination of forwarding tables, access control lists, and quality of service (QoS) policies. These mechanisms help ensure that traffic is delivered in a timely, secure, and prioritized manner. The distinction between routing and forwarding is important routing determines the path, while forwarding executes it.In addition to addressing and routing, the Network Layer is also responsible for fragmentation and reassembly. Networks can have different Maximum Transmission Unit (MTU) sizes, and when a packet is larger than the MTU of a particular network, it must be fragmented into smaller pieces. The Network Layer at the receiving end reassembles these fragments into the original packet. This process is vital for interoperability across heterogeneous network environments and is handled transparently to higher layers. Lastly, the Network Layer also incorporates error handling and diagnostics, though to a more limited extent than the lower layers. Protocols such as ICMP (Internet Control Message Protocol) operate at this layer to send error messages and operational information. For example, ICMP is used in the popular "ping" and "traceroute" utilities to test connectivity and path traversal. These diagnostic tools are invaluable for network administrators in managing and troubleshooting network issues.

Point-to-point Networks

A point-to-point network refers to a type of communication system where two devices or systems are directly connected to each other in Figure 4.1. This type of network can be seen as one of the simplest forms of communication, where the devices or endpoints are linked through a single dedicated communication link or channel. Here's a detailed breakdown of point-to-point networks: A point-to-point network involves direct communication between two endpoints, such as computers, routers, or other devices. It provides a dedicated path for data transmission between the two devices. Unlike more complex networks, such as broadcast or multicast networks, which allow communication among multiple devices, point-to-point networks are solely concerned with direct communication between two endpoints.

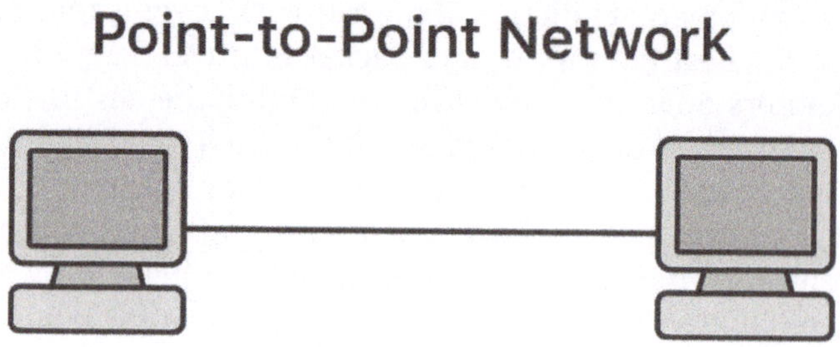

Figure 4.1: Represent the Point-to-point networks.

Key Characteristics

Dedicated Communication Link

A dedicated communication link refers to a direct, exclusive connection between two devices or endpoints. Unlike shared networks where bandwidth is divided among multiple devices, a dedicated link ensures that the full bandwidth is available solely for communication between the two endpoints. This isolation leads to more predictable and stable performance as there is no competition for resources. Such links are often used in high-demand environments where consistent data transfer rates and reliability are paramount, such as in telecommunication networks or private point-to-point connections. These links can be either physical (e.g., fiber optics, leased lines) or virtual, depending on the technological setup. The dedicated nature of the link ensures minimal interference from external devices or networks, making it ideal for critical applications where downtime or fluctuation in connection quality could result in significant disruptions.

Data Transmission

Data transmission in a dedicated communication link involves the movement of information between two connected devices, typically in a specific direction. The system may support either unidirectional or bidirectional data flow depending on the design. Unidirectional transmission sends data from one endpoint to another, often used in scenarios like broadcasting or one-way data updates. Bidirectional transmission allows for data flow in both directions, enabling two-way communication, such as in telecommunication networks, video conferencing, or real-time applications. The advantage of dedicated links is that they ensure high-quality, uninterrupted data transmission, with no interference from other network traffic. Additionally, the use of dedicated channels increases the efficiency of the communication process by optimizing throughput and minimizing latency. These systems are often tailored to specific needs, making them crucial for applications requiring high bandwidth, low latency, and secure data transmission.

Simplicity

The simplicity of a dedicated communication link architecture lies in its straightforward setup and operation. Unlike complex networks that require intricate routing and switching protocols, dedicated links provide a direct, exclusive path for data transmission between two endpoints. This makes them particularly suitable for environments where minimal infrastructure is needed. Without the need for intermediary devices such as routers or switches, dedicated communication links are less prone to configuration errors and network congestion, offering a more stable and reliable connection. Furthermore, the absence of network layers typically involved in shared networks reduces the overhead associated with managing traffic, ensuring faster and more predictable data delivery. This simplicity also makes these systems easier to maintain and troubleshoot. Such straightforward architectures are often favored in scenarios where high-performance, secure, and real-time communication is necessary, such as in banking, defense, and industrial control systems.

Types of Point-to-Point Networks

There are several types of point-to-point networks, based on the underlying technology used for the communication link:

Physical Point-to-Point Networks

A physical point-to-point network refers to a direct, dedicated communication link between two devices using tangible infrastructure such as copper wires, fiber-optic cables, or wireless connections. These connections are exclusive and can be customized to ensure a reliable and consistent data flow. An example is DSL (Digital Subscriber Line), which offers a dedicated connection between the user and the service provider's network, allowing for high-speed internet access. Leased lines, another example, are a service provided by telecommunication companies where a specific physical line is set aside for a client's exclusive use, often offering higher bandwidth and more reliable performance than typical broadband connections. These types of physical links provide guaranteed bandwidth and minimal interference, which is beneficial for businesses and critical applications requiring stable, uninterrupted communication, especially in environments like private offices or data centers.

Virtual Point-to-Point Networks

Virtual point-to-point networks are logically established connections that use software to create an appearance of a dedicated link, even though the same physical infrastructure is often shared with multiple users. These networks utilize technologies like VPN (Virtual Private Network), MPLS (Multiprotocol Label Switching), or L2TP (Layer 2 Tunneling Protocol) to provide secure and isolated communication over a common internet backbone. In a VPN, for example, users can establish an encrypted tunnel over the internet to ensure privacy and security while maintaining the illusion of a dedicated line. MPLS and L2TP allow for efficient traffic routing and the establishment of virtual point-to-point connections that mimic the functionality of physical networks but without requiring dedicated infrastructure. While these networks do not guarantee the same level of exclusivity or reliability as physical networks, they offer flexibility, scalability, and lower costs, making them suitable for businesses and individuals seeking secure, efficient communication over public networks.

Advantages of Point-to-Point Networks

High Performance

Point-to-point networks provide high performance due to the dedicated nature of their connections. Since the bandwidth is not shared with other users or devices, there is minimal congestion, leading to faster data transfer rates and lower latency. This results in high throughput and efficient communication between the connected devices. Such performance is essential for applications that require fast and consistent data transfer, such as real-time communication systems, high-definition video streaming, or financial transactions. Additionally, because there's no competition for bandwidth, users can expect more predictable and stable performance, ensuring a seamless experience even during peak usage times. The dedicated nature of point-to-point connections ensures that the full capacity of the link is available for the connected devices, optimizing network performance.

Reliability

Reliability is one of the key advantages of point-to-point networks. The dedicated connection between two devices minimizes the risk of interference, congestion, and packet loss that often occurs in shared networks. Since no other users or devices are competing for the same bandwidth, point-to-point networks tend to maintain a stable and consistent connection. This is especially important in mission-critical applications, where disruptions or downtime can result in significant losses. Moreover, because the devices are directly linked, issues such as data collisions or network congestion due to external traffic are less likely to occur. This makes point-to-point networks highly suitable for applications requiring high availability and reliability, such as business-critical communications, remote monitoring systems, or secure financial transactions.

Security

Point-to-point networks are often more secure than shared networks, mainly because they offer a dedicated communication channel between two devices. As there is no involvement of multiple users or devices on the same connection, the risk of unauthorized access or eavesdropping is significantly reduced. In private point-to-point networks, encryption and other security measures can be applied directly to protect sensitive data transmitted across the link. The isolation of the communication path also makes it difficult for potential attackers to intercept or manipulate the data. This makes point-to-point networks ideal for organizations that handle sensitive information, such as government agencies, financial institutions, or enterprises that require secure communication channels. Private leased lines or VPNs are often used in these cases to ensure a higher level of security compared to typical shared networks.

Simpler Design

The design and setup of point-to-point networks are generally simpler than shared network configurations. Since there are only two devices involved, the complexity of managing multiple devices or connections is eliminated. This makes the network architecture easier to plan, implement, and maintain. Troubleshooting is also more straightforward, as any issues that arise typically involve only the two connected devices or the direct link between them. This can significantly reduce the time and effort required to resolve network issues.

Additionally, with a simpler design, the network can be more easily scaled or adjusted to meet changing needs, making point-to-point networks an attractive option for businesses or organizations with straightforward connectivity requirements. This simplicity also leads to lower operational costs as fewer resources are needed for maintenance and management.

Disadvantages of Point-to-Point Networks

Scalability

One of the major disadvantages of point-to-point networks is their poor scalability. As the number of devices or endpoints grows, the number of required point-to-point connections increases exponentially. Each device needs a dedicated link to communicate with others, making network expansion complicated and costly. For example, if an organization has multiple branches, it would need a unique connection for each branch. This approach does not allow easy growth, and the network's complexity increases with every added endpoint. As businesses expand and require more devices to be connected, the infrastructure needed to support these additional connections becomes a challenge. The inability to scale effectively without a significant increase in network infrastructure makes point-to-point networks unsuitable for larger organizations or rapidly growing environments.

Cost

Point-to-point networks can incur substantial costs due to the need for dedicated connections between each pair of devices. Whether using physical lines like leased lines or fiber-optic cables, each individual connection comes with its own associated costs. This expense can escalate quickly, especially when the network needs to support multiple connections. For example, a business with several remote offices or branches will require a unique link for each location. These individual connections not only incur setup fees but also maintenance and operational costs. Moreover, the cost increases as network traffic and demand for bandwidth rise, making it an inefficient and expensive option for businesses that need to scale or upgrade their infrastructure frequently. Thus, while point-to-point networks provide secure and direct communication, the financial burden can be a significant disadvantage.

Limited Flexibility

Point-to-point networks are limited in terms of flexibility compared to other network topologies such as mesh or broadcast networks. In point-to-point networks, each communication path is dedicated to specific endpoints, which means that adding new devices or expanding communication capabilities requires establishing new, dedicated links. If any one of these endpoints fails or experiences issues, communication between the connected devices is disrupted, potentially causing network downtime or communication failure. Unlike in broadcast networks, where a single failure does not necessarily affect the entire system, point-to-point setups offer no backup or redundancy unless specifically engineered with additional infrastructure. This lack of flexibility can be a significant disadvantage, particularly in environments where high availability and continuous communication are critical. The inability to quickly reconfigure or adapt to changes in network requirements makes point-to-point networks less ideal for dynamic or high-demand applications.

Applications of Point-to-Point Networks

Private Leased Lines

Private leased lines are dedicated communication channels that are used by businesses for secure and reliable data transmission between two points, such as between a company's headquarters and a branch office. These lines provide a direct, private connection that offers high speeds, low latency, and greater security compared to shared public networks. Private leased lines are essential for organizations that require constant data flow without interruptions or interference from external traffic. This type of connection is ideal for critical business applications such as VoIP (Voice over Internet Protocol), video conferencing, and secure data transfers. Additionally, they eliminate the risks associated with public internet connections, such as data breaches and downtime, providing peace of mind to businesses handling sensitive information. As the demand for reliable and high-performance networks increases, private leased lines remain a top choice for many enterprises.

Backbone Networks

In large-scale network architectures, backbone networks play a crucial role in connecting various subnetworks or segments across extensive geographic areas. These high-capacity point-to-point connections form the central framework that ensures fast and efficient data transfer across different network nodes. Backbone networks typically use high-speed communication technologies such as fiber optics to link multiple regions, data centers, or branch offices. The primary function of a backbone network is to facilitate the seamless exchange of data between smaller, distributed networks while maintaining reliability and minimizing delays. In many cases, backbone networks handle vast amounts of internet traffic and enable large organizations or service providers to offer high-speed services to their customers. These networks are also essential for connecting critical infrastructure and ensuring that all parts of an enterprise or a service provider's network are adequately linked, robust, and capable of handling large data volumes.

Satellite Communication

Satellite communication systems rely heavily on point-to-point connections, where the ground station communicates directly with satellites in orbit, enabling global communication. This technology is essential for remote areas that lack terrestrial infrastructure, providing essential connectivity for data, voice, and video transmissions. In satellite communication, point-to-point links facilitate the seamless exchange of signals between the satellite and ground stations, which can be located thousands of miles apart. These links are particularly beneficial in military, emergency, or maritime communications where traditional cables and networks are not feasible. Additionally, satellite communication is instrumental in broadcasting television signals, internet access, and communication services for rural or isolated regions. The use of point-to-point satellite links ensures that communication remains uninterrupted, even in remote locations, making it a critical infrastructure component for global connectivity and real-time data exchange.

Telecommunication

Point-to-point communication in telecommunications involves direct transmission of data, voice, and video signals between two endpoints. This method forms the foundation of traditional telephony, such as the Public Switched Telephone Network (PSTN), which connects users through dedicated circuits. In this model, each call or communication session involves a direct link between the caller and receiver, ensuring quality and minimal interference. Point-to-point communication is used in various telecommunication applications, including mobile networks, internet access, and video conferencing systems. With the evolution of technologies, such as fiber optics and 5G, these direct connections now offer much higher bandwidth, enabling faster data transfer and improved voice/video quality. Point-to-point systems remain essential for telecommunication infrastructure, delivering a reliable communication channel for both individual users and businesses, ensuring consistent, high-quality service without congestion or delay.

VPN Connections

Virtual Private Networks (VPNs) extensively utilize point-to-point connections to create secure and private communication channels over the internet. VPN technology uses encryption and tunneling protocols to establish virtual point-to-point links between remote devices or sites, ensuring secure data transmission over potentially unsecured public networks. By creating an encrypted tunnel, VPNs prevent eavesdropping and data breaches while enabling businesses and individuals to securely access sensitive information and resources. Point-to-point links in VPNs are essential for remote work scenarios, connecting employees to their corporate networks from anywhere in the world. These secure connections are crucial for businesses that rely on cloud-based services, remote access to internal systems, or inter-office communication over the internet. VPNs protect user privacy, provide data integrity, and enable organizations to comply with data protection regulations, making them an indispensable tool in modern enterprise IT security strategies.

Protocols Used in Point-to-Point Networks

Several protocols are commonly associated with point-to-point communication in Figure 4.2:

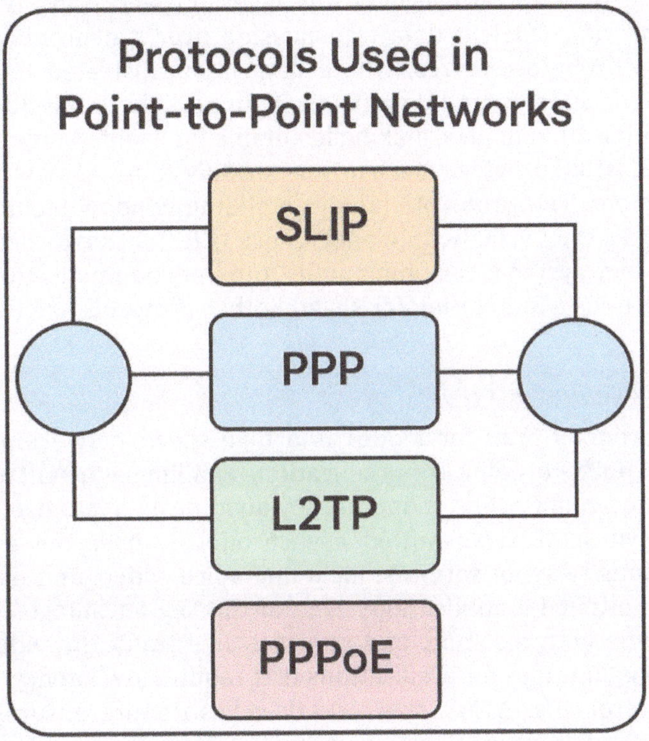

Figure 4.2: Protocols Used in Point-to-Point Networks.

PPP (Point-to-Point Protocol)

PPP (Point-to-Point Protocol) is a widely used data link protocol designed to establish direct communication between two network nodes over point-to-point links. Its primary purpose is to enable the transmission of packets across a direct connection, such as a dial-up link or a dedicated leased line. PPP provides essential features like authentication, encryption, and compression. It supports multiple network layer protocols, making it versatile for a range of applications, including internet connections and VPNs. PPP operates by framing data into packets and providing mechanisms for error detection and correction. It also includes the Link Control Protocol (LCP) for managing the link's establishment, maintenance, and termination. PPP ensures secure and efficient data transfer by negotiating various parameters such as compression and encryption protocols, making it an essential technology in legacy dial-up connections and broadband access technologies like DSL.

HDLC (High-Level Data Link Control)

HDLC (High-Level Data Link Control) is a bit-oriented synchronous data link protocol commonly used in leased-line communication for point-to-point connections. It operates at the data link layer (Layer 2) and is employed to ensure reliable and efficient data transmission over synchronous serial links. HDLC defines frame structures, where data is encapsulated in a frame that contains control, address, and data fields. It supports both full-duplex and half-duplex communication modes, making it suitable for a wide range of networking environments. HDLC provides mechanisms for flow control, error detection, and link management. The protocol employs a sliding window technique for flow control and uses the Cyclic Redundancy Check (CRC) for error detection. HDLC is used in various systems, including point-to-point communication over leased lines, and serves as a foundation for several other protocols like PPP and Frame Relay.

ATM (Asynchronous Transfer Mode)

ATM (Asynchronous Transfer Mode) is a high-speed networking technology designed for point-to-point communication, enabling efficient data transfer across dedicated connections. It operates by dividing data into fixed-size packets called cells, which are transmitted asynchronously over the network. ATM supports various types of services, including voice, video, and data, making it suitable for multimedia applications. One of the key advantages of ATM is its ability to handle both real-time and non-real-time traffic, providing Quality of Service (QoS) guarantees for applications that require low latency, such as voice or video conferencing. ATM's fixed-length cell structure ensures predictable performance, and it uses virtual circuits to establish logical point-to-point connections. It has been used in wide-area networks (WANs), particularly in high-speed environments such as backbone networks. Despite being less common today due to the rise of Ethernet-based technologies, ATM was crucial in the development of broadband networks.

Logical Addressing

Logical Addressing refers to the method of identifying devices or nodes on a network using an address that is independent of the underlying physical hardware. It is primarily used in network layer protocols (such as the Internet Protocol, IP) to ensure that data can be routed across different networks. Logical addressing is contrasted with physical addressing, where each device is identified by a unique hardware address (such as a MAC address). Here's a detailed explanation of logical addressing:

Logical addressing is a system used to identify devices or nodes on a network, which allows them to communicate across various networks (such as LANs, WANs, or the Internet).A logical address is assigned to each device, often by a network administrator or a dynamic address allocation system like DHCP (Dynamic Host

Configuration Protocol).The primary purpose of logical addressing is to facilitate the routing of data packets between devices on different networks.

Key Components of Logical Addressing

Logical Address

A logical address is a network identifier assigned to a device within a specific network. Unlike physical addresses, which are unique to hardware, logical addresses are used to specify a device's location in a network. In IP-based networks, this address is typically an IP address. The primary purpose of a logical address is to facilitate communication between devices in different networks or subnets. Logical addresses enable devices to identify each other over the network, ensuring that data is sent to the correct destination. For example, in IPv4, a device's IP address uniquely identifies it within a particular network or the entire internet. Logical addressing is hierarchical, meaning it allows for both local and global addressing within smaller subnets or larger networks. It serves as the foundation for routing and facilitates scalability in large networks, making it critical for managing network traffic efficiently.

Subnet Mask

A subnet mask is a key component in network addressing that helps define the structure of a network by dividing it into smaller segments called subnets. It works by identifying which part of an IP address refers to the network and which part refers to the host (individual devices). The subnet mask is a 32-bit number that corresponds to the length of the network portion of the address, using a series of binary ones (1s) followed by binary zeros (0s). The ones indicate the network portion, while the zeros represent the host portion. This segmentation allows networks to be broken down into manageable pieces, optimizing IP address allocation and improving network efficiency. The subnet mask also aids in determining whether a destination IP address is within the same network or requires routing to a different network. It plays a crucial role in controlling network traffic and managing IP address space.

Routing

Routing is the process of forwarding data packets between different networks, ensuring that data reaches its destination, even if it has to travel across multiple networks. Routers, which are specialized networking devices, use logical addresses to make decisions about where to send packets. The primary role of routing is to determine the best path for a packet from its source to its destination. Logical addresses, such as IP addresses, are key in this process as they provide a standardized way for devices to identify each other across networks. Routers examine the destination address of a packet and use routing tables to decide how to forward the packet. This enables communication across wide-area networks (WANs), such as the internet, by connecting smaller, local networks. Routing is essential for enabling communication between devices on different networks and for ensuring that data reaches its correct destination in a timely and efficient manner.

Structure of Logical Addressing

Logical addressing is essential in computer networking as it helps in identifying devices on different networks. The structure of logical addressing is designed hierarchically, typically divided into three parts: the network portion, the host portion, and sometimes a subnet portion. Each of these parts plays a specific role in determining the exact location and identity of a device within a network.

1. Network Portion: This part of the logical address specifies the network to which a device belongs. It identifies the range or group of devices that are part of a larger network. For example, in IP addressing, the network portion allows routers to know which network the data should be forwarded to, thus guiding the routing process.

   Example-Network Portion: 192.168.1

2. Host Portion: The host portion identifies the individual device within a network. It ensures that each device connected to a specific network can be uniquely addressed. This enables the accurate delivery of data to the correct host.

   Example-Host Portion: 10

3. Subnet Portion (optional): In some cases, the logical address also includes a subnet portion. This additional division enables a network to be further subdivided into smaller subnetworks, improving network management, efficiency, and security. Subnetting helps in reducing network congestion and optimizing resource allocation within the organization.

Example-Subnet Mask: 255.255.255.0

This mask helps in identifying the network portion (192.168.1) and the host portion (10).

Classes of IP Addressing

In IPv4 addressing, logical addresses are divided into classes to represent different sizes of networks:

Class A (1.0.0.0 to 127.255.255.255)

Class A addresses are designated for very large networks, with the range spanning from 1.0.0.0 to 127.255.255.255. In this addressing scheme, the first octet of the address is used to identify the network portion, while the remaining three octets are used for the host portion. This class allows for a significant number of hosts per network, up to 16,777,214 hosts, making it suitable for large organizations, ISPs, or any entity requiring a vast number of devices. The class is also recognized by its first bit, which is set to 0, ensuring it remains distinct from other address classes. A notable feature is that Class A includes both private and public IP addresses, allowing it to be used across global and internal networks, though in practice, public Class A addresses are limited due to the shortage of available IP addresses in this range.

Class B (128.0.0.0 to 191.255.255.255)

Class B addresses are intended for medium-sized networks, encompassing the address range from 128.0.0.0 to 191.255.255.255. In this class, the first two octets represent the network portion, with the remaining two octets designated for hosts. This structure allows for approximately 65,536 possible networks, each capable of supporting up to 65,534 hosts. Class B addresses are often used by universities, large businesses, or government agencies, as they balance the need for a moderate number of networks and hosts. Class B addresses begin with a binary pattern of 10 in the first octet, which helps distinguish them from Classes A and C. Like Class A, Class B also includes both public and private addresses, with the private Class B address range being 172.16.0.0 to 172.31.255.255, allowing for internal network utilization without utilizing public address space.

Class C (192.0.0.0 to 223.255.255.255)

Class C addresses are designed for smaller networks, spanning the address range from 192.0.0.0 to 223.255.255.255. In this scheme, the first three octets serve as the network portion, leaving the final octet for the host portion. This allows for a large number of individual networks, but each network can only support up to 254 hosts. Class C addresses are often used for small to medium-sized businesses or smaller subnets within larger networks. With the ability to accommodate over 2 million networks, Class C is ideal for cases where many smaller, segmented networks are needed. The binary pattern of 110 in the first octet ensures that Class C addresses are easily identified. Additionally, Class C includes a private address range, 192.168.0.0 to 192.168.255.255, which is widely used for local area networks (LANs), allowing for private addressing on internal networks.

Class D (224.0.0.0 to 239.255.255.255)

Class D addresses are reserved for multicast groups and span the address range from 224.0.0.0 to 239.255.255.255. Unlike Class A, B, and C addresses, which are used for unicast communication (one-to-one), Class D addresses enable multicast communication (one-to-many). In multicast communication, a message is sent from a source to multiple receivers, reducing bandwidth and enhancing efficiency in scenarios like live video streaming, online gaming, or real-time data dissemination. Class D addresses are not assigned to individual devices or networks for regular communication, but instead are used to identify multicast groups, allowing multiple hosts to join a specific group and receive data sent to that group. The first four bits of a Class D address are set to 1110, distinguishing it from other address classes. This class does not have a network or host division since its sole purpose is to facilitate multicast communication.

Class E (240.0.0.0 to 255.255.255.255)

Class E addresses, spanning the range from 240.0.0.0 to 255.255.255.255, are reserved for experimental and future use. These addresses are not assigned for general public or private network usage and are not utilized for regular communication. The purpose of Class E is to accommodate experimental protocols or network technologies that might be developed in the future. While Class E addresses are not actively used in current IPv4 networks, they provide flexibility for addressing needs that may arise as technology evolves. The first four bits of a Class E address are set to 1111, making it distinct from the other address classes. Although initially reserved for experimental purposes, Class E addresses are unlikely to be used on a large scale, as the adoption of IPv6, with its significantly larger address space, is expected to address any future needs for unique addressing schemes.

IPv6 and Logical Addressing

IPv6 (Internet Protocol version 6) was developed to address the limitations of IPv4, primarily its finite address space. IPv4 uses a 32-bit address, which provides approximately 4.3 billion unique IP addresses. This was sufficient in the early days of the internet, but the rapid growth of internet-connected devices quickly led to the exhaustion of available IPv4 addresses. In contrast, IPv6 uses a 128-bit address, allowing for a virtually unlimited number of unique IP addresses. This is achieved by breaking the address into eight 16-bit blocks, each represented as a 4-digit hexadecimal number. This expanded address space not only accommodates the growing number of devices but also ensures that every device connected to the internet can be assigned a unique, globally routable IP address. The large address pool also helps in addressing issues like network fragmentation and allows for more efficient and scalable networking solutions.

IPv6 Addressing Scheme

IPv6 addresses are structured into eight groups of four hexadecimal digits, separated by colons. Each 16-bit block in the address is represented by four hexadecimal digits (each representing 4 bits), which helps in reducing the overall length of the address compared to a binary format. For example, an IPv6 address might look like this:2001:0db8:85a3:0000:0000:8a2e: 0370:7334. This structure provides a total of 128 bits, significantly enhancing the scalability and flexibility of internet addressing. The address space offered by IPv6 is so vast that it is capable of supporting trillions of devices, far surpassing the limitations of IPv4's 32-bit system. This new structure also brings advantages such as improved routing efficiency, simpler network configuration (with features like Stateless Address Autoconfiguration), and better support for modern technologies like IoT and mobile devices, where the need for unique addressing is critical.

IPv6 Address Space

One of the most significant improvements IPv6 offers over IPv4 is its vast address space. IPv4, using a 32-bit address, provides about 4.3 billion unique IP addresses, which seemed more than adequate in the early days of the internet. However, the exponential growth of connected devices, coupled with the limited number of available IPv4 addresses, has led to a shortage. In contrast, IPv6 uses 128-bit addresses, which results in 340 undecillion (3.4×10^38) unique IP addresses. This staggering number ensures that every device, from smartphones to sensors in the Internet of Things (IoT), can have a globally unique IP address. The expanded address space also supports efficient address aggregation and routing, reducing the complexity of network management. As a result, IPv6 is expected to accommodate the ever-growing number of devices for the foreseeable future, ensuring the internet remains scalable and efficient as the digital ecosystem continues to evolve.

Subnetting and Logical Addressing

Subnetting is the process of dividing a larger network into smaller sub-networks (subnets), each of which has its own logical address range. The logical address is used to define both the network and the specific device (host) within that network:

1. The subnet mask helps determine the boundary between the network portion and the host portion of the address.
2. Subnetting allows for more efficient use of available IP addresses and can reduce the size of routing tables. For example, if a company has the IP address 192.168.1.0/24, it can split this into smaller subnets using a different subnet mask, such as 255.255.255.128, which creates two subnets (192.168.1.0/25 and 192.168.1.128/25).

Role of Logical Addressing in Routing

Logical addressing plays a crucial role in the routing process by enabling routers to determine how to forward packets across networks. Unlike physical addresses (e.g., MAC addresses), logical addresses, such as IP addresses, are used to identify devices on different networks. Routers rely on logical addresses to understand the destination of a packet and decide the optimal route for its delivery. When a packet reaches a router, the router checks the destination logical address and looks up the best available path in its routing table. This ensures that the packet reaches its intended destination, even if it traverses multiple networks or intermediate routers. The use of logical addressing allows for more efficient and scalable network communication, particularly when dealing with large and complex networks, as each logical address corresponds to a unique network entity, facilitating end-to-end communication.

Routing Table

A routing table is a critical component within a router, serving as a guide for determining the best path for forwarding packets to their destinations. This table contains a collection of entries, each mapping a network destination (identified by its logical address) to a specific route or interface. The routing table is constantly updated, either through static configuration by network administrators or dynamically via routing protocols such as OSPF, BGP, or RIP. These updates enable routers to adapt to changes in network topology, ensuring that the packet forwarding process remains accurate and efficient. By referencing the routing table, routers can evaluate various network paths based on factors like distance, cost, and network performance, allowing for optimized packet delivery. This decision-making process is vital for ensuring that data travels through the most appropriate and reliable network route to reach its intended endpoint.

Packet Forwarding

Packet forwarding is the process by which routers examine the destination logical address of incoming packets and determine the most appropriate route for the packet's journey. This process begins when a packet arrives at a router, and the router reads the packet's destination IP address. The router then searches its routing table to find the next-hop address or interface that brings the packet closer to its final destination. Based on this lookup, the router forwards the packet along the correct path, ensuring it reaches its target network. In scenarios involving multiple routers, each router along the path repeats this process, gradually moving the packet closer to its destination. The efficiency and accuracy of packet forwarding are crucial for network performance, as it minimizes delays and ensures reliable data delivery across various networks. Effective packet forwarding ensures that data can traverse complex networks seamlessly.

Network Layer

Logical addressing is a function of the network layer (Layer 3) in the OSI model, which is responsible for facilitating end-to-end communication between devices across different networks. At this layer, logical addresses like IP addresses are assigned to devices, allowing them to be uniquely identified on a global scale. The network layer is responsible for routing packets across intermediate routers and network paths, ensuring that data reaches its destination. It abstracts the underlying physical networks and provides a uniform addressing scheme, enabling seamless communication between devices that may reside on different local area networks (LANs) or wide area networks (WANs). The network layer encapsulates data from the transport layer into packets and forwards them based on logical addresses. This abstraction simplifies network management and facilitates data transmission over a large, distributed network infrastructure, playing a pivotal role in the overall functionality of modern communication systems.

Dynamic vs. Static Logical Addressing

A device is assigned a permanent logical address, such as an IP address. This method is often used for servers, routers, and devices that need a consistent address.Logical addresses are dynamically assigned by a network service, such as DHCP. This is commonly used in home networks, where devices like laptops and smartphones may frequently join and leave the network.This Table 4.1 highlights the key differences between static and dynamic addressing methods, providing insight into their respective use cases and advantages.

Table 4.1: Comparison dynamic versus static logical addressing.

Aspect	Static Addressing	Dynamic Addressing
Definition	A permanent logical address is manually assigned to a device.	Logical addresses are assigned dynamically, often by a network service like DHCP.
Usage	Used for servers, routers, and devices requiring consistent addresses.	Commonly used for devices in home or office networks, such as laptops and smartphones.
Configuration	Manually configured by the network administrator.	Automatically assigned by a network service, such as DHCP.
IP Address Assignment	Fixed and unchanging IP address for the device.	IP address changes whenever the device connects to the network or after lease expiry.
Address Consistency	Consistent over time, providing stability for services like web hosting.	Address may change over time as devices disconnect and reconnect.
Scalability	Less scalable, requires manual management for each device.	Highly scalable as devices can join and leave the network without manual intervention.
Security	More secure for certain devices (e.g., servers) as addresses remain constant.	May be less secure if the IP address is frequently changing.
Suitability	Ideal for fixed devices that need reliable addressability (e.g., servers, printers).	Ideal for devices that frequently join/leave the network (e.g., laptops, smartphones).

Address Resolution Protocol (ARP)

While logical addresses (e.g., IP addresses) are used for communication across networks, devices on a local network need to know the physical (MAC) address of other devices in order to send data frames within the same network. ARP maps an IP address to its corresponding MAC address on the local network. When a device wants to communicate with another device on the same network, it sends an ARP request to find the MAC address associated with the logical IP address.

Advantages of Logical Addressing

Scalability

Logical addressing is a fundamental concept for scaling networks, particularly when combined with technologies like routing protocols and subnetting. By utilizing logical addresses, networks can be expanded without significant changes to physical infrastructure. For instance, subnetting allows network administrators to divide large networks into smaller, more manageable subnets, optimizing both the network's performance and security. Additionally, routing protocols such as OSPF or BGP facilitate the distribution of logical addresses across vast distances, ensuring that data can be transmitted across different network segments efficiently. This scalability is essential in today's global networks, where millions of devices must be connected and managed seamlessly. The ability to scale logically addresses the growing demand for internet connectivity and ensures networks can accommodate an increasing number of users, devices, and applications without needing a complete overhaul of the underlying physical infrastructure.

Flexibility

One of the primary advantages of logical addressing is its flexibility. Logical addresses, such as IP addresses, can be reassigned or modified without changing the underlying physical hardware. This enables a network to adapt to changing conditions, like network reorganization, addition of new devices, or changing geographical locations, without requiring physical adjustments. For example, a device's IP address can be changed to another subnet without physically relocating the device or replacing any hardware. This flexibility is essential for dynamic environments, particularly in large-scale networks or cloud infrastructures, where addressing schemes may need to be altered frequently. Moreover, it supports easier management and maintenance, as network administrators can reconfigure the network remotely, enhancing operational efficiency. The decoupling of logical addressing from physical hardware also allows for network virtualization and other advanced network management techniques, making it a critical component of modern network design.

Inter-network Communication

Logical addressing is critical for enabling communication between different networks, particularly in the context of the Internet. Without logical addressing, devices on different networks would have no means of identifying or communicating with each other, making inter-network communication impossible. Logical addresses, such as IP addresses, provide a unique identifier for devices, ensuring they can be reached from any other device connected to the Internet, regardless of their physical location. The Internet, as a vast global network, relies heavily on logical addressing to route data between disparate networks. This ability to identify devices across multiple networks makes logical addressing indispensable for connecting the world's millions of devices and enabling a seamless flow of data between them. Furthermore, logical addressing supports protocols like DNS (Domain Name System), which translates human-readable domain names into machine-readable IP addresses, facilitating smooth and effective communication on the Internet.

Routing

Routing is a key function of logical addressing, allowing data to traverse multiple networks and devices to reach its intended destination. Logical addresses, particularly IP addresses, enable routers to make intelligent decisions about the best path for data to travel from the source to the destination across interconnected networks. Routers use routing tables and algorithms, such as RIP, OSPF, or BGP, to determine the optimal route based on factors like network topology, traffic, and distance. Logical addresses facilitate the identification of source and destination devices in these routing processes, ensuring that data packets are directed along the correct paths, even across multiple hops and devices. This routing functionality is essential for the operation of the Internet and large-scale enterprise networks, ensuring that information can be transferred efficiently and reliably across diverse networks. In essence, logical addressing serves as the cornerstone for ensuring data is accurately delivered across complex, interconnected systems.

Logical Addressing

Logical addressing refers to the use of addresses that identify a device or network location in a way that is independent of the physical hardware. It is a concept used primarily in the Network Layer (Layer 3) of the OSI model, where it plays a crucial role in enabling devices to communicate across different networks in Figure 4.3. Logical addresses help route packets from one device to another, often across multiple networks or the internet. These addresses are hierarchical and can be dynamically assigned, unlike physical addresses (such as MAC addresses), which are fixed to the hardware. Logical addressing is used to uniquely identify devices or network locations in a network. It serves as the address for devices on IP networks (e.g., IPv4 or IPv6) and is independent of the physical network topology. The logical address is typically structured to reflect both the network and the device (host) within that network, providing a systematic and organized way to address devices on a large scale.

Examples of Logical Addressing

IPv4: An example of logical addressing in IPv4 would be 192.168.1.10. This address uniquely identifies a device within the 192.168.1.0 network.

IPv6: An example of logical addressing in IPv6 would be 2001:0db8:85a3:0000:0000:8a2e: 0370:7334. This is a longer address with 128 bits, designed to accommodate a larger number of devices.

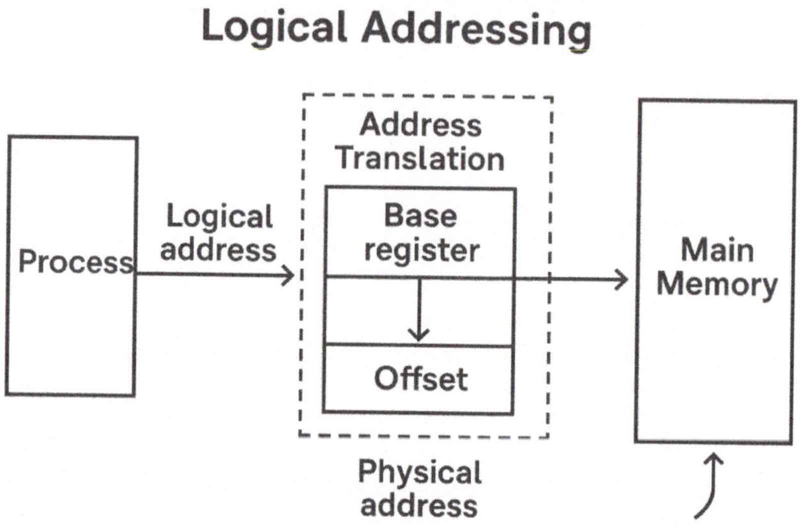

Figure 4.3: Process of Logical Addressing.

Advantages of Logical Addressing

Scalability

Logical addressing is a fundamental concept for scaling networks, particularly when combined with technologies like routing protocols and subnetting. By utilizing logical addresses, networks can be expanded without significant changes to physical infrastructure. For instance, subnetting allows network administrators to divide large networks into smaller, more manageable subnets, optimizing both the network's performance and security. Additionally, routing protocols such as OSPF or BGP facilitate the distribution of logical addresses across vast distances, ensuring that data can be transmitted across different network segments efficiently. This scalability is essential in today's global networks, where millions of devices must be connected and managed seamlessly. The ability to scale logically addresses the growing demand for internet connectivity and ensures networks can accommodate an increasing number of users, devices, and applications without needing a complete overhaul of the underlying physical infrastructure.

Flexibility

One of the primary advantages of logical addressing is its flexibility. Logical addresses, such as IP addresses, can be reassigned or modified without changing the underlying physical hardware. This enables a network to adapt to changing conditions, like network reorganization, addition of new devices, or changing geographical locations, without requiring physical adjustments. For example, a device's IP address can be changed to another subnet without physically relocating the device or replacing any hardware. This flexibility is essential for dynamic environments, particularly in large-scale networks or cloud infrastructures, where addressing schemes may need to be altered frequently. Moreover, it supports easier management and maintenance, as network administrators can reconfigure the network remotely, enhancing operational efficiency. The decoupling of logical addressing from physical hardware also allows for network virtualization and other advanced network management techniques, making it a critical component of modern network design.

Inter-network Communication

Logical addressing is critical for enabling communication between different networks, particularly in the context of the Internet. Without logical addressing, devices on different networks would have no means of identifying or communicating with each other, making inter-network communication impossible. Logical addresses, such as IP addresses, provide a unique identifier for devices, ensuring they can be reached from any other device connected to the Internet, regardless of their physical location. The Internet, as a vast global network, relies heavily on logical addressing to route data between disparate networks. This ability to identify devices across multiple networks makes logical addressing indispensable for connecting the world's millions of devices and enabling a seamless flow of data between them. Furthermore, logical addressing supports protocols like DNS (Domain Name System), which translates human-readable domain names into machine-readable IP addresses, facilitating smooth and effective communication on the Internet.

Routing

Routing is a key function of logical addressing, allowing data to traverse multiple networks and devices to reach its intended destination. Logical addresses, particularly IP addresses, enable routers to make intelligent decisions about the best path for data to travel from the source to the destination across interconnected networks. Routers use routing tables and algorithms, such as RIP, OSPF, or BGP, to determine the optimal route based on factors like network topology, traffic, and distance. Logical addresses facilitate the identification of source and destination devices in these routing processes, ensuring that data packets are directed along the correct paths, even across multiple hops and devices. This routing functionality is essential for the operation of the Internet and large-scale enterprise networks, ensuring that information can be transferred efficiently and reliably across diverse networks. In essence, logical addressing serves as the cornerstone for ensuring data is accurately delivered across complex, interconnected systems.

Structure of Logical Addressing (IPv4 Addressing)

IPv4 addresses are 32 bits in length, often represented in dotted decimal format (e.g., 192.168.1.10).The IPv4 address is divided into two parts:

1. Network Portion: The network portion identifies the network to which the device belongs, helping routers determine the appropriate path for data transmission. The host portion, on the other hand, identifies the individual device (host) within the network. This division enables network administrators to manage and segment networks, making it possible to route traffic between different networks and devices effectively. Understanding the structure of IPv4 addressing is crucial for configuring and managing IP networks.
2. Host Portion: the network portion and the host portion. The network portion identifies the network to which a device belongs, and the host portion identifies the specific device within that network. The combination of these two parts ensures proper routing of data to the correct destination. Network administrators configure network masks, or subnet masks, to determine how many bits arc assigned to the network portion versus the host portion, allowing for flexible network design and scalability.

The subnet mask helps determine the size of the network portion and the host portion of the address. For example, with a subnet mask of 255.255.255.0, the first 24 bits represent the network address, and the last 8 bits represent the host address.

IPv6 Addressing

IPv6 addressing is based on a 128-bit address, providing a vastly larger address space compared to the 32-bit IPv4 system. The 128 bits are divided into 8 groups of 16 bits, and each group is represented as four hexadecimal digits, separated by colons (e.g., 2001:0db8:85a3:0000:0000:8a2e:0370:7334). The hexadecimal notation makes it easier to represent long binary sequences in a more concise format.IPv6 was designed to overcome the limitations of IPv4, particularly the exhaustion of address space. With 128 bits, IPv6 can provide approximately 340 undecillion (3.4×10^38) unique addresses, which is exponentially more than IPv4. This vast address space enables the internet to support a much greater number of devices and allows for future growth without concerns about address depletion. IPv6's extensive addressing is especially important with the rise of the Internet of Things (IoT), where billions of devices need unique identifiers.

IPv6 Addressing Structure

An IPv6 address is composed of 128 bits, split into eight 16-bit blocks. Each block is represented by four hexadecimal digits (e.g., 2001:0db8:85a3:0000:0000:8a2e:0370:7334), which makes the address more manageable than its binary counterpart. These 16-bit blocks are separated by colons, and leading zeros in each block can be omitted to simplify the address representation. For example, an address like 0db8 can be written simply as db8. This reduces redundancy and enhances readability. The structure of IPv6 addresses includes two key components: the network portion and the host portion. The network portion typically refers to the first part of the address, while the host portion identifies a specific device within that network. In practice, this allows for efficient addressing and routing, and also helps with subnetting, which is crucial for network organization and optimization. IPv6's extended address space facilitates efficient routing and better organization of the global internet infrastructure.

IPv6 Address Space

IPv6 provides a vastly larger address space compared to its predecessor IPv4. While IPv4 uses a 32-bit address, resulting in around 4.3 billion unique addresses, IPv6's 128-bit address space offers approximately 340 undecillion unique addresses. This is a fundamental improvement, ensuring that the world's growing number of devices can be addressed without running into limitations. The enormous address space of IPv6 enables each device, even in highly dense environments like cities or data centers, to have its own unique IP address. This feature is crucial for modern technologies such as the Internet of Things (IoT), where billions of devices, from home appliances to sensors, require unique identifiers to communicate. The nearly infinite address pool also supports future scalability, providing ample room for expanding networks, new technologies, and unforeseen innovations in the digital realm. IPv6's address space is key to accommodating the expanding internet and ensuring long-term sustainability.

IPv6 Prefixes and Network Design

In IPv6, addresses are divided into two main parts: the network prefix and the host identifier. The network prefix, typically indicated by a subnet mask, is used to define the network portion of the address, while the host identifier identifies a specific device within the network. This is similar to how IPv4 addresses use subnetting to separate network and host portions.IPv6 addressing also introduces the concept of prefixes, which are similar to subnet masks in IPv4. The prefix is used to identify the network portion of the address, with the remaining bits used for the host portion. A common prefix length in IPv6 is /64, meaning the first 64 bits represent the network, while the remaining 64 bits are reserved for the host. This allows for a large number of devices to be addressed within a single network, making IPv6 especially useful for large-scale networks. Additionally, prefix-based routing helps simplify network configuration and management, enabling more efficient allocation of IP addresses.

Subnetting and Logical Addressing

Subnetting is a method of dividing a network into smaller sub-networks or subnets. This is done by adjusting the subnet mask, which determines how many bits in the IP address correspond to the network portion and how many bits correspond to the host portion.

Subnetting

Subnetting is the practice of breaking a large network into smaller, more manageable sub-networks, called subnets. It involves modifying the network mask, which dictates how many bits in the IP address are dedicated to the network portion and how many bits are left for the host portion. By performing subnetting, an organization can create multiple subnets within the same IP address range. This allows for better resource allocation, reducing network congestion and improving overall performance. Subnetting is essential for organizations with a large number of devices, as it optimizes network management by grouping devices into logical units. It also enhances security by limiting the broadcast domain to smaller sections of the network, thereby reducing the scope of potential security breaches. Subnetting plays a crucial role in both IPv4 and IPv6 addressing schemes, helping administrators effectively manage and organize their networks.

Logical Addressing

Logical addressing is the method of assigning unique IP addresses to devices within a network, ensuring proper communication and data routing. Unlike physical addressing, which relies on hardware-based identifiers like MAC addresses, logical addressing uses IP addresses to define a device's location in a network. Logical addressing plays a central role in the hierarchical structure of networks, where networks are organized into segments or subnets to improve efficiency and scalability. This method enables communication across different types of networks, whether local or distributed, by ensuring that each device has a unique identifier. Logical addressing is crucial for routers and other networking devices, as they use IP addresses to route packets of data across different networks. By using logical addressing, devices can efficiently communicate with one another over both private and public networks, such as the internet, forming the backbone of modern network communication.

Example

IP Address: 192.168.1.0/24

This represents a network with 192.168.1 as the network portion and a /24 subnet mask, which leaves 8 bits for host addresses. If you need to divide this network into two smaller subnets, you could use a subnet mask of /25, resulting in two subnets:

1. Subnet 1: 192.168.1.0/25 (range: 192.168.1.1 to 192.168.1.126)
2. Subnet 2: 192.168.1.128/25 (range: 192.168.1.129 to 192.168.1.254).

Routing and Logical Addressing

Routing is the process of determining the best path for data packets to travel across networks. Logical addresses, like IP addresses, are crucial for the routing process:

Routing

Routing is the process through which data packets are directed across networks from the source to the destination. It involves selecting the most efficient path for the data to traverse, considering factors such as network topology, available routes, and current network conditions. Routers, specialized network devices, are responsible for this process. They use protocols like RIP, OSPF, and BGP to exchange information about network paths and make decisions. Routers operate using routing tables, which contain entries that map network destinations to next-hop addresses. These tables are dynamically updated based on network changes. Routing is essential for large-scale networks like the internet, as it enables efficient and reliable data transmission. By determining the optimal route, routing ensures that data arrives at its intended destination without unnecessary delays, maintaining the flow of information across interconnected systems.

Logical Addressing

Logical addressing refers to the use of IP addresses to identify devices on a network and facilitate communication between them. Unlike physical addresses, such as MAC addresses, logical addresses are designed to work at higher layers of the OSI model, specifically in the network layer. The most commonly used logical addressing scheme is the Internet Protocol (IP) address, which consists of a network portion and a host portion. The network portion identifies the specific network a device is part of, while the host portion identifies the individual device within that network. Logical addressing allows devices across different networks to communicate with each other by providing a unique identifier that can be used for routing purposes. The flexibility of logical addressing enables devices to be located and addressed regardless of their physical location, making it a crucial component of modern networking and the internet.

Router

A router is a networking device responsible for forwarding data packets between different networks. It examines the destination IP address in each packet and determines the best path to reach that destination. Routers are crucial in large-scale networks, such as the internet, as they ensure that data can travel across different segments of a network or between multiple networks. To make forwarding decisions, routers rely on routing tables, which contain information about the network's topology. These tables are dynamically updated using routing protocols like OSPF (Open Shortest Path First) or BGP (Border Gateway Protocol). Routers may also perform network address translation (NAT) to map private IP addresses to public ones for internet access. In essence, routers serve as traffic managers, directing packets through the network to their destination while ensuring efficient and reliable communication between devices.

Forwarding

Forwarding refers to the process of transferring a data packet from one device to another based on routing decisions. Once a router has determined the most appropriate path for a packet using its routing table, it forwards the packet to the next device on the route. This process is repeated at each hop, where each intermediate router performs the same routing decision-making process until the packet reaches its final destination. Forwarding decisions are typically made based on the destination IP address, and the router chooses the next hop by checking the best match in its routing table. Efficient forwarding ensures that packets are transmitted across networks in an optimal and timely manner. In the case of high-traffic networks, forwarding also involves congestion management to prevent packet loss and delays. Ultimately, forwarding enables data to travel across different networks, connecting remote devices and systems.

Dynamic vs. Static Logical Addressing

The Table 4.2 compares Static and Dynamic Logical Addressing, highlighting the differences in address assignment, usage, flexibility, and management. Static logical addressing involves manually assigning fixed addresses to devices, commonly used for network infrastructure like servers and printers, ensuring address consistency. On the other hand, dynamic logical addressing allows devices to automatically obtain addresses via protocols like DHCP, commonly used for client devices such as laptops and smartphones, where the address can change over time. Static addressing offers stability but requires more manual management, while dynamic addressing simplifies network administration by automatically assigning and managing IP addresses, though it can result in address changes that may impact security and device identification.

Table 4.2: Comparison on Dynamic versus Static Logical Addressing.

Feature	Static Logical Addressing	Dynamic Logical Addressing
Definition	Devices are assigned a fixed, permanent address.	Devices are assigned an address temporarily, often automatically.
Address Assignment	Manually configured or fixed by network admin.	Automatically assigned via DHCP (Dynamic Host Configuration Protocol).
Usage	Common for servers, printers, routers, and other infrastructure devices.	Common for client devices like laptops, desktops, and smartphones.
Address Stability	Address remains the same unless manually changed.	Address can change over time, especially after device restarts or lease expiration.
Management Complexity	Requires manual configuration and management.	Easier to manage as addresses are assigned automatically.
Address Flexibility	Inflexible, as the address remains constant.	Flexible, as addresses can change as needed.
Examples	Static IP addresses for a web server.	Dynamic IP addresses for a home laptop or smartphone.
Security Considerations	More secure due to fixed addresses.	Less secure, as addresses can change and be difficult to track.

Address Resolution Protocol (ARP)

ARP is used to map a logical address (e.g., an IP address) to a physical address (e.g., MAC address) within a local network.When a device needs to send data to another device on the same local network, it uses ARP to determine the MAC address of the destination device based on its IP address.ARP broadcasts a request across the local network, and the device with the matching IP address replies with its MAC address.

Private vs. Public Logical Addresses

The Table 4.3 highlights the key differences between Public and Private Logical Addresses. Public addresses are globally unique and routable across the internet, assigned by organizations like IANA or regional internet registries (RIRs). They are essential for devices or services that need to be directly accessed from anywhere on the internet, such as web servers or cloud applications. In contrast, private addresses are reserved for use within private networks and cannot be routed on the internet. They fall within specific address ranges (e.g., 192.168.x.x, 10.x.x.x) and are typically used within local networks like home or office LANs. To connect a private network to the internet, a process like Network Address Translation (NAT) is required, which translates private IP addresses to a public address. This distinction is crucial for understanding how devices are networked internally and how they interact with the external world.

Table 4.3: Comparison on Private versus Public Logical Addresses.

Aspect	Public Addresses	Private Addresses
Definition	Unique IP addresses that are globally routable across the internet.	Reserved IP addresses used within private networks, not routable on the internet.
Assignment Authority	Assigned by IANA (Internet Assigned Numbers Authority) or RIRs (Regional Internet Registries).	Reserved by IANA for internal network use.
Example Ranges	Any IP address outside the reserved private ranges (e.g., 8.8.8.8, 192.0.2.1).	192.168.x.x, 10.x.x.x, 172.16.x.x to 172.31. x.x.
Routing	Routable over the internet.	Not routable over the internet. Requires NAT to access the internet.
Usage	Used for devices that need to be accessed globally (e.g., web servers, email servers).	Used for devices within a local network, such as computers, printers, and internal servers.
Example Usage	Websites, public-facing services, cloud applications.	Home or office LANs, private enterprise networks.

Classes of IP Addressing (IPv4)

IP addresses in IPv4 are categorized into different classes based on the size of the network:

Class A

Class A IP addresses are allocated for very large networks. The address range for Class A starts from 1.0.0.0 and goes up to 127.255.255.255. The first octet (the first 8 bits) represents the network portion of the address, and the remaining three octets (24 bits) are used for host addresses. This allows for a vast number of hosts within a network. Class A can accommodate up to 16 million hosts, which makes it ideal for large organizations or government networks. A notable feature of Class A is that the first bit of the address is always 0, so the address range starts at 1. The Class A range includes some reserved addresses such as 127.x.x.x, which is used for loopback testing (localhost).

Class B

Class B IP addresses are designed for medium-sized networks, and the address range spans from 128.0.0.0 to 191.255.255.255. Class B addresses allocate 16 bits for the network portion and 16 bits for the host portion. This structure allows for up to 65,536 possible hosts within a network, providing a balance between network size and the number of hosts. Networks using Class B IP addresses are typically medium-sized corporations or institutions that require a substantial number of IP addresses but not as many as Class A. The first two bits of a Class B address are fixed as '10', making the address range start at 128. This division ensures that Class B networks can handle a significant number of hosts while maintaining efficient address allocation.

Class C

Class C IP addresses are used for small networks, where fewer hosts are needed. The address range for Class C spans from 192.0.0.0 to 223.255.255.255. The network portion is represented by 24 bits (three octets), while the remaining 8 bits are reserved for host addresses, allowing for up to 254 hosts in a single network. This makes Class C ideal for smaller organizations, local networks, or individual departments that don't require a large number of IP addresses. The first three bits of a Class C address are fixed as '110', and the network address typically starts at 192.0.0.0. Class C is the most common class of IP addresses used by private networks, and its smaller scale is suited for local area networks (LANs).

Class D

Class D IP addresses are reserved for multicast groups, which allow for the transmission of data to multiple devices simultaneously. The range for Class D addresses spans from 224.0.0.0 to 239.255.255.255. Unlike the previous classes, Class D addresses do not have a network/host structure, as they are used for multicast communication. A multicast address enables one-to-many communication, which is typically used in streaming media or conferencing applications, where data is sent to a group of recipients rather than a single device. The first four bits of a Class D address are fixed as '1110', and these addresses are not assigned to any specific network or organization. Class D addresses are essential for network applications that require group communication among multiple recipients.

Class E

Class E IP addresses are reserved for experimental purposes and research use. The address range for Class E spans from 240.0.0.0 to 255.255.255.255. These addresses are not used for general network assignments and are not intended for public use. The first four bits of a Class E address are fixed as '1111', which allows for the identification of experimental and future protocols. While Class E addresses are technically valid, they are not allocated for regular internet use, and their use is largely confined to experimental networks or for research in areas like network protocols and future network innovations. This class ensures that there is a designated space for exploring new technologies without interfering with publicly routable IP addresses.

Basic Internetworking Concepts

Internetworking involves the connection of different types of networks using standardized protocols, ensuring data can flow seamlessly across diverse systems. Below is an explanation of key internetworking concepts including IP, CIDR, ARP, RARP, DHCP, and ICMP.

IP (Internet Protocol)

Internet Protocol (IP) is a fundamental communication protocol that operates in the networking layer of the OSI model. It is used to address and route data packets between devices across networks, ensuring that data reaches its intended destination. IP assigns unique addresses to each device on a network, which is essential for identifying and communicating with devices across diverse networks, including local and wide-area networks. The protocol is responsible for packet forwarding, addressing, and routing to ensure that information is transmitted efficiently and correctly. IP plays a crucial role in the global Internet infrastructure, forming the foundation for network communication and enabling devices to communicate seamlessly over the internet. With the rapid growth of connected devices, the evolution of IP versions like IPv4 and IPv6 has become crucial to address the growing demand for IP addresses and network scalability.

IPv4 (Internet Protocol version 4)

IPv4, or Internet Protocol version 4, is the most commonly used version of IP. It uses a 32-bit address space, which allows for approximately 4.3 billion unique IP addresses. These addresses are divided into different classes (A, B, C, etc.), depending on the network size and range needed. IPv4 addresses are represented in a dotted decimal format, such as "192.168.1.1," where each segment is an 8-bit value, resulting in four octets. While IPv4 has been the backbone of the Internet for decades, the rapid expansion of devices and services led to the exhaustion of available IP addresses. This limitation has driven the development of IPv6. Despite this, IPv4 remains widely in use and continues to function as the dominant protocol in most networks. Its adoption and implementation have been a key factor in the growth and accessibility of the Internet.

IPv6 (Internet Protocol version 6)

IPv6, or Internet Protocol version 6, was developed as the successor to IPv4 to overcome the limitations of address space exhaustion. IPv6 uses a 128-bit address space, which allows for a virtually unlimited number of unique addresses (approximately 340 undecillion addresses), addressing the issue of IPv4 address scarcity. IPv6 addresses are written in hexadecimal notation, consisting of eight groups of four hexadecimal digits separated by colons, such as "2001:0db8 :85a3:0000:0000:8a2e:0370:7334." One of the key advantages of IPv6 is its ability to support the growing number of Internet-connected devices, providing ample address space for future network expansion. Additionally, IPv6 includes improvements such as better security, more efficient routing, and automatic configuration of devices. Despite its benefits, IPv6 adoption has been gradual, and many networks still rely on IPv4 due to compatibility and infrastructure considerations.

Key Characteristics of IP

Routing

Routing in IP refers to the process of determining the path that data packets take across the network from the source to the destination. Routers use routing tables, which store information about network paths, to forward packets to the correct destination. IP enables routers to identify the most efficient route, considering factors such as network topology and traffic conditions. During routing, data packets may pass through multiple routers, and each router uses the destination IP address to forward the packet to the next hop in the path. This process continues until the packet reaches its final destination. Routing is essential for ensuring that data is transmitted efficiently and reliably across large-scale networks, such as the internet. It also accommodates changes in network infrastructure, adapting routes dynamically to account for failures or congestion in the network.

Addressing

IP addressing is a fundamental aspect of networking that assigns unique identifiers to devices on a network. These IP addresses are used to differentiate devices and enable communication between them. There are two main types of IP addresses: IPv4 and IPv6. IPv4 uses a 32-bit address scheme, while IPv6 utilizes a 128-bit address, allowing for a vastly larger number of unique addresses. Each

IP address consists of a network portion, which identifies the network to which the device belongs, and a host portion, which specifies the individual device within that network. IP addresses can be assigned statically, where the address is manually configured, or dynamically, using protocols like DHCP. Proper addressing ensures that data sent across the network reaches the correct device, allowing for seamless communication and efficient data routing. Addressing is crucial for both local and global networking, including internet communications.

CIDR (Classless Inter-Domain Routing)

CIDR is a modern method of allocating IP addresses that replaces the older class-based system (Class A, B, C). It was introduced to improve the efficiency of IP address space usage. The primary advantage of CIDR is that it allows for variable-length subnet masking (VLSM), enabling more flexible and precise network designs. Unlike the rigid class-based system, CIDR eliminates the fixed size of subnet blocks and provides a way to create subnet sizes that closely match the network's requirements. This results in better utilization of IP addresses and avoids wasting valuable address space. CIDR also supports hierarchical routing, which improves the management and scalability of routing tables, especially for large networks. The introduction of CIDR was a crucial step in extending the life of IPv4 by enabling more efficient address allocation and reducing the exhaustion of available IP addresses.

Format of CIDR

CIDR notation combines an IP address and a subnet mask, which is represented by a slash (/) followed by the number of bits allocated for the network portion of the address. This notation allows for precise definition of the network and host segments of the address. For example, the CIDR notation "192.168.0.0/24" means that the first 24 bits (or the first three octets) are used for the network part of the address, while the remaining 8 bits are used for host addresses within that network. This format allows network administrators to create subnets of various sizes based on their specific needs. CIDR notation has become the standard for expressing IP address ranges, providing a more efficient method for representing IP blocks compared to the traditional class-based system. By using this flexible format, networks can be designed more efficiently, reducing waste and improving address allocation.

Benefits of CIDR

The adoption of CIDR brought several significant benefits to networking, the most notable being the more efficient use of IP address space. Unlike the traditional class-based system that assigned fixed-size blocks of IP addresses, CIDR allows networks to be assigned more appropriate-sized address blocks, reducing waste and maximizing the available IP space. This is particularly important with the limited supply of IPv4 addresses. CIDR also helps to reduce the size of routing tables used by routers in the internet backbone, making routing more efficient. By allowing multiple IP address ranges to be aggregated into a single routing table entry, CIDR simplifies routing and enhances network performance. Additionally, CIDR supports the allocation of smaller or larger subnets as needed, enabling network administrators to optimize their network designs and avoid the depletion of IP addresses. Overall, CIDR played a key role in making internet routing more scalable and manageable.

ARP (Address Resolution Protocol)

ARP (Address Resolution Protocol) is a network protocol used to map an IP address to a MAC (Media Access Control) address within a local network. It operates at Layer 2 (Data Link Layer) of the OSI model. When a device needs to communicate with another device within the same local network, it must know the destination device's MAC address. Since devices typically know each other by IP addresses, ARP resolves this mismatch by providing the MAC address corresponding to the IP address.

Process:When a device wants to send data to another device on the same network but does not know its MAC address, it sends an ARP request. This request is broadcasted to all devices on the network, asking who has the corresponding IP address. The device that holds the matching IP address sends an ARP reply with its MAC address. This enables the requesting device to update its ARP table for future communication.

RARP (Reverse Address Resolution Protocol)

RARP (Reverse Address Resolution Protocol) is a network protocol used by a device to obtain its IP address from a network server, knowing only its MAC (Media Access Control) address. It works in the reverse manner of ARP (Address Resolution Protocol), which is used to map an IP address to a MAC address. Devices that are unable to store or configure their IP address, such as diskless workstations, rely on RARP to request an IP address from a RARP server within the local network. The process involves the device sending a broadcast RARP request to the network, which includes its MAC address. A RARP server then responds with the corresponding IP address assigned to that MAC address. Despite its utility, RARP had limitations, such as requiring static server configurations and limited flexibility. It was eventually replaced by more dynamic and versatile protocols like DHCP (Dynamic Host Configuration Protocol), which simplified the assignment of IP addresses.

Limitation of RARP: RARP, although useful in earlier network environments, had significant limitations that led to its replacement by more advanced protocols like DHCP (Dynamic Host Configuration Protocol). One of the key drawbacks of RARP was its reliance on a static mapping server, which needed to be manually configured with the MAC-to-IP address mapping. This static nature made it cumbersome to manage, especially in dynamic or large networks where devices frequently joined or left the network. Additionally, RARP only worked in local network environments and could not easily handle a range of dynamic IP assignments for multiple devices. In contrast, DHCP provides a more efficient, automated, and flexible way of assigning IP addresses. DHCP also supports other network configuration parameters, such as DNS servers and gateways, which RARP could not offer. As a result, RARP became obsolete and was phased out in favor of DHCP for IP address management.

DHCP (Dynamic Host Configuration Protocol)

DHCP (Dynamic Host Configuration Protocol) is a network management protocol used to automatically assign IP addresses and other essential network configuration settings to devices within a network. It streamlines the process of configuring devices to ensure they can communicate with other devices over the network. DHCP reduces the need for manual configuration, making network management simpler and more efficient, particularly in larger networks. It can assign a range of parameters, including IP addresses, default gateway, DNS servers, and more. When a device connects to the network, it communicates with a DHCP server to receive this information. DHCP is essential for maintaining network functionality and scalability without the need for a network administrator to manually configure each device. It supports both IPv4 and IPv6 addressing, which allows it to function in modern and legacy network environments.

DHCP Process: The DHCP process involves a series of steps that enable devices to dynamically obtain network configuration information. When a device first connects to a network, it sends out a DHCP Discover message, looking for a DHCP server. Upon receiving this request, the DHCP server responds with a DHCP Offer message, which includes an available IP address, subnet mask, default gateway, and DNS server addresses. The device then chooses the offer and responds with a DHCP Request message, confirming its acceptance of the offered configuration. Finally, the DHCP server sends a DHCP Ack (acknowledgment) message, completing the process and officially assigning the device its IP address and other network settings. This sequence of messages ensures that devices are properly configured for seamless network communication without requiring manual intervention.

Advantages of DHCP

The primary advantage of DHCP is its ability to automate the process of IP address assignment, significantly reducing the manual effort involved in configuring network devices. By centralizing IP address management, DHCP prevents conflicts that might occur when administrators manually assign addresses to each device. Furthermore, it allows for more efficient management of the IP address pool, particularly in large or dynamic networks, as IP addresses can be reused when devices disconnect or change networks. DHCP also supports both IPv4 and IPv6 addressing, providing flexibility for both modern and older networks. In addition to reducing the administrative burden, DHCP ensures that devices are assigned correct and consistent network configurations, reducing errors and improving overall network reliability. This automated process allows network administrators to focus on higher-level tasks rather than routine configuration chores.

ICMP (Internet Control Message Protocol)

ICMP (Internet Control Message Protocol) is an essential protocol in the Internet Protocol (IP) suite, operating at the network layer. It is primarily used for diagnostic and error-reporting purposes. When network devices, such as routers or computers, encounter issues with packet transmission, ICMP helps to notify the sender about these issues. ICMP messages are crucial for diagnosing network problems, helping administrators and users troubleshoot connectivity issues. For instance, it is used to report errors such as unreachable destinations or expired Time-to-Live (TTL). While ICMP is not directly involved in the delivery of data packets, it serves as a valuable tool for maintaining the health of the network. It is lightweight and versatile, ensuring that data flow interruptions can be promptly identified and addressed. Commonly recognized ICMP-based utilities include "ping" and "traceroute," which provide insights into network performance.

Uses of ICMP

ICMP serves multiple important purposes within a network, particularly for network diagnostics and error handling. One of its primary uses is the Echo Request and Echo Reply messages, commonly associated with the "ping" command. This function allows users to check the reachability of a network device, such as a server or router, by sending an Echo Request. If the destination is reachable, the device replies with an Echo Reply. This simple interaction helps to verify the operational status of a network device and assess the network latency. Another critical use is the Destination Unreachable message, which is sent when a packet cannot be delivered to its intended destination. This could happen for various reasons, such as incorrect routing or an unavailable server. Additionally, ICMP provides the Time Exceeded message, which informs the sender when a packet's Time-to-Live (TTL) field expires, often used for traceroute operations to map out the path packets take across a network.

Echo Request and Echo Reply

The Echo Request and Echo Reply messages are two of the most widely used types of ICMP messages. These messages form the core of the "ping" utility, which is a diagnostic tool used to check the availability of a network host. When a sender sends an Echo Request message to a target IP address, the receiving host responds with an Echo Reply message if it is reachable. This interaction allows network administrators and users to confirm that a device is connected to the network and assess its response time or round-trip time (RTT). Ping is a simple but powerful tool that helps identify connectivity issues and measure network performance. The time between sending the Echo Request and receiving the Echo Reply gives an estimate of the network's latency. While ICMP Echo Requests and Replies are basic, they provide valuable insight into the operational status of a network and the devices on it.

Destination Unreachable

The Destination Unreachable ICMP message is sent when a router or host is unable to deliver a packet to its destination. This message is crucial for troubleshooting network issues, as it informs the sender that the intended recipient cannot be reached. Various factors can trigger this message, including network routing errors, misconfigured devices, or a non-existent IP address. The Destination Unreachable message can be further categorized into several codes that provide more detailed information about why the destination is unreachable. For example, it may indicate that the destination network is unreachable, the port is closed, or the protocol is unrecognized. When a network device receives this message, it can take appropriate action to address the issue, such as re-routing the packet, notifying the user, or attempting to find an alternative route. Overall, this ICMP message helps to detect and diagnose issues related to packet delivery.

Time Exceeded

The Time Exceeded ICMP message is generated when a packet's Time-to-Live (TTL) field expires, typically as a result of a long journey through the network. Each packet has a TTL field that specifies the number of hops (routers) the packet can make before being discarded. When this field reaches zero, the router sends a Time Exceeded message back to the sender. This functionality is essential for preventing packets from circulating endlessly in the network due to routing loops or misconfigurations. Time Exceeded messages are commonly used in network diagnostic tools such as traceroute. Traceroute works by sending packets with incrementally increasing TTL values, allowing it to map out the series of routers a packet passes through to reach its destination. By examining the Time Exceeded messages along the way, users can trace the path a packet takes and identify points of failure or delays in the network.

ICMP Message Types

Type 0: Echo Reply

ICMP Type 0, also known as the Echo Reply message, is used as a response to an Echo Request message (ICMP Type 8). This message serves as an acknowledgment that the destination device has received the ICMP Echo Request. When a device sends an Echo Request to another device to check its reachability, the receiving device responds with an Echo Reply. The message includes the data sent in the original Echo Request to confirm that the device is still operational and reachable on the network. The Echo Reply is commonly used by the ping command, which is used for network diagnostics. This message does not indicate any errors or problems; instead, it merely serves to confirm that the destination is reachable. The Echo Reply message contains the same data as the Echo Request, enabling the sender to measure round-trip time and ensure proper network connectivity.

Type 3: Destination Unreachable

ICMP Type 3, known as the Destination Unreachable message, is sent by a router or destination host to inform the sender that their packet could not reach the intended destination. There are several subtypes within Type 3, each specifying the reason for the failure. Common causes for this message include network or host unreachable conditions, issues with protocol or port unavailability, or when the packet is dropped because it exceeds the allowable time to live (TTL). This message is vital for error handling in network communication, as it alerts the sender that the destination is unreachable under the current network conditions. Network troubleshooting tools, like traceroute, rely on ICMP Type 3 messages to identify where packets are being dropped in the network. The Destination Unreachable message helps administrators pinpoint network issues, such as incorrect routing or connectivity problems, so that corrective actions can be taken.

Type 8: Echo Request

ICMP Type 8, also known as the Echo Request message, is used to initiate a network diagnostic procedure by sending a request to another host or device to check its reachability. This message is often used by the ping command to determine whether a device is online and responsive. When an Echo Request is sent, the receiver is expected to reply with an Echo Reply (ICMP Type 0), indicating that the device is reachable. The Echo Request includes a sequence number and a timestamp, which allows the sender to measure the round-trip time (RTT) for the packet to travel to the destination and back. This process is essential for network monitoring and troubleshooting, as it provides a simple method to verify network connectivity and identify delays. If no response is received within a specified timeout period, it indicates potential connectivity issues between the sender and receiver.

Summary of Protocols

These protocols form the backbone of communication on the internet and within local networks, ensuring devices can connect, address, resolve, and communicate efficiently in Table 4.4.

Table 4.4: Summary of Protocols.

Protocol	Purpose	Layer	Examples
IP	Addressing and routing data across networks	Network (Layer 3)	IPv4, IPv6
CIDR	Efficient allocation of IP addresses	Network (Layer 3)	192.168.1.0/24
ARP	Resolves IP addresses to MAC addresses	Data Link (Layer 2)	ARP request/reply
RARP	Resolves MAC addresses to IP addresses	Data Link (Layer 2)	Deprecated protocol
DHCP	Automatically assigns IP addresses to devices	Application (Layer 7)	DHCP Discover, Offer, Request
ICMP	Sends error messages and diagnostics		

Routing

Routing refers to the process of selecting the optimal path for data packets to travel across a network from the source to the destination. Routers are responsible for routing, as they determine the best route for the data based on factors like network topology, destination address, and routing algorithms. Routing is generally performed at the network layer (Layer 3) of the OSI model. There are two main types of routing in Figure 4.4:

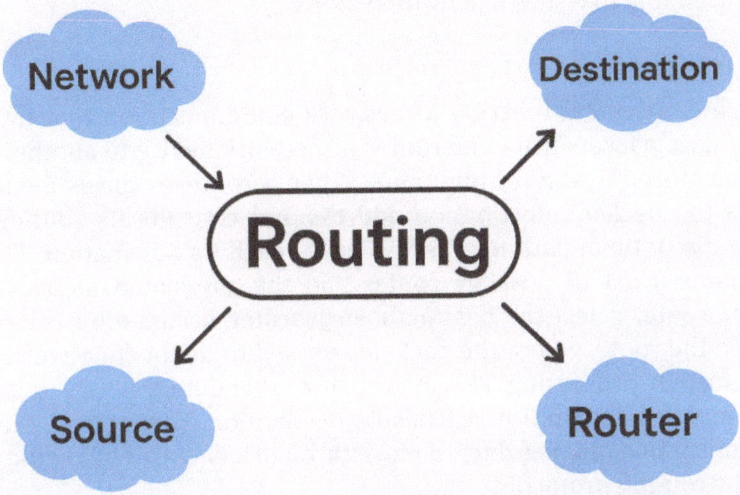

Figure 4.4: Types of routing.

Static Routing

Static routing is a method where routes are manually configured by the network administrator. In this method, the administrator assigns fixed paths for data transmission between devices in the network. These routes are stored in the routing table and remain constant unless manually changed by the administrator. Static routing is suitable for small or simple networks with minimal changes in topology. One advantage is that it does not require additional resources for routing decisions since the path is predefined. However, static routing has limitations, especially in larger or more complex networks where the network topology frequently changes. If a network link fails, static routes will not adapt automatically, leading to potential downtime. Additionally, managing static routes across large networks can be time-consuming and prone to errors.

Dynamic Routing

Dynamic routing, in contrast, uses specialized protocols to allow routers to automatically exchange routing information with each other. These protocols, such as RIP (Routing Information Protocol), OSPF (Open Shortest Path First), and BGP (Border Gateway Protocol), enable routers to adjust routes based on current network conditions. Dynamic routing is highly adaptable and can quickly respond to changes in network topology, such as a failed link or a newly added route. As a result, it is particularly beneficial in larger, more complex networks. The key advantage is that it reduces the need for manual intervention, as routes are updated automatically. However, dynamic routing can be resource-intensive, requiring more CPU and memory on routers. It also involves the potential risk of incorrect routing decisions if the routing protocol's algorithms or configurations are flawed, leading to issues like routing loops.

Forwarding

Forwarding is a critical function in network communication that involves the transfer of data packets from one router or network device to another based on information stored in the routing table. When a router receives a data packet, it inspects the packet's destination address and consults its routing table to determine the optimal path for the packet to reach its destination. The routing table contains a list of possible routes and the associated metrics for each, helping the router select the best path. Forwarding occurs after the router has determined the route, where the packet is passed to the next network device or router for further processing. This step ensures that data travels across different networks and devices until it reaches its destination. Forwarding, therefore, is the mechanism that enables data to move through a network following the paths specified by routing protocols.

Delivery

Delivery refers to the final step in the packet transmission process, where the packet is delivered to the correct destination device on the network. This process involves determining the correct interface or link to forward the packet to, eventually reaching the device (host) that requested it. The packet's destination address, typically an IP address, plays a crucial role in this process. Routers and other network devices examine the destination address, checking their routing tables to determine the most efficient path. If the packet's final destination is within a local network, it will be forwarded directly to the appropriate device through the correct link. If the destination is outside the local network, the packet will traverse multiple routers and network segments before reaching the final device. Proper delivery ensures the successful transfer of data, enabling applications and services on the destination device to process the packet and complete the communication process.

Static vs. Dynamic Routing

Both static and dynamic routing have their roles, with static routing being more suited for simple, stable environments and dynamic routing being better for large, dynamic networks where scalability and automatic adaptation to changes are essential in Table 4.5.

Table 4.5: Comparison on Static versus Dynamic Routing.

Feature	Static Routing	Dynamic Routing
Configuration	Manual (static IP addresses, routes)	Automatic (using routing protocols)
Network Size	Best for small networks	Ideal for large, complex networks
Adaptability	No automatic adjustment to network changes	Automatically adjusts to changes (e.g., link failure)
Routing Protocols	None	RIP, OSPF, EIGRP, BGP
Scalability	Not scalable	Highly scalable
Overhead	Low (no protocol exchange)	Higher (protocol exchange overhead)
Complexity	Simple	More complex to configure and maintain
Example Use Cases	Small office, fixed network	Enterprise networks, large-scale environments

Static Routing

In static routing, the network administrator manually configures routes in the router's routing table. The router will follow these pre-configured paths to forward traffic, and these paths will remain unchanged unless the administrator makes adjustments. The configuration involves specifying the destination networks and the corresponding next-hop IP address. Static routing is often used in simple or small networks where the traffic paths are predictable and do not change frequently. The routes defined in static routing are fixed and require manual updates to accommodate any changes in the network topology.

Example: A simple static route configuration might look like this on a router:

ip route 192.168.2.0 255.255.255.0 192.168.1.1

This means that any packet destined for the 192.168.2.0 network will be forwarded via the 192.168.1.1 gateway.

Advantages of Static Routing

The simplicity of static routing makes it an ideal solution for small, stable networks. Since the routes are predefined by the administrator, there is no need for complex routing protocols to manage the paths, reducing the computational overhead. Additionally, static routing provides predictable and consistent routing behavior, making it easier to troubleshoot network issues. Furthermore, the absence of dynamic protocols eliminates the risks of unwanted routing behavior, such as route flapping or convergence delays, typically seen in dynamic routing protocols.

Disadvantages of Static Routing

Despite its advantages, static routing has several drawbacks. One of the primary limitations is its lack of scalability, making it unsuitable for large networks. The administrator must manually configure and update routes, which becomes increasingly cumbersome as the network grows. Static routes also do not automatically adapt to changes in the network, such as link failures or changes in the topology. In case of a network issue, the static routes must be manually updated, resulting in potential network downtime until the routes are reconfigured.

Use Cases for Static Routing

Static routing is most effective in small networks where the routing paths are stable and do not change frequently. It is also useful in networks where specific paths need to be followed for security, performance, or policy reasons. For example, static routes are often deployed in networks where traffic must follow specific secure paths, such as in environments with sensitive data or stringent security policies. Additionally, static routing is commonly used in branch offices or remote sites with minimal network complexity.

Dynamic Routing

Dynamic routing uses routing protocols to automatically exchange routing information between routers. The routers adjust their routing tables based on real-time network conditions, such as changes in topology or link status.

Example: In OSPF, routers send hello packets to each other to form neighbor relationships. After exchanging routing information, routers build a link-state database and compute the shortest path to each destination using Dijkstra's algorithm.

Common Dynamic Routing Protocols:

RIP (Routing Information Protocol)

RIP (Routing Information Protocol) is one of the oldest and simplest dynamic routing protocols, classified as a distance-vector protocol. It uses hop count as its metric to determine the best path to a destination. RIP has a maximum hop count of 15, which limits its scalability to larger networks. Each router in a RIP network periodically broadcasts its routing table to its neighbors, allowing other routers to update their routes accordingly. RIP is relatively easy to configure and is well-suited for smaller or less complex networks. However, its performance degrades in larger networks due to its limited metric and slow convergence time. Despite these limitations, RIP is still used in smaller environments or as a learning tool for understanding dynamic routing protocols.

OSPF (Open Shortest Path First)

OSPF (Open Shortest Path First) is a link-state dynamic routing protocol, commonly used in large enterprise networks. Unlike RIP, which uses hop count as its metric, OSPF uses the cost of a route, which is calculated based on factors such as bandwidth. OSPF employs Dijkstra's algorithm to determine the shortest path to a destination, ensuring that routers in the network have a synchronized view of the entire topology. This results in faster convergence compared to distance-vector protocols like RIP. OSPF is highly scalable and efficient in large networks, as it supports hierarchical network designs with areas, reducing the size of routing tables and enhancing performance. Its robustness and scalability make it ideal for large networks with frequent route changes and complex topologies.

EIGRP (Enhanced Interior Gateway Routing Protocol)

EIGRP (Enhanced Interior Gateway Routing Protocol) is a Cisco proprietary dynamic routing protocol that blends the features of both distance-vector and link-state protocols. EIGRP uses a metric called the "composite metric," which includes bandwidth, delay, load, and reliability, to determine the best path. It uses Diffusing Update Algorithm (DUAL) to ensure loop-free and efficient routing within the network. EIGRP is faster and more efficient than RIP, as it converges quickly and only sends updates when there are changes in the network, reducing the amount of bandwidth used. It also supports both IPv4 and IPv6 routing and is commonly used in large Cisco-based networks due to its flexibility, scalability, and ability to handle complex topologies. EIGRP is also easier to configure than OSPF in some scenarios, especially within Cisco environments.

BGP (Border Gateway Protocol)

BGP (Border Gateway Protocol) is the primary routing protocol used to route traffic between different autonomous systems (ASes) on the internet. Unlike OSPF and EIGRP, which are interior gateway protocols (IGPs) used within a single AS, BGP is a path-vector protocol that uses policies and rules to select the most efficient route. BGP makes routing decisions based on a variety of factors such as path length, network policies, and rule-based attributes like AS path, prefix length, and next-hop address. It is highly scalable and supports the vast inter-domain routing needs of the global internet. BGP is also known for its stability and flexibility, allowing internet service providers (ISPs) to define routing policies and control traffic flow across multiple networks. Its use is essential for managing large-scale, global networks.

Use Cases

Dynamic routing protocols like RIP, OSPF, EIGRP, and BGP are essential in modern, complex network environments where static routing is impractical due to the dynamic nature of network topologies. They are especially useful in larger networks where the number of devices and routes is too large to manage manually. These protocols adapt automatically to network changes such as link failures, route adjustments, or bandwidth changes, ensuring that data continues to flow efficiently without human intervention. For instance, BGP is used to manage internet routing across different ISPs, while OSPF and EIGRP are widely deployed in large enterprise networks where frequent topology changes occur. Additionally, dynamic routing protocols improve fault tolerance, optimize network performance, and support scalability, which is critical for growing organizations and service providers.

Routing Algorithms and Protocols

Routing algorithms and protocols are essential components of computer networks that define the method of selecting paths for data transmission across a network in Figure 4.5. There are two main types of routing protocols: static and dynamic.

Routing Algorithms

Routing algorithms define the way routes are selected based on various metrics such as distance, network topology, and load. They can be categorized into the following types:

Distance Vector Routing

Distance vector routing algorithms determine the best path to a destination based on the number of hops, or the distance, from the source to the destination. Each router in the network maintains a table, often called a routing table, that lists the best-known distance to each destination. Routers periodically share these tables with their neighbors, allowing them to update their own routing tables based on the new information received. This process is called "distance vector" because routers exchange information about the distance to various destinations. A key characteristic of distance vector routing is its simplicity. A common example of a distance vector protocol is the Routing Information Protocol (RIP), which uses hop count as its primary metric. RIP is widely used in smaller networks due to its ease of implementation, though it is less efficient in larger or more complex networks due to its slow convergence time and lack of scalability.

Link-State Routing

Link-state routing algorithms maintain a complete view of the network topology, which helps in selecting the best path to a destination. Each router independently discovers its neighbors and builds a map of the entire network, typically using a method called "flooding." Routers then use algorithms, like Dijkstra's algorithm, to calculate the shortest path to each destination. This method ensures that each router has up-to-date information about the network's structure. A well-known example of a link-state routing protocol is Open Shortest Path First (OSPF). OSPF is commonly used in large enterprise networks because it provides fast convergence and scalability compared to distance vector protocols. By maintaining an accurate map of the network, link-state protocols like OSPF can quickly adapt to network changes, such as link failures or topology alterations, ensuring optimal routing paths are always used.

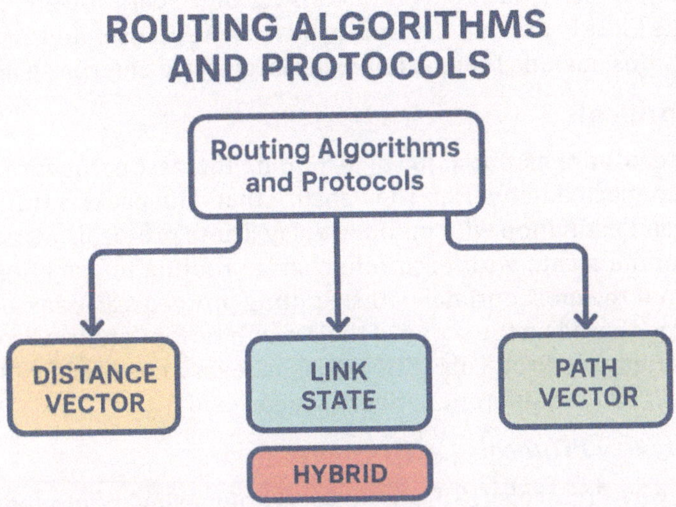

Figure 4.5: Routing Algorithms and Protocols.

Path-Vector Routing

Path-vector routing algorithms maintain a table of complete paths, rather than just distances, to reach various destinations. These algorithms determine the best path by analyzing various path attributes, such as the sequence of routers that must be traversed to reach the destination. Each entry in the table represents a path to a destination, and routers exchange path information with their neighbors to update their own routing tables. Border Gateway Protocol (BGP) is the most widely used path-vector routing protocol. BGP is essential for routing data between different autonomous systems on the internet, making it a core protocol for inter-domain routing. One of the key advantages of path-vector routing is its ability to handle complex network topologies and ensure that routing decisions consider various path attributes, including policy-based routing, path length, and other metrics like AS path length, which is useful for controlling routing decisions between different organizations.

Hybrid Routing

Hybrid routing algorithms combine the features of both distance vector and link-state routing protocols to offer a balance between efficiency and scalability. These protocols take advantage of the simplicity of distance vector algorithms for small, local networks, while also using the topological knowledge provided by link-state algorithms for better performance in larger networks. One widely known example of a hybrid routing protocol is Enhanced Interior Gateway Routing Protocol (EIGRP), which was developed by Cisco. EIGRP uses a combination of distance vector and link-state principles, allowing it to adapt to changing network conditions while minimizing the convergence time. EIGRP employs a sophisticated metric system that accounts for bandwidth, delay, load, and reliability, offering flexibility in choosing the most efficient path. Hybrid protocols like EIGRP provide scalability, fast convergence, and more accurate routing decisions, making them suitable for large-scale enterprise networks.

Routing Protocols

Routing protocols are essential for determining the best paths for data transfer across interconnected networks. They ensure that data packets travel efficiently and reach their destination with minimal delay. These protocols work by enabling routers to communicate with each other, share routing information, and make decisions about the most optimal paths. Routing protocols are classified into two main categories based on the scope of their use: Interior Gateway Protocols (IGP) and Exterior Gateway Protocols (EGP). Each category has specific functions and protocols designed for different network scenarios.

Interior Gateway Protocols (IGP)

Interior Gateway Protocols (IGPs) are used within a single Autonomous System (AS), typically controlled by one organization. Their primary function is to determine the best route for data within the internal network. IGPs operate based on the network topology and ensure efficient data transfer within an AS. Common example of IGPs include Routing Information Protocol (RIP), Open Shortest Path First (OSPF), and Enhanced Interior Gateway Routing Protocol (EIGRP). These protocols vary in complexity and performance, with OSPF and EIGRP generally offering better scalability and reliability compared to RIP.

Exterior Gateway Protocols (EGP)

Exterior Gateway Protocols (EGPs) are used to route traffic between different Autonomous Systems (AS). Unlike IGPs, which operate within a single AS, EGPs enable communication between multiple networks that may be owned by different organizations. The most well-known example of an EGP is the Border Gateway Protocol (BGP), which plays a crucial role in the global internet routing infrastructure. BGP allows different ASs to exchange routing information and ensures the efficient transfer of data between various networks, making it integral to the functioning of the internet. EGPs are designed to handle larger, more complex networks and provide stability and flexibility in inter-network routing.Each protocol has its own strengths and weaknesses depending on the network requirements, such as speed, scalability, or fault tolerance.

Congestion Control Algorithms

Congestion control algorithms are used to manage the amount of data in a network to avoid congestion, where the network becomes overwhelmed by too much data. This leads to delays, packet loss, and reduced network performance in Figure 4.6. Common congestion control algorithms include:

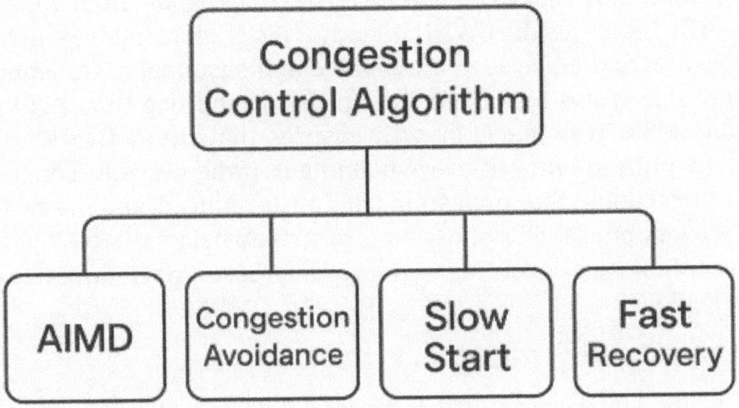

Figure 4.6:Types of Congestion Control Algorithms.

TCP Congestion Control

TCP Congestion Control is a crucial mechanism within the Transmission Control Protocol (TCP) designed to ensure efficient and reliable data transmission over networks by managing network congestion. It prevents congestion from overwhelming the network and causing packet loss or delays. The primary objective is to maximize throughput while minimizing the chances of congestion-induced disruptions. This process involves various phases that dynamically adjust the congestion window (CWND) based on network feedback. The algorithm operates in multiple stages, including Slow Start, Congestion Avoidance, Fast Retransmit, and Fast Recovery. These phases allow TCP to adapt to changing network conditions, ensuring the efficient and orderly transmission of data across the network.

Slow Start

Slow Start is the first phase of TCP congestion control, where the algorithm begins with a small congestion window (CWND), typically starting at one or two maximum segment sizes (MSS). During this phase, the CWND grows exponentially with each acknowledgment (ACK) received, effectively doubling the window size for every round trip time (RTT). This exponential increase helps TCP quickly utilize available network bandwidth without overwhelming the network. However, as the CWND grows, the network may approach its capacity, prompting the transition to the next phase, Congestion Avoidance. Slow Start continues until the congestion window exceeds a predefined threshold known as the slow start threshold (ssthresh), at which point the growth rate of the CWND slows down to prevent congestion.

Congestion Avoidance

Congestion Avoidance is the second phase in TCP congestion control, triggered once the congestion window (CWND) surpasses the slow start threshold (ssthresh). Unlike Slow Start, where the CWND grows exponentially, in Congestion Avoidance, TCP increases the CWND linearly. This gradual increase helps prevent rapid congestion and ensures a more stable and sustainable transmission rate. The window size grows by a fixed amount per round trip time (RTT), which is typically one MSS. This linear growth ensures that the network's capacity is incrementally utilized without overwhelming it. If the network congestion level reaches a critical point, the congestion window is reduced, and the system enters the Fast Recovery phase. This phase aims to strike a balance between throughput and network stability by avoiding aggressive increases in window size that could lead to packet loss.

Fast Retransmit and Fast Recovery

Fast Retransmit and Fast Recovery are TCP mechanisms designed to handle packet loss efficiently, enhancing the overall performance of congestion control. When a sender receives three duplicate acknowledgments (ACKs) for the same packet, it assumes that the packet has been lost and triggers Fast Retransmit. The lost packet is retransmitted immediately without waiting for the timeout period, which helps in minimizing delay and improving throughput. After Fast Retransmit, the protocol enters the Fast Recovery phase, where the congestion window (CWND) is adjusted to avoid further congestion. The CWND is reduced but not drastically; rather, it's adjusted to a point that allows for recovery without excessively throttling the connection. Fast Recovery enables the sender to continue transmitting data, ensuring that throughput is maintained while preventing excessive congestion.

Additive Increase/Multiplicative Decrease (AIMD)

Additive Increase/Multiplicative Decrease (AIMD) is the core mechanism behind TCP's congestion control strategy. AIMD dynamically adjusts the congestion window (CWND) based on the network's current congestion state. In the Additive Increase phase, TCP increases the CWND slowly, adding a small amount for each round-trip time (RTT) to avoid overloading the network. This ensures that as network conditions improve, more bandwidth is used, which helps maximize throughput. However, when packet loss occurs, typically signaled by duplicate acknowledgments or a timeout, the Multiplicative Decrease phase kicks in. During this phase, the CWND is reduced by a factor (usually halved), signaling a reduction in the sender's transmission rate to alleviate congestion. AIMD allows TCP to balance between aggressive data transmission and cautious reaction to congestion, optimizing network utilization while minimizing the risk of congestion collapse.

Random Early Detection (RED)

Random Early Detection (RED) is an active queue management (AQM) technique used in networking, particularly in routers, to manage congestion. The primary goal of RED is to prevent congestion by detecting early signs and responding before the network becomes overwhelmed. It works by monitoring the queue length in routers and randomly dropping packets when the average queue length exceeds a predefined threshold. This early packet drop signals the sender to reduce its transmission rate, preventing further congestion. By randomly dropping packets, RED avoids global synchronization, where all sources reduce their rates simultaneously, which can lead to underutilization of the network. RED is effective in improving network stability and fairness, especially in environments with varying traffic patterns. The key advantage of RED is that it can be tuned to optimize performance by adjusting the threshold and dropping probability, thereby preventing buffer overflow and maintaining network efficiency.

Explicit Congestion Notification (ECN)

Explicit Congestion Notification (ECN) is an enhancement to the traditional congestion control mechanisms in networking. Unlike methods that drop packets to signal congestion, ECN works by marking packets with a congestion indication flag. When network routers detect congestion, they set the ECN field in the IP header of the packet, rather than dropping it. This ECN-marked packet is forwarded to the receiver, which then notifies the sender to reduce the transmission rate. ECN helps to minimize the negative effects of packet loss, such as retransmissions, thus improving network performance. By marking packets instead of discarding them, ECN enables a more efficient way to manage congestion without introducing the overhead associated with packet loss. It is commonly used in TCP and other transport protocols, providing a more graceful congestion management solution that helps maintain throughput and reduce delays, benefiting both real-time and bulk data applications.

Active Queue Management (AQM)

Active Queue Management (AQM) refers to a set of techniques that routers use to manage packet queues and control congestion proactively before it becomes critical. Rather than waiting for the queue to overflow, AQM algorithms monitor the queue length and make decisions to drop or mark packets based on certain conditions. One common AQM technique is Random Early Detection (RED), which helps manage congestion by dropping packets early when the queue reaches a threshold. By doing so, AQM techniques like RED can signal the sender to decrease its transmission rate and prevent further buildup of packets, ensuring that the network remains stable and efficient. AQM algorithms aim to improve network performance by reducing buffer bloat, minimizing delays, and ensuring fairness among different flows. These mechanisms are essential in scenarios were maintaining low latency and avoiding congestion are critical, such as in real-time communication and video streaming applications.

IPv6 (Internet Protocol version 6)

IPv6 is the most recent iteration of the Internet Protocol designed to overcome the limitations of IPv4, particularly the exhaustion of available IP addresses. It was introduced to provide a larger address space, better security features, and improved network performance. IPv6 is crucial in the era of an ever-growing number of internet-connected devices, from smartphones to IoT devices. With its 128-bit address length, IPv6 can accommodate an enormous number of unique IP addresses, ensuring that the internet can continue to scale. Additionally, IPv6 simplifies networking processes, improves security, and enhances mobility, addressing the limitations of IPv4 and paving the way for more efficient and secure internet communication in the future. The Key Features of IPv6:

One of the key advantages of IPv6 is its larger address space. While IPv4 is limited to approximately 4.3 billion unique addresses using 32-bit addresses, IPv6 uses 128-bit addresses, which allows for around 3.4 × 10^38 unique IP addresses. This expansion is crucial for supporting the increasing number of devices and applications relying on internet connectivity, from smart home devices to industrial systems. The larger address space ensures that there will be no shortage of IP addresses for the foreseeable future. This feature is essential for enabling the full realization of the Internet of Things (IoT), where billions of devices need to be uniquely identified on the network.

Simplified Header Format

IPv6 features a simplified header format compared to IPv4. In IPv4, the header contains several fields that are either rarely used or redundant, which can add processing overhead on routers. IPv6 reduces this complexity by eliminating unnecessary fields, resulting in more efficient packet processing. For example, IPv6 headers have a fixed length of 40 bytes, which allows for faster packet forwarding. With a more streamlined header, routers are able to process IPv6 packets more quickly, reducing delays and improving overall network performance. This improvement is particularly beneficial in high-speed and large-scale networks, where efficiency is crucial for optimal data transmission.

Auto-Configuration

One of the significant features of IPv6 is its support for Stateless Address Autoconfiguration (SLAAC). This allows devices on an IPv6 network to automatically assign themselves an IP address without the need for a DHCP (Dynamic Host Configuration Protocol) server. SLAAC simplifies network administration and improves the user experience by enabling plug-and-play functionality for devices. When a device connects to an IPv6-enabled network, it can automatically configure its own address based on the network prefix. This feature is particularly useful in scenarios where rapid device deployment or mobility is needed, such as in IoT environments or large enterprise networks, where manual IP address assignment would be time-consuming.

Improved Security

IPv6 was designed with security in mind, offering several enhancements over IPv4. One of the most notable security features is the mandatory inclusion of IPsec, which provides encryption and integrity protection for data transmitted over the network. While IPsec is optional in IPv4, IPv6 requires it as part of the standard, ensuring that data transmission is secure by default. This mandatory security feature helps protect against threats such as eavesdropping and data tampering. In addition, IPv6's support for privacy extensions provides further protection by allowing devices to generate random addresses, preventing tracking based on fixed IP addresses. These built-in security features make IPv6 a more robust and secure protocol for modern networking needs.

Better Mobility

IPv6 enhances mobile device communication with support for Mobile IPv6 (MIPv6). This feature enables mobile devices to maintain active connections even as they move between different networks. Unlike IPv4, which typically requires a new IP address whenever a device changes networks, IPv6 allows for seamless handoffs without losing connectivity. Mobile IPv6 uses a process where the device's home address remains constant while it obtains a temporary care-of address when connecting to different networks. This improves the performance of mobile applications, such as VoIP or video conferencing, by reducing the interruption in service when users switch between cellular networks or Wi-Fi networks, thus ensuring uninterrupted connectivity.

Multicast *and Anycast Support*

IPv6 introduces enhanced support for multicast and anycast communication, which significantly improves network efficiency. Multicast allows data to be sent to multiple devices simultaneously, reducing bandwidth usage compared to sending individual copies of data to each device. This is particularly useful for streaming media, video conferencing, and other group communication applications. Anycast, on the other hand, allows data to be sent to the nearest device in a group of potential recipients. This reduces latency and improves response times by directing traffic to the most efficient destination. Both multicast and anycast support make IPv6 a more efficient and scalable protocol, especially in large-scale networks and content delivery applications.

IPv6 Addressing

IPv6 addressing is designed to provide a larger address space compared to IPv4, accommodating the growing number of devices on the internet. IPv6 addresses are 128-bit in length and are written as eight groups of four hexadecimal digits separated by colons. This expanded address space resolves the exhaustion issues faced by IPv4. IPv6 addresses are categorized into several types based on their function in network communication. These include global unicast addresses, link-local addresses, multicast addresses, and anycast addresses, each serving specific purposes in routing and communication across networks. By implementing IPv6, the internet is better equipped to handle the demands of modern networking and the increasing number of devices, ensuring efficient routing and more secure communication.

Global Unicast Address

The Global Unicast Address (GUA) in IPv6 functions similarly to a public IP address in IPv4. It is globally unique, meaning no two devices in the world should have the same GUA. These addresses are routable across the internet, and they follow a hierarchical structure that aids efficient routing. A GUA typically begins with the prefix "2000: :/3" and is allocated by the IANA (Internet Assigned Numbers Authority) to organizations based on their needs. The Global Unicast Address ensures that every device on the internet can be uniquely identified and accessible, contributing to the scalability and sustainability of the internet infrastructure. It is primarily used for external communication between devices across different networks and the broader internet.

Link-Local Address

A Link-Local Address in IPv6 is used for communication within a single network segment or link, meaning it is not routable beyond the local network. These addresses are automatically configured on all IPv6-enabled interfaces and do not require any manual configuration or DHCP server. The link-local address is prefixed with "fe80::/10" and can be used for tasks like neighbor discovery, local communications, and router advertisements within a local network segment. They are essential for functions such as autoconfiguration and local diagnostics. Link-local addresses are non-routable, ensuring they stay within the local network, which helps in maintaining security and reducing unnecessary traffic across different network segments.

Multicast Address

In IPv6, a Multicast Address is used to send data packets to multiple destinations simultaneously, improving the efficiency of the communication process. Instead of sending individual copies of a message to each recipient, multicast allows the sender to transmit a single packet that can be received by multiple devices that are part of a multicast group. These addresses are identified with the prefix "ff00: :/8". Multicast addresses are particularly useful in applications such as streaming media, conference calls, and any situation where the same information needs to be delivered to multiple recipients at once. The multicast model helps reduce network congestion and optimize bandwidth utilization by eliminating redundant transmissions.

Anycast Address

The Anycast Address in IPv6 is an address that can be assigned to multiple devices, but unlike multicast, packets sent to an anycast address are routed to the nearest device in terms of routing distance. This makes anycast ideal for services that require load balancing and fault tolerance, such as DNS servers and content delivery networks (CDNs). Anycast addresses provide a mechanism to route traffic to the closest available service node, ensuring faster response times and improving the overall reliability of internet services. When a packet is sent to an anycast address, it is delivered to the first reachable node in the group, based on the network topology and routing protocol.

Transition from IPv4 to IPv6

The transition from IPv4 to IPv6 has been a slow yet crucial process due to the vast number of systems still running IPv4. IPv4, with its 32-bit address space, offers about 4.3 billion unique IP addresses, which has proven insufficient for the growing number of devices connecting to the internet. IPv6, on the other hand, uses a 128-bit address space, offering an almost unlimited supply of IP addresses to accommodate the expanding Internet of Things (IoT) and other connected technologies. While IPv6 adoption is essential for the long-term scalability of the internet, its deployment faces hurdles, particularly in legacy systems that rely on IPv4. Despite these challenges, IPv6 adoption is progressing steadily, with various transition mechanisms in place to ensure interoperability between IPv4 and IPv6 networks, including dual-stack configurations, tunneling, and translation techniques.

IPv6 Transition Mechanisms

Several transition mechanisms have been designed to ease the migration from IPv4 to IPv6. One of the most common approaches is the dual-stack method, where both IPv4 and IPv6 are run on the same device or network infrastructure simultaneously. This approach allows for compatibility with both IP versions during the transition period. Another method is tunneling, which involves encapsulating IPv6 packets within IPv4 packets to enable communication over an IPv4-only network. Tunneling ensures that IPv6 traffic can still be sent across IPv4 infrastructure until full IPv6 support is in place. Additionally, translation techniques are used to convert IPv6 packets into IPv4 packets and vice versa, allowing devices running different IP versions to communicate seamlessly. These mechanisms help bridge the gap between IPv4 and IPv6 networks, ensuring a smooth transition while minimizing disruptions to existing services.

Importance of IPv6 for Future-Proofing the Internet

IPv6 is essential for the future-proofing of the internet, particularly as the number of connected devices continues to rise exponentially. The explosive growth of the Internet of Things (IoT), smart devices, and the expansion of mobile networks are pushing the demand for IP addresses beyond the capacity of IPv4. IPv6 addresses this challenge by offering an address space that is 340 undecillion times larger than IPv4's, providing virtually unlimited IP addresses. This vast address pool allows for more devices to connect directly to the internet, facilitating the continued growth and innovation of digital technologies. Moreover, IPv6 introduces improved security features, better network efficiency, and enhanced support for mobility. Its adoption ensures that the internet can scale to meet future needs, making it crucial for the long-term sustainability of global communication infrastructure. Without IPv6, the internet could face address exhaustion and network fragmentation in the near future.

Conclusion

The Network Layer plays a pivotal role in ensuring the successful transmission of data across networks, especially within the vast interconnected framework of the internet. This layer is responsible for the logical addressing of devices, which is primarily achieved through protocols such as IP (Internet Protocol), facilitating the identification and communication of devices within a network. By using techniques such as CIDR (Classless Inter-Domain Routing), it efficiently manages address allocation and ensures optimal use of the IP address space. Additionally, the Network Layer handles the routing, forwarding, and delivery of data packets through both static and dynamic routing protocols, ensuring that data reaches its intended destination even in complex network environments. Key protocols like ARP (Address Resolution Protocol) and RARP (Reverse Address Resolution Protocol) allow for address mapping between different layers of the network. Furthermore, the role of protocols such as ICMP (Internet Control Message Protocol) and DHCP (Dynamic Host Configuration Protocol) enhances network management, allowing for troubleshooting and efficient configuration. The need for IPv6 adoption is also becoming increasingly important as the demand for IP addresses grows, providing an extended address space to support future network expansion. Finally, congestion control algorithms help prevent network overload, ensuring reliable data transmission. A deep understanding of the Network Layer is fundamental for building and maintaining robust, efficient, and scalable networks.

Exercise Questions

- What is the primary function of the Network Layer in networking?
- Define IP and explain its role in logical addressing.
- How does CIDR differ from traditional IP addressing?
- What are the functions of ARP and RARP in networking?
- Explain the difference between static and dynamic routing.
- What is the significance of ICMP in network communication?
- Describe the role of DHCP in managing network configurations.
- What are congestion control algorithms, and why are they necessary?
- What is the purpose of IPv6, and how does it differ from IPv4?
- List the key components that fall under the Network Layer in the OSI model.

CHAPTER

5

TRANSPORT LAYER

The Transport Layer is a critical layer in the OSI (Open Systems Interconnection) model, responsible for providing end-to-end communication services between hosts in a network. It sits above the Network Layer and beneath the Application Layer, playing a central role in ensuring that data is transmitted reliably, efficiently, and in the correct order. Its main function is to establish, maintain, and terminate communication sessions, as well as to ensure that data packets are delivered without errors, loss, or duplication. The Transport Layer is vital for providing a robust communication infrastructure, making it a cornerstone in the functionality of modern networks. One of the key responsibilities of the Transport Layer is the segmentation of large chunks of data from the Application Layer into smaller packets, which are then sent through the network. This segmentation ensures that data is broken into manageable pieces for more efficient transmission. It also adds headers to these packets, which contain necessary information like the source and destination port numbers, sequence numbers, and checksums for error detection. Once the packets reach their destination, the Transport Layer is also responsible for reassembling these segments into the original data, ensuring data integrity and completeness. The Transport Layer utilizes two main protocols: Transmission Control Protocol (TCP) and User Datagram Protocol (UDP). TCP is connection-oriented, meaning it requires a connection to be established between the sender and receiver before data transmission begins. It ensures reliable data delivery by implementing mechanisms like acknowledgment, flow control, and error checking. On the other hand, UDP is connectionless, offering a faster, but less reliable alternative to TCP. UDP is used in situations where speed is crucial, and the occasional loss of data is acceptable, such as in streaming media or online gaming.

Another key aspect of the Transport Layer is flowing control. This mechanism ensures that data is sent at a rate that the receiver can handle, preventing buffer overflow and packet loss. Flow control is particularly important in environments with varying network conditions, where the rate of data transmission may need to be adjusted dynamically to avoid congestion. Both TCP and UDP offer different levels of flow control, with TCP providing more sophisticated mechanisms like the sliding window protocol to manage the flow of data between sender and receiver. Error detection and correction are also critical functions of the Transport Layer. For TCP, this includes mechanisms like checksums and retransmission of lost or corrupted packets. The checksums help ensure the integrity of the data being transmitted, while the acknowledgment and retransmission mechanisms allow TCP to recover from packet loss. UDP, while faster and less reliable, can still perform basic error checking via checksums, but it does not offer the same error recovery features as TCP. This trade-off between speed and reliability is a key consideration when selecting the appropriate transport protocol for specific applications. Lastly, the Transport Layer also handles congestion control, which is essential for maintaining the efficiency and stability of the network. Congestion occurs when the volume of data sent exceeds the network's capacity, leading to packet loss and delays. TCP uses algorithms like Slow Start, Congestion Avoidance, and Fast Retransmit to detect and respond to congestion, adjusting the transmission rate to avoid overwhelming the network. This proactive management of congestion helps ensure that the network remains functional even under heavy traffic conditions, contributing to the overall performance and stability of the internet and other networks.

Process-to-Process Delivery

Process-to-Process Delivery refers to the communication mechanism in the Transport Layer that ensures data is transmitted from one process (application) on a source host to the correct process (application) on the destination host. This delivery process is central to the functioning of the Transport Layer and involves several key steps and mechanisms. Here's a detailed breakdown:

Role of Ports in Process-to-Process Delivery

Ports play a crucial role in process-to-process delivery in the Transport Layer of the OSI model. Each application running on a system is assigned a unique port number, which allows the Transport Layer to identify and route data to the correct application. When data is transmitted over a network, the Transport Layer encapsulates it into segments, adding both source and destination port numbers. These port numbers serve as identifiers for specific applications on the sending and receiving systems. By including the port numbers in the segment header, the Transport Layer ensures that incoming data is directed to the appropriate application process. This is vital for enabling communication between different applications across a network, as it allows multiple applications to run concurrently on a single device without data interference. Therefore, port numbers act as a fundamental mechanism for accurate and reliable communication in networked systems.

Transport Layer's Responsibility

The Transport Layer is responsible for providing reliable end-to-end communication between processes running on different hosts in a network.

It ensures that data from a source process reaches the corresponding process on the destination host accurately. This is achieved by establishing logical connections between the two processes, utilizing source and destination IP addresses along with port numbers to identify the specific processes involved. The Transport Layer manages the segmentation of large data into smaller units, known as segments, and oversees their reassembly at the receiving end. It also handles flow control, error detection, and retransmission of lost or corrupted data, ensuring reliable data delivery. This layer supports two main protocols: Transmission Control Protocol (TCP), which offers reliable, connection-oriented communication, and User Datagram Protocol (UDP), which provides faster, connectionless communication, though without guaranteed delivery. Through these mechanisms, the Transport Layer ensures that data reaches the right destination process efficiently.

Segmentation of Data

The Transport Layer is responsible for ensuring reliable data transmission between processes on different machines. To achieve this, it takes large chunks of data from the Application Layer and breaks them into smaller, manageable units known as segments. This process is crucial because large data sizes cannot be efficiently transmitted in one go due to network constraints. Each segment is equipped with a header that contains vital information to ensure that the data is delivered correctly and in order. Segmentation allows for better error handling, retransmission of lost segments, and efficient use of network resources. It also enables parallel transmission, optimizing data delivery. By dividing data into smaller units, the Transport Layer enhances reliability, ensuring that the communication channel is used efficiently, even when network conditions are less than optimal. This process ensures data integrity, proper sequence handling, and overall connection management between the sender and receiver.

Source and Destination Port Numbers

In the context of data transmission, the Transport Layer assigns unique identifiers called port numbers to each end-point in communication. These numbers are essential for differentiating between multiple processes running on the same device. The source port number identifies the sending process, and the destination port number directs the data to the correct receiving process at the remote system. Port numbers enable the Transport Layer to establish communication sessions between specific applications on the sender and receiver. For instance, when a web browser communicates with a web server, the source port may be dynamically allocated by the operating system, while the destination port typically corresponds to port 80 for HTTP or port 443 for HTTPS. The use of port numbers ensures that data is routed to the right application, even when multiple applications are communicating over the same network connection. Without port numbers, the Transport Layer would be unable to distinguish between different processes on either end of the communication.

Sequence Numbers

Sequence numbers play a crucial role in maintaining the correct order of data segments during transmission. When the Transport Layer segments data into smaller packets, there is a risk that the segments may arrive out of order due to varying network conditions or congestion. To mitigate this issue, each segment is assigned a unique sequence number. This number helps the receiving system reassemble the segments in the correct order, ensuring that the data stream appears continuous. Sequence numbers also help in identifying lost or duplicated segments, as each segment is expected to have a specific sequence number. For example, in the Transmission Control Protocol (TCP), sequence numbers allow the receiver to determine which data segments have been successfully received and which need to be retransmitted. This system ensures that data is delivered in the exact order as intended, thereby enhancing the reliability and integrity of the communication process.

Acknowledgments

Acknowledgments are a fundamental feature of reliable transport protocols, especially in protocols like TCP. They serve as a mechanism to confirm that a segment has been successfully received by the destination. Each time the receiver gets a segment, it sends an acknowledgment (ACK) back to the sender, indicating that the data has been successfully received. This feedback loop ensures that both sides of the communication are synchronized and can handle potential transmission errors. In case a segment is lost or corrupted during transmission, the sender can use the acknowledgment mechanism to detect the issue and retransmit the lost data. Acknowledgments are also used in flow control to prevent overwhelming the receiver with too much data at once. The process of acknowledgment not only ensures the correctness of the data transfer but also contributes to overall network efficiency, as it helps the sender adjust the transmission rate based on the receiver's capacity to handle the data.

Multiplexing

Multiplexing in the Transport Layer is a technique that enables multiple applications or processes to share the same network channel effectively in Figure 5.1. When data is sent from various applications, the Transport Layer collects data from each application and attaches a unique port number to identify the source application. These segments are then combined into a single data stream and transmitted over the network. This allows for the simultaneous transmission of data from multiple applications, efficiently utilizing network resources. Multiplexing is crucial because it reduces the need for multiple physical connections, thereby optimizing bandwidth usage. It ensures that data from different processes is correctly separated and efficiently sent over the network. This method helps in making the communication between different applications seamless and orderly, without interference, ensuring that the network's capacity is used to its maximum potential.

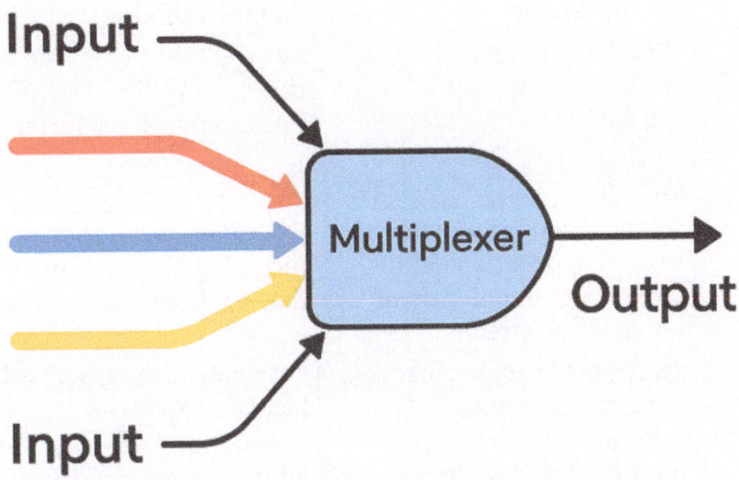

Figure 5.1: Process of Multiplexing.

Demultiplexing

Demultiplexing occurs at the receiver side of the Transport Layer and is the process of separating incoming data streams and directing them to the appropriate application. When data segments arrive at the destination, the Transport Layer examines the port numbers associated with each segment. By referencing these port numbers, it can determine which application or process the data belongs to. Demultiplexing ensures that each process on the receiving end gets the exact data it requested, maintaining the integrity and organization of the communication in Figure 5.2. This process is vital for supporting multiple applications simultaneously on the same host, enabling smooth and accurate data delivery. If the port number is not recognized or the segment is malformed, the Transport Layer may discard the data or handle the error accordingly. Through demultiplexing, the Transport Layer ensures that data reaches its intended destination efficiently, providing clear communication across processes. This comparison highlights the complementary roles of multiplexing and demultiplexing in the Transport Layer in Table 5.1.

Table 5.1: Difference between the multiplexing and demultiplexing.

Aspect	Multiplexing	Demultiplexing
Definition	The process of combining multiple data streams into a single stream for transmission.	The process of separating a combined data stream into individual data streams at the receiver.
Location	Occurs at the sender side.	Occurs at the receiver side.

Aspect	Multiplexing	Demultiplexing
Purpose	To allow multiple applications to share the network efficiently by combining their data streams.	To direct the received data to the appropriate application or process based on port numbers.
Role	Assigns unique port numbers to each application data stream and bundles them into a single stream.	Examines port numbers in the incoming data stream to deliver data to the correct application.
Process	Transport Layer segments data, attaches header information (such as port numbers), and multiplexes them.	Transport Layer checks the header for port numbers and forwards the data to the appropriate process/application.
Example	A server sending data from multiple applications (e.g., HTTP and FTP) over the same connection.	A receiver receiving data for different applications (e.g., one for HTTP and another for FTP) from a single stream.

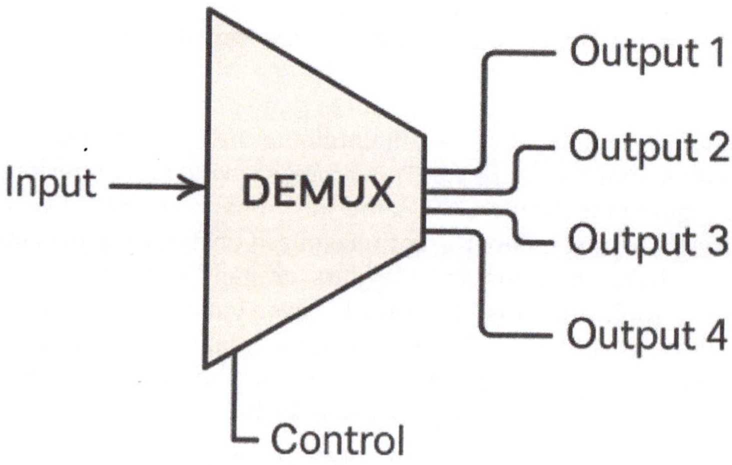

Figure 5.2: Process of Demultiplexing.

Connection Establishment (for Connection-Oriented Protocols)

In connection-oriented protocols like TCP (Transmission Control Protocol), establishing a connection is a crucial step before data transmission can occur. The process ensures reliable communication by confirming both the sender and receiver are ready to exchange data. This is achieved using a method called the three-way handshake, which is designed to synchronize both ends of the communication channel. This is done using the three-way handshake:

SYN

The SYN (synchronization) request is the initial step in the process of establishing a connection between two devices in a network, typically used in the Transmission Control Protocol (TCP). This request is sent by the sender to the receiver to indicate the desire to establish a connection. The sender generates a packet with the SYN flag set, which serves as a signal that the sender is ready to initiate communication. This packet includes an initial sequence number, which is used to synchronize the sequence of data that will be transmitted once the connection is established. The SYN packet does not carry any actual data; its sole purpose is to set up a reliable communication channel. Once the SYN request is received by the receiver, the next phase of the process, which involves acknowledging the request, can begin.

SYN-ACK

In response to the SYN request, the receiver sends a SYN-ACK (synchronization acknowledgment) packet. This packet serves two purposes: acknowledging the receipt of the sender's SYN request and sending a synchronization signal back to the sender. The SYN-ACK packet has both the SYN and ACK flags set. The receiver includes its own sequence number in the packet, which is necessary to synchronize the communication from both ends. The receiver's acknowledgment number is set to one more than the sequence number received in the SYN packet, indicating that the receiver is ready to proceed with establishing the connection. This response confirms that the receiver has successfully received the sender's request and is willing to establish a communication link. After sending the SYN-ACK, the receiver waits for the sender's final acknowledgment to complete the three-way handshake and establish the connection.

ACK

The final step in the three-way handshake is the ACK (acknowledgment) packet, sent by the sender to the receiver. This packet serves to confirm the receipt of the receiver's SYN-ACK response. It acknowledges that the sender has received the receiver's synchronization acknowledgment and is now ready to begin transmitting actual data. The ACK packet includes the sender's sequence number incremented by one, as well as the acknowledgment number set to one more than the sequence number received in the SYN-ACK. By sending the ACK packet, the sender completes the handshake process, and the connection is considered fully established. From this point on, both sides can begin exchanging data in a reliable, orderly manner. The three-way handshake (SYN, SYN-ACK, ACK) ensures that both the sender and receiver are synchronized and agree on the communication parameters before data transfer begins.

Flow Control in TCP

Flow control in TCP is a vital mechanism to prevent data congestion between the sender and the receiver. It ensures that the sender does not overwhelm the receiver with excessive data, which could lead to packet loss. The mechanism is implemented using a sliding window protocol. In this approach, the receiver advertises a window size, which represents the amount of data it is capable of handling without overflowing its buffer. The sender is restricted to sending only the amount of data that fits within the receiver's window, ensuring that the receiver can process the data in a timely manner. This dynamic window size adjusts according to the receiver's capacity, providing an efficient flow of data while maintaining reliability. This process is fundamental for maintaining optimal throughput and avoiding congestion, especially in variable network conditions where receiver buffers can change in size due to varying load.

Buffer Management in TCP

Buffer management is a critical aspect of flow control in TCP that ensures the smooth handling of incoming data. The receiver maintains a buffer to temporarily store incoming data until it can be processed. The size of this buffer determines how much data the receiver can handle at once, which directly influences the flow control window. If the buffer fills up, the receiver will notify the sender to slow down or stop sending data, avoiding data loss. Proper buffer management ensures that the receiver is not overwhelmed by too much data in a short time. It also ensures that the data is processed in the correct order, preserving the integrity of the communication. Buffer size can dynamically adjust in some implementations, further optimizing data flow. By effectively managing buffers, TCP can maintain reliable, ordered data delivery, ensuring that the receiver can process data at its own pace without losing information.

Error Detection and Reliability

The Transport Layer also ensures that the data delivered is error-free and reliable. It does this through various techniques, depending on the protocol:

Checksums

A checksum is a value derived from a data set using a mathematical algorithm and is used to detect errors in data transmission. During data transfer, the sender computes the checksum of the data before transmission and sends it along with the data. Upon receiving the data, the receiver recalculates the checksum and compares it with the value sent by the sender. If the two values match, the data is assumed to be intact and uncorrupted. If there is a mismatch, it indicates that the data may have been altered during transmission, signaling the need for retransmission or error correction. This error-detection mechanism helps ensure that the data reaches its destination without corruption and enables the network to maintain data integrity, particularly in unreliable transmission mediums.

Acknowledgments (ACK)

Acknowledgments (ACK) are a critical part of data transmission protocols, particularly in connection-oriented protocols like Transmission Control Protocol (TCP). In such systems, after receiving a segment of data, the receiving host sends an ACK to inform the sender that the segment was successfully received. This feedback loop is crucial for ensuring reliable delivery of data across networks. If the sender does not receive the expected ACK within a specified time frame, it assumes that the segment was lost or corrupted, and thus, it retransmits the segment. ACKs help manage the flow of data and ensure that all data is delivered in the correct order without loss, making them essential for reliable communication in protocols designed for applications that require accuracy and consistency.

Sequence Numbers

Sequence numbers are integral to ensuring the correct order and integrity of data transmission, particularly in protocols like TCP. Each segment of data transmitted over the network is assigned a unique sequence number. This allows the receiver to correctly reorder the segments when they arrive, even if they take different paths or experience network delays. Sequence numbers also help detect lost segments; if a segment is missing, its absence can be noted based on the sequence numbers, prompting the retransmission of the missing data. Furthermore, they aid in preventing duplication of data. Sequence numbers ensure that data is received and reassembled in the correct order, crucial for maintaining the logical structure of communication, especially when larger amounts of data are being transferred over networks that may experience delays, retransmissions, or packet loss.

Data Reassembly

Data reassembly refers to the process by which the data segments received over a network are reconstructed into the original message at the receiving end. This is a crucial function in communication protocols like Transmission Control Protocol (TCP), which ensures reliable, ordered delivery of data. Each segment sent over the network contains sequence numbers in its header, which help the receiving system understand the correct order in which to assemble the message. The Transport Layer is responsible for keeping track of these sequence numbers, ensuring that the message is reassembled accurately, even if it was divided into multiple smaller segments. This process helps maintain the integrity of the original data and ensures that the application at the receiving end can access the complete, correctly ordered message.

Out-of-order Segments

In a network communication system, out-of-order segments occur when data segments arrive at the destination in a sequence different from the one, they were sent. This can happen due to various factors such as network congestion, routing variations, or packet retransmissions. The Transport Layer is responsible for handling such situations, ensuring that the data is properly re-ordered before it is passed to the destination process. In protocols like TCP, each segment contains a sequence number, which helps the receiver identify the order of the segments. When out-of-order segments are detected, the Transport Layer buffers the segments until all prior segments have been received. Once all segments are in the correct order, the complete message is passed to the application. This guarantees the accurate reconstruction of the original message, even if segments were received out of sequence.

Connection Termination (for Connection-Oriented Protocols)

Connection termination in connection-oriented protocols, such as TCP (Transmission Control Protocol), is an essential process that ensures the orderly and reliable closure of a communication channel. In TCP, the termination procedure is carried out through a four-way handshake, which facilitates the mutual acknowledgment of data transmission completion between the sender and receiver. This process ensures that both parties are aware that no further data will be exchanged, avoiding potential issues like lost or incomplete data. The first step involves the sender transmitting a FIN (finish) signal, notifying the receiver that it has completed its data transmission. This signal signifies the sender's intent to close the connection. Upon receiving the FIN, the receiver acknowledges it and responds with its own FIN signal, indicating its readiness to close the connection from its side as well. Finally, the sender acknowledges the receiver's FIN, at which point the connection is fully terminated, and both sides can release any resources associated with the connection.

Connectionless Communication (for UDP)

UDP (User Datagram Protocol) is a connectionless communication protocol that operates without establishing or maintaining a dedicated connection between the sender and receiver. Unlike TCP (Transmission Control Protocol), there is no handshaking process to establish a connection, and once the data is sent, there is no termination process to formally close the connection. Data is transmitted in discrete packets, known as datagrams, that are sent independently. This means that UDP does not provide guarantees regarding the delivery of data, its order, or its integrity. If a datagram is lost, there is no mechanism in place to request a retransmission. As a result, UDP is preferred in applications where speed is more critical than reliability, such as in real-time applications like video streaming, Voice over IP (VoIP), and online gaming. These applications can tolerate occasional packet loss as long as the communication remains fast and responsive, minimizing latency.

Use of Process-to-Process Delivery

File Transfer

In the process of file transfer, the Transport Layer plays a critical role in ensuring that the file data is delivered to the correct destination process. When a file is transferred between applications, such as using the File Transfer Protocol (FTP), the Transport Layer establishes communication through a reliable connection. This is accomplished by using port numbers to uniquely identify the source and destination processes on the sending and receiving machines. For instance, if an application is sending a large file, the Transport Layer guarantees the correct ordering of packets, manages any retransmissions in case of data loss, and ensures the integrity of the transmitted data. The reliable, error-checked delivery of the file to the correct destination process is facilitated by the Transport Layer's protocols, such as TCP, which ensures the file is fully reconstructed at the receiving end, ready for the intended application to process and use.

Web Browsing

In web browsing, the Transport Layer is responsible for ensuring the reliable communication between the web browser and the web server. When a user types in a website address, the Transport Layer uses the Hypertext Transfer Protocol (HTTP) over Transmission Control Protocol (TCP) to establish a connection. This connection facilitates the secure transmission of web pages, images, and other resources from the server to the browser. The Transport Layer ensures that the data reaches the correct destination process, i.e., the web browser, through the use of port numbers. For example, HTTP typically uses port 80, while HTTPS (the secure version) uses port 443. By managing packet sequencing, error recovery, and flow control, the Transport Layer ensures that the web pages are delivered correctly and completely to the browser. This seamless communication process enables users to access and interact with websites reliably and efficiently.

Email

When an email is sent or received, the Transport Layer ensures that the message is reliably delivered to the correct email client by using TCP. This is achieved through the use of specific port numbers that are associated with various email protocols. For example, the Simple Mail Transfer Protocol (SMTP), used for sending emails, typically operates over port 25. The Transport Layer is responsible for managing the establishment of a connection between the sending and receiving servers, ensuring that email data is transferred accurately and in the correct sequence. If an email is being received, protocols like Post Office Protocol (POP3) or Internet Message Access Protocol (IMAP) are used, often over ports 110 or 143. The Transport Layer's role is to maintain the reliability of the email transmission, handle retransmissions if necessary, and ensure that the email reaches the correct email client, ready for the recipient to read.

Port Numbers in Process-to-Process Delivery

Well-known Ports

Well-known ports are reserved for specific protocols and services, ensuring that network communication occurs smoothly and predictably. These ports range from 0 to 1023 and are assigned by the Internet Assigned Numbers

Authority (IANA) to standard applications. For example, port 80 is reserved for HTTP (Hypertext Transfer Protocol), which is responsible for web traffic. Port 443 is assigned to HTTPS (Hypertext Transfer Protocol Secure) for encrypted communication, providing security for online transactions. Additionally, port 25 is commonly used for SMTP (Simple Mail Transfer Protocol), which handles email transmission. These well-known ports are crucial in defining the way services interact within a network. The operating system ensures that the correct application listens on the corresponding well-known port for incoming requests, preventing conflicts and ensuring seamless communication for various internet-based services in Table 5.2.

Ephemeral Ports

Ephemeral ports, also known as dynamic ports, are temporary ports assigned by an operating system for the duration of a communication session. These ports are used for outbound connections or as part of a two-way communication between client and server. Typically, the range for ephemeral ports is between 1024 and 49151, though the exact range may vary depending on the operating system. When a client initiates a request, the operating system dynamically selects an available ephemeral port and associates it with the connection. Once the communication session ends, the port is released and can be reused by other applications. The use of ephemeral ports is essential for enabling multiple simultaneous connections without conflicts, as each session requires a unique port number for its duration. This dynamic allocation allows for efficient resource management and avoids the need for fixed ports for each client-server interaction.

Table 5.2: Comparison between the Well-known Ports and Ephemeral Ports.

Feature	Well-known Ports	Ephemeral Ports
Definition	Reserved ports for specific services (e.g., HTTP, HTTPS, SMTP).	Temporary, dynamic ports assigned by the OS for session-based communication.
Port Range	0 to 1023	1024 to 65535
Assignment	Assigned and fixed for well-known services.	Assigned dynamically by the operating system as needed.
Usage	Used by specific protocols like HTTP, HTTPS, FTP, SMTP.	Used for the client-side communication in a connection session.
Management	Managed by IANA (Internet Assigned Numbers Authority).	Managed by the Transport Layer protocol.
Duration	Permanent until reassigned for another service.	Temporary, lasts only for the duration of a session.

Feature	Well-known Ports	Ephemeral Ports
Examples	Port 80 (HTTP), Port 443 (HTTPS), Port 25 (SMTP).	Ports assigned dynamically during sessions, like 49152-65535.
Visibility	Known and fixed, can be accessed publicly.	Typically, not visible outside the local system or session.
Connection Type	Typically used for server-side listening ports.	Typically used for client-side connections.

Transport layer protocols (UDP and TCP)

The Transport Layer is the fourth layer in the OSI (Open Systems Interconnection) model and is responsible for providing communication services directly to the application layer. It facilitates data transfer between end systems and ensures reliable or unreliable delivery of data depending on the protocol used. The two primary transport layer protocols are TCP (Transmission Control Protocol) and UDP (User Datagram Protocol). Below is a detailed comparison of both.

Transmission Control Protocol (TCP)

TCP is a connection-oriented, reliable transport layer protocol designed for applications that require guaranteed delivery of data in Figure 5.3. It establishes a connection between the sender and receiver before transmitting data and ensures that data is delivered in the correct order and without errors.

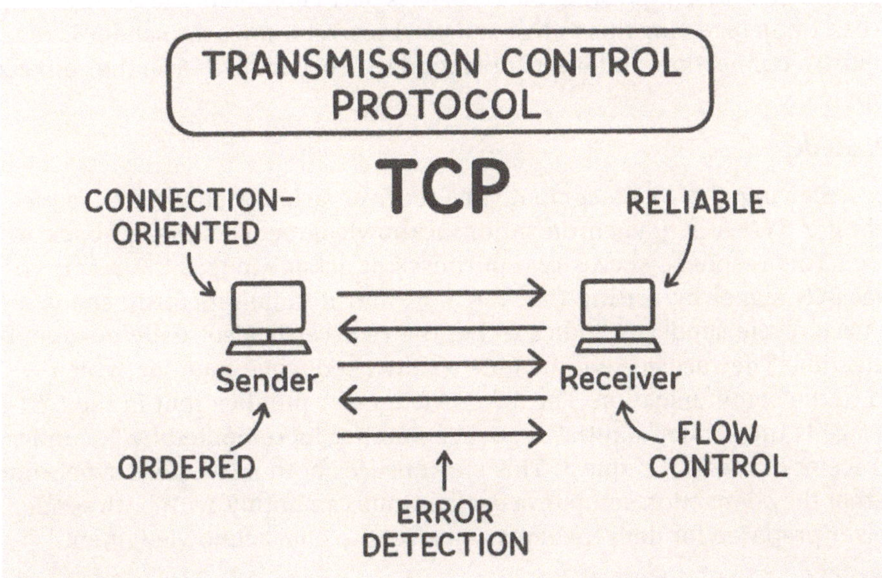

Figure 5.3: Key features of the of Transmission Control Protocol (TCP).

Key Features of TCP

TCP (Transmission Control Protocol) is a connection-oriented protocol, which means that a reliable connection must be established between the sender and the receiver before any data is transmitted. This is achieved through a process known as the three-way handshake. The handshake begins when the sender sends a SYN (synchronize) packet to the receiver, requesting a connection. In response, the receiver acknowledges the request by sending a SYN-ACK (synchronize-acknowledge) packet. Finally, the sender sends an ACK (acknowledge) packet to confirm the establishment of the connection. Only after this handshake process is complete can the actual data transfer begin. The three-way handshake ensures that both the sender and receiver are ready to communicate, preventing data loss and ensuring that both parties are synchronized before the actual transmission starts. This makes TCP ideal for applications that require reliability and orderly data delivery, such as web browsing and file transfer. Three-Way Handshake:

SYN

The SYN (synchronization) flag is used in the TCP three-way handshake to initiate a connection between a client and server. When the sender wishes to establish a connection, it sends a TCP segment with the SYN flag set to the receiver. This signal indicates the sender's intent to establish a reliable communication session and to synchronize the sequence numbers. The sender typically selects an initial sequence number for the connection, which will be used for the data that is sent once the connection is established. This SYN segment is the first step in the handshake process, requesting the receiver's participation in the communication process. Upon receiving this SYN signal, the receiver knows the sender is ready to establish a connection, and it must respond to proceed further in the connection setup.

SYN-ACK

After receiving the SYN segment, the receiver acknowledges the request by sending a SYN-ACK (synchronization acknowledgment) message back to the sender. This response serves two purposes: it acknowledges the receipt of the initial SYN signal by setting the ACK flag, and it simultaneously sends a SYN flag back to the sender to indicate that the receiver is also ready to establish a connection. The receiver will include its own sequence number, which will be used in the communication. The acknowledgment number sent in the SYN-ACK message is the sender's initial sequence number incremented by 1, confirming the receipt of the SYN request. This step ensures both parties are synchronized and that the connection setup process continues smoothly, with both sender and receiver prepared for data transmission after the final acknowledgment.

ACK

The sender responds to the SYN-ACK message with an ACK (acknowledgment) segment, completing the three-way handshake process and establishing the connection. The ACK segment from the sender acknowledges the reception of the receiver's SYN-ACK, signaling the establishment of a reliable communication link between both parties. In this message, the sender sets the ACK flag and includes an acknowledgment number, which is the receiver's sequence number incremented by 1, confirming that the SYN-ACK was successfully received. At this point, the sender and receiver have synchronized their sequence numbers, and the connection is officially established. The ACK message marks the conclusion of the handshake, and both parties are now ready to begin exchanging data over the established TCP connection. This three-step process ensures that both sender and receiver are prepared for reliable, ordered data transmission.

Reliable Data Transfer

TCP (Transmission Control Protocol) guarantees reliable data transfer by ensuring that data packets are acknowledged upon successful receipt. If a packet is lost or corrupted during transmission, TCP detects the failure and initiates a retransmission. Acknowledgment packets (ACKs) are sent back to the sender as a confirmation that the data has been successfully received. If the sender does not receive an acknowledgment within a specified time frame, it assumes that the packet was lost and resends it. This process ensures that all data is reliably transferred, even in the presence of network issues, and that the receiver receives the complete and accurate data. Retransmission mechanisms play a crucial role in TCP's ability to provide a reliable, error-free communication channel, making it suitable for applications where data integrity is critical, such as file transfers and web browsing.

Flow Control

TCP uses flow control to manage the rate at which data is sent, ensuring that the receiver does not become overwhelmed by incoming packets. One of the primary mechanisms for flow control in TCP is the sliding window protocol. This allows the sender to send a specific amount of data before waiting for an acknowledgment from the receiver. The size of the window is determined by the receiver's buffer capacity, which indicates how much data it can handle at once. As the receiver processes the data and sends back acknowledgments, the sender can slide the window forward, transmitting additional data. This dynamic adjustment of the window size ensures that the receiver's buffer is not overwhelmed, preventing data loss and ensuring efficient use of the network. Flow control helps avoid congestion and ensures that the sender adjusts its data transmission rate according to the receiver's ability to process it.

Error Detection

TCP uses checksums to detect errors in transmitted data, ensuring data integrity. The checksum is a calculated value based on the content of the segment, and it is included in the packet header. When the receiver receives the packet, it performs the same checksum calculation on the data and compares it to the checksum value sent with the packet. If the values match, the data is considered valid. If they do not match, indicating that the data has been corrupted during transmission, the receiver discards the packet and does not send an acknowledgment. In such cases, the sender retransmits the corrupted data, ensuring that the correct data is eventually delivered. This process of error detection, coupled with retransmission mechanisms, makes TCP highly reliable in environments where data integrity is critical, such as in file transfers, database communication, and web browsing.

Ordered Data Delivery

One of the key features of TCP is its ability to ensure ordered data delivery. In a typical network, data packets may take different routes to reach their destination, which can cause them to arrive out of order. TCP handles this issue by assigning sequence numbers to each data packet before transmission. These sequence numbers allow the receiver to reorder the packets as they arrive, ensuring that the data is reassembled in the correct order. If any packets are missing, the receiver can request retransmission of the lost packets. This ordered delivery mechanism is crucial for applications where the sequence of data is important, such as video streaming, file transfers, and voice communications, where the integrity and sequence of the data are essential for proper functioning. By guaranteeing ordered delivery, TCP ensures that the transmitted data is meaningful and usable by the receiver.

Congestion Control

TCP incorporates congestion control to manage the flow of data across the network, adjusting transmission rates based on current network conditions. Congestion control aims to prevent network congestion, which can occur when too much data is sent into the network too quickly, causing packet loss, delays, and reduced throughput. TCP uses several algorithms for congestion control, including slow-start, congestion avoidance, and fast recovery. In slow-start, the transmission rate starts small and gradually increases as the network allows. Congestion avoidance further adjusts the rate to prevent congestion, while fast recovery helps to quickly recover from lost packets due to congestion. These algorithms dynamically respond to changing network conditions, ensuring that TCP adapts to the current level of congestion. As a result, TCP can maintain a stable and efficient data flow, even in congested networks, making it highly effective for applications that require high data reliability and throughput.

Segmentation and Reassembly

TCP handles large amounts of data by dividing it into smaller segments before transmission. This process is known as segmentation. Each segment includes a header that contains important information, such as the sequence number and checksum, to help the receiver correctly reassemble the data. On the receiving end, TCP reassembles the segments into the original data stream, ensuring that all parts of the data are correctly ordered and intact. Segmentation is essential because networks often have limitations on the maximum size of data that can be transmitted in a single packet, known as the Maximum Transmission Unit (MTU). By breaking down large data into smaller chunks, TCP can efficiently use the network's resources and avoid issues related to packet size limitations. This segmentation and reassembly process ensures that large files, such as web pages or videos, can be transmitted reliably across networks with varying capacity.

Applications Using TCP

Web Browsing (HTTP/HTTPS)

TCP (Transmission Control Protocol) is fundamental to web browsing, where HTTP (Hypertext Transfer Protocol) and HTTPS (secure version of HTTP) operate. Web browsers rely on TCP to establish reliable connections with web servers, ensuring that data packets arrive in sequence without errors. When a user requests a webpage, the browser sends an HTTP or HTTPS request to the server over a TCP connection. TCP guarantees the reliable transmission of content, such as HTML files, images, videos, and scripts, between the client and server. The three-way handshake mechanism in TCP ensures a reliable connection, while the flow and congestion control features manage data traffic. HTTPS adds an additional layer of security by encrypting the data sent over TCP, making it suitable for secure transactions. Therefore, TCP ensures web browsing is both reliable and secure, which is crucial for a smooth and protected user experience.

Email (SMTP, IMAP)

TCP plays a vital role in email communication, supporting protocols like SMTP (Simple Mail Transfer Protocol) and IMAP (Internet Message Access Protocol). SMTP is used for sending emails, while IMAP is used for retrieving and managing messages on a mail server. When sending an email, SMTP relies on TCP to establish a reliable connection between the sender's email client and the mail server. TCP ensures that the email data is transferred reliably, acknowledging each segment of data to avoid loss or corruption. Similarly, IMAP uses TCP to establish a reliable connection for retrieving emails. The mail server and client ensure that messages are synchronized correctly. By using TCP's mechanisms for error detection, flow control, and reliability, both SMTP and IMAP protocols guarantee that emails are transmitted and retrieved accurately, without loss or duplication, enhancing the integrity of email communication.

File Transfer (FTP)

FTP (File Transfer Protocol) is a common application that uses TCP for transferring files between computers over a network. FTP enables users to upload or download files from a server to a client system, supporting a wide range of file types. The protocol relies on TCP to ensure the reliable transmission of data, leveraging its error-checking and acknowledgment mechanisms. When a file is transferred, TCP ensures that the data is received in the correct order, and any lost packets are retransmitted, providing a secure and consistent file transfer.

FTP operates on two separate TCP connections: one for command communication (port 21) and one for transferring the file data (dynamic port for data transfer). TCP guarantees that files are completely transferred without errors, which is essential for maintaining the integrity of large files or data sets. As such, FTP is a robust solution for file transfers requiring reliability and accuracy.

Remote Login (SSH, Telnet)

TCP is crucial for remote login applications like SSH (Secure Shell) and Telnet, which enable users to access and manage remote systems over a network. Telnet, though now largely replaced by SSH, originally used TCP to establish a reliable connection between the user's terminal and the remote host. TCP ensures that the connection is secure, with all commands and responses arriving in sequence and without loss. SSH, which has replaced Telnet due to its added security features, also relies on TCP to create a reliable, encrypted communication channel for remote logins. TCP's reliability and sequencing features ensure that commands are executed in the correct order and that any lost data is retransmitted. This reliability is crucial for both interactive and automated processes, ensuring uninterrupted communication between local and remote systems. TCP, therefore, plays an essential role in maintaining the integrity and reliability of remote login protocols like SSH and Telnet.

User Datagram Protocol (UDP)

UDP is a connectionless, unreliable transport layer protocol that is used in applications where speed is more critical than reliability. Unlike TCP, UDP does not establish a connection before data transfer and does not guarantee delivery or order of data. The Key Features of UDP:

Connectionless

UDP (User Datagram Protocol) is a connectionless protocol, meaning that it does not require a connection to be established before transmitting data. In contrast to connection-oriented protocols like TCP, UDP sends data packets independently without a handshake or synchronization between the sender and receiver. As a result, there is no need for the protocol to first establish a connection, making it faster and more efficient for specific applications. The lack of connection establishment allows UDP to minimize overhead, but it comes with the drawback of not ensuring reliable delivery or maintaining any state information. This characteristic makes UDP suitable for real-time applications, such as video streaming or online gaming, where speed and latency are more critical than reliability. However, this also means that packet loss, duplication, or out-of-order delivery can occur without any inherent mechanism to correct such issues.

Unreliable

UDP is considered an unreliable protocol because it does not guarantee the delivery of data packets. Unlike TCP, which implements various mechanisms such as retransmissions, sequencing, and acknowledgments to ensure reliable data transmission, UDP simply sends packets to the destination and does not track or confirm their receipt. As a result, packets can be lost, corrupted, or arrive out of order without any attempt by UDP to correct or recover from these issues. The lack of reliability makes UDP unsuitable for applications that require guaranteed data delivery, such as file transfers or web browsing. However, for certain use cases like streaming or VoIP (Voice over IP), where timely delivery is more important than complete accuracy, UDP's unreliability is less of a concern. In these scenarios, occasional packet loss may be tolerated for the sake of low-latency and real-time communication.

No Acknowledgments

One of the key characteristics of UDP is the absence of acknowledgment mechanisms. In protocols like TCP, each packet sent is typically acknowledged by the receiver to confirm successful delivery. If the acknowledgment is not received, the sender will retransmit the data. UDP, however, does not implement this process, meaning that once data is sent, the sender does not wait for a confirmation from the receiver. This lack of acknowledgment significantly reduces the protocol's overhead, leading to faster data transmission. With fewer control messages exchanged between sender and receiver, UDP can be more efficient in environments where real-time performance is essential, such as video conferencing or live broadcasts. However, this comes at the cost of reliability, as there is no guarantee that the data was successfully received, making UDP unsuitable for applications where data integrity is a priority.

Lower Latency

UDP is designed for low-latency communication. Since it does not require a connection to be established or managed, and it lacks mechanisms such as error correction and retransmission, the protocol can transmit data with minimal delay. This results in lower latency compared to TCP, which must establish a connection, exchange handshakes, and perform error recovery during transmission. In scenarios such as online gaming, voice calls, or video streaming, low latency is critical for maintaining real-time communication and a smooth user experience. UDP's efficiency, in this regard, allows it to be well-suited for time-sensitive applications where the data must be delivered quickly and without the overhead of connection setup or packet loss recovery. While this makes UDP ideal for real-time communication, it sacrifices the reliability that might be necessary for non-real-time applications, such as file transfers or web browsing.

No Flow or Congestion Control

UDP does not implement flow control or congestion control mechanisms, which are crucial features of connection-oriented protocols like TCP. Flow control ensures that the sender does not overwhelm the receiver by sending data too quickly, while congestion control prevents the network from becoming congested with too many packets. UDP's lack of these features means that it will transmit data as fast as the network can handle, without adjusting the sending rate based on network conditions or receiver capacity. This can lead to potential problems in cases where the network is congested or the receiver cannot process the data as quickly as it is sent. For real-time applications that require constant data flow, such as live video or voice communications, the lack of flow or congestion control may not be an issue, but for other types of data transmission, it can cause packet loss or delays, especially under heavy network load.

Error Detection

UDP provides basic error detection through the use of checksums. A checksum is a small-sized piece of data derived from the content of the packet, which is used to verify the integrity of the transmitted data. When a packet is received, the checksum is checked to ensure that the data has not been altered or corrupted during transmission. If an error is detected, the packet is discarded. However, UDP does not perform any error correction or retransmission of lost or corrupted data. This means that if an error is detected, the receiver simply ignores the packet, and there is no attempt by UDP to request the packet again. This makes UDP less reliable in environments where data integrity is essential, but it also reduces the overhead required for error correction, which is why it is used in applications where occasional data loss can be tolerated, such as media streaming or gaming.

Message Boundaries

One important feature of UDP is that it maintains message boundaries. This means that when data is sent over UDP, it is transmitted as discrete, independent packets, and the receiver must interpret the boundaries of these messages. Unlike TCP, which is a stream-oriented protocol and does not preserve message boundaries, UDP ensures that each packet represents a full message. This can be beneficial in applications where the integrity of individual messages is important, such as in real-time data transmission like video and audio streaming. However, this also means that the receiver must be able to correctly reconstruct the original message from the sequence of UDP packets. In some cases, if the message is larger than the maximum packet size, it must be split into multiple packets, and the application layer must handle reassembly, which can add complexity.

Applications Using UDP

Streaming Media (e.g., video and audio streaming)

UDP is widely used in streaming media applications like video and audio streaming because of its low-latency nature and ability to handle real-time data transmission. Unlike TCP, UDP does not require extensive error checking or retransmission of lost packets, which makes it more suitable for applications where speed is crucial, and occasional data loss is acceptable. For example, streaming services such as YouTube or Spotify leverage UDP for delivering real-time media content to users. Since these applications prioritize smooth playback over perfect data integrity,

UDP allows for efficient transmission, minimizing buffering delays and enabling continuous content delivery. While some loss of packets may occur, the streaming experience remains uninterrupted as buffering algorithms can compensate for small glitches in the media stream. This combination of speed and tolerance for occasional errors makes UDP the preferred choice for real-time media delivery.

Voice over IP (VoIP)

Voice over IP (VoIP) applications, such as Skype and WhatsApp calls, use UDP to deliver voice and video communications in real time. VoIP systems require low-latency transmission to ensure seamless conversations between users. UDP's connectionless protocol allows it to transmit voice data packets rapidly without waiting for acknowledgments or retransmitting lost packets, which is crucial for maintaining natural-sounding conversations. While UDP's lack of built-in error correction may result in occasional packet loss, this minor degradation is typically less noticeable in voice communication compared to video streaming. Additionally, many VoIP applications use jitter buffers to smooth out the effects of delayed or lost packets, further enhancing call quality. The primary advantage of UDP in VoIP systems is its ability to reduce delay, which is vital for real-time conversations. Consequently, UDP's efficiency in minimizing transmission delays makes it an ideal protocol for VoIP.

Online Gaming

UDP is extensively used in online gaming for its ability to provide fast, real-time communication between the client and server. In multiplayer games, data such as player movements, actions, and game events must be transmitted with minimal latency to ensure a responsive gaming experience. Unlike TCP, UDP does not establish a connection or wait for acknowledgments, which reduces the transmission delay. Although UDP may result in packet loss, most games are designed to handle such situations, prioritizing speed over perfect data delivery. In fast-paced games, such as first-person shooters or battle royale games, the need for immediate updates outweighs the occasional loss of data packets, which can be corrected by the game itself through predictive algorithms. UDP's low overhead and minimal delay make it ideal for interactive gaming environments where real-time updates and a seamless experience are critical.

DNS (Domain Name System)

The Domain Name System (DNS) often utilizes UDP to resolve domain names into IP addresses. DNS queries are typically small and require quick responses, making UDP the ideal choice due to its low-latency, connectionless nature. When a user attempts to access a website, the DNS request is sent to a server using UDP, which then provides the corresponding IP address. The simplicity of UDP allows DNS servers to handle large volumes of requests efficiently, as it avoids the overhead associated with establishing and maintaining connections, unlike TCP. Moreover, DNS responses are usually small, so the possibility of packet loss is minimal and can often be tolerated without significant impact on performance. If a DNS query does not receive a response, it can be retried without any major consequences, further emphasizing UDP's suitability for this application.

DHCP (Dynamic Host Configuration Protocol)

Dynamic Host Configuration Protocol (DHCP) uses UDP to dynamically assign IP addresses to devices on a network. When a device connects to a network, it broadcasts a DHCP Discover message to find DHCP servers, which reply with an offer of an IP address. The use of UDP in DHCP ensures that devices can quickly communicate with DHCP servers without the need for a lengthy connection setup. DHCP messages, such as Discover, Offer, Request, and Acknowledgment, are all sent via UDP, as the protocol allows for fast transmission of small packets. DHCP clients do not require reliable delivery or acknowledgment of each packet, as the process involves a sequence of messages that can be retried if necessary. The low overhead and quick exchange of information make UDP ideal for DHCP, where speed and minimal delay are more important than reliability.

Real-time Applications (Where Low Latency is Critical)

Real-time applications that require low-latency communication often rely on UDP for efficient data transmission. These applications include video conferencing, online trading, live broadcasting, and financial systems where quick updates and interactions are critical. UDP's connectionless nature and lack of handshakes or retransmission delays make it highly suitable for environments where real-time performance is paramount. For instance, in live video conferences, UDP enables instant transmission of video and audio streams, ensuring that participants can interact in real time with minimal delay. Similarly, in financial applications like stock trading, UDP ensures that market data and transactions are processed as quickly as possible, allowing users to act on real-time information. While occasional packet loss may occur, real-time applications are typically designed to tolerate such issues, as delays would have a much more detrimental impact on user experience than the loss of small amounts of data.

Comparison of TCP and UDP

TCP is ideal for applications where data integrity and order are crucial, such as file transfers, web browsing, and email communication in Table 5.3.UDP, on the other hand, is better suited for real-time applications where speed is more important than reliability, such as video streaming, VoIP, and online gaming.The choice between TCP and UDP depends on the specific requirements of the application, including the need for reliability, error correction, and the importance of timely data delivery.

Table 5.3: Comparison between the TCP and UDP.

Feature	TCP	UDP
Connection Type	Connection-oriented (requires handshake)	Connectionless (no handshake)
Reliability	Reliable, ensures delivery and order	Unreliable, no guarantee of delivery or order
Error Checking	Checksums, retransmission of lost packets	Checksums, no retransmission
Flow Control	Yes, uses sliding window mechanism	No flow control
Congestion Control	Yes, adapts transmission rate	No congestion control
Speed	Slower due to error checking, retransmission, and congestion control	Faster, due to lack of reliability mechanisms
Use Case	Applications requiring reliable communication	Applications that require low latency and can tolerate some data loss
Protocol Overhead	Higher, due to additional mechanisms for error recovery and flow control	Lower, as it does not require connection management

Multiplexing

There are various types of multiplexing techniques, and they are generally classified based on how the multiplexing occurs at different layers of the network stack:

Time Division Multiplexing (TDM)

Time Division Multiplexing (TDM) is a technique that divides the available bandwidth of a communication channel into distinct time slots, which are allocated to different signals or users. In TDM, each user or signal gets a dedicated time slot to transmit its data, allowing multiple signals to share the same transmission medium. These time slots are interspersed in a cyclical manner, ensuring that no two signals interfere with each other. The time slots are typically of equal duration, and the process repeats continuously, enabling the sequential transmission of multiple signals. TDM is commonly used in digital communication systems like telephone networks, where it allows efficient use of bandwidth by ensuring that users take turns to access the communication channel. This technique is highly effective for systems that need to transmit fixed-size data packets with minimal delay and interference. Each signal is assigned a specific time slot in which it can transmit data. The Key Features:

1. Each sender transmits its signal in a predefined time slot.
2. The time slots are usually small, and the system rapidly cycles between the different sources.
3. TDM can be synchronous or asynchronous. In synchronous TDM, time slots are allocated at fixed intervals, whereas in asynchronous TDM, time slots are assigned dynamically as needed.
4. Application: Used in digital communication systems, such as satellite communication, where different data streams are transmitted at different time slots.

Frequency Division Multiplexing (FDM)

Frequency Division Multiplexing (FDM) is a technique where the total bandwidth of a communication channel is split into multiple, smaller frequency bands. Each signal or user is assigned a unique frequency band within the total available bandwidth, allowing multiple signals to be transmitted simultaneously without causing interference. This method ensures that each signal occupies a distinct portion of the frequency spectrum. FDM is commonly used in analog communication systems, such as radio broadcasting and cable television, where different channels are transmitted over the same medium. The frequency bands are typically separated by guard bands to minimize interference between adjacent channels. FDM's key advantage is its ability to handle multiple signals concurrently, making it suitable for continuous transmission of data in systems where signals need to be sent at the same time. The system requires careful management of frequency allocation to avoid overlap and interference. The Key Features:

1. Each signal occupies a unique frequency band.
2. The frequency bands do not overlap, which ensures that signals do not interfere with each other.
3. FDM is commonly used in analog communications.
4. Application: Used in radio and television broadcasting, where different stations operate on different frequency bands.

Code Division Multiplexing (CDM)

Code Division Multiplexing (CDM) is a method that allows multiple data streams to be transmitted simultaneously over the same communication channel by assigning a unique code to each signal. Each user or data stream is encoded using a distinct spreading code, which is used to modulate the signal. When the signals are transmitted, they overlap in both time and frequency. However, each receiver can extract its desired signal by correlating the received signal with the corresponding code, effectively "filtering out" the other signals. CDM is a form of multiplexing commonly used in cellular networks, such as CDMA (Code Division Multiple Access) systems, where multiple users share the same frequency spectrum. The main advantage of CDM is its ability to provide high capacity and security, as the data streams are spread across a wide frequency band, reducing the likelihood of interference. Additionally, it allows efficient use of the available bandwidth. The Key Features:

1. All signals are sent over the same frequency at the same time.
2. The signals are encoded with unique codes, and receivers use the codes to differentiate between the signals.
3. CDM is used in Code Division Multiple Access (CDMA) systems.
4. Application: Widely used in cellular networks, such as the 3G and 4G wireless communication systems.

Multiplexing in the Transport Layer

In the transport layer, multiplexing is a technique that enables multiple communication sessions to share a single network connection, optimizing resource utilization. This is essential in network protocols like TCP (Transmission Control Protocol) and UDP (User Datagram Protocol), where each process or application running on a host must be able to communicate independently. Multiplexing relies on port numbers to differentiate between various data streams. A port number is a 16-bit identifier that, when paired with an IP address, uniquely identifies a specific application or service on a host. This allows the transport layer to manage multiple communication sessions concurrently, even if they share the same physical network connection. By using different port numbers, applications like web servers, email clients, and file transfer protocols can run simultaneously without interfering with each other, enabling efficient use of the network's bandwidth and improving overall performance in multi-tasking environments.

Multiplexing in TCP

Multiplexing in TCP is a technique used to allow multiple communication sessions to take place simultaneously over a single network connection. This is accomplished by utilizing port numbers, which are 16-bit integers that help distinguish between different applications or services running on a machine. In a TCP header, both the source port and destination port are specified to ensure that each segment of data reaches the appropriate process on the receiving end. When a packet is sent over the network, the destination machine uses the destination port number to direct the data to the correct application or service. This approach ensures that different services, such as web servers, email servers, or file transfer applications, can operate concurrently on a single machine without interference, maximizing the use of available network resources. Multiplexing is essential for achieving efficient communication and resource sharing in a multi-tasking network environment. The Key Features:

1. Each TCP connection is uniquely identified by the source IP address, source port, destination IP address, and destination port.

2. Multiple processes or applications running on the same machine can communicate over the network using distinct port numbers.
3. The Transport Layer makes use of multiplexing to direct incoming packets to the correct application based on the destination port.

Example: When you browse a website, your browser communicates over port 80 (HTTP) or port 443 (HTTPS). If you use a different service, such as FTP, that will use port 21.

Multiplexing in UDP

Multiplexing in UDP (User Datagram Protocol) refers to the ability of the protocol to handle multiple applications or processes on a single host. Each process that wants to send or receive data through UDP uses a specific port number, which helps the protocol direct the data to the correct application. The port numbers allow multiple applications to share a single network connection, each identified by a unique combination of IP address and port number. UDP, being a connectionless protocol, does not establish a session or connection before transmitting data, unlike TCP. It uses port numbers to ensure that data is sent to the appropriate application but does not ensure reliability, ordering, or integrity of the data. This lack of guarantees is one of UDP's key characteristics, making it suitable for applications that require speed over reliability, such as video streaming or online gaming. The Key Features:

1. Like TCP, UDP uses source and destination port numbers to identify the communication endpoints.
2. Each application using UDP will have a unique port number, and the operating system will use these numbers to deliver the data to the correct application.
3. UDP multiplexes data streams by placing the appropriate port number in the header of each datagram.

Example: In a video streaming application, multiple video streams can be sent using different ports. Each stream would be directed to a specific application on the receiver's system using the corresponding port.

Multiplexing in General (Socket-Level Multiplexing)

Multiplexing refers to the technique of combining multiple signals or data streams into one medium to optimize the use of resources. In the context of network communication, multiplexing allows multiple communication sessions to share a single channel or connection. Socket-level multiplexing is a mechanism used in network programming where multiple input/output (I/O) operations on different sockets are managed simultaneously. It enables efficient communication by allowing a program to handle multiple network connections over a single thread or process without the need for creating separate threads for each connection. With socket-level multiplexing, a single process can monitor multiple sockets for activity using techniques like select (), poll (), or e-poll(). These functions allow the program to wait for events like data availability or readiness to send data, without blocking execution. This method is commonly used in servers that handle large volumes of concurrent connections, ensuring resource efficiency and scalability.

Multiplexing Process in Data Communication

The multiplexing process in Figure 5.4 can be broken down into the following steps:

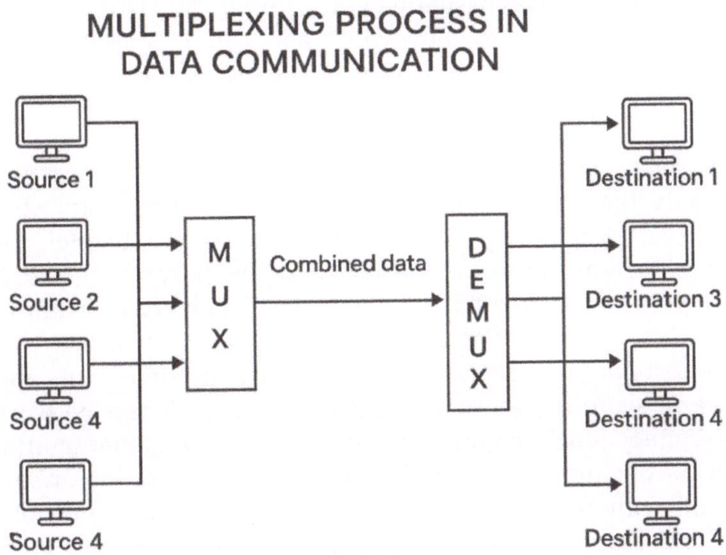

Figure 5.4: Multiplexing Process in Data Communication.

Segmentation

In data communication, segmentation is the process of dividing large chunks of data into smaller, manageable units. These smaller units are referred to as segments in TCP (Transmission Control Protocol) or datagrams in UDP (User Datagram Protocol). Each segment contains part of the original message, along with control information, including sequence numbers and error-checking data, ensuring that data is correctly transmitted and reconstructed at the destination. Segmentation allows the sender to efficiently handle large messages by breaking them down into smaller parts, making them easier to route through networks and manage at the transport layer. This step is crucial for ensuring that data is transmitted in an organized, reliable manner, and it is an essential aspect of both reliable and connectionless protocols.

Port Assignment

Port assignment is the process of designating a specific port number for each segment or datagram as it is created during the segmentation phase. These port numbers are critical for ensuring that data is routed correctly at the destination. Each application or service running on a device is identified by a unique port number, which serves as a virtual "address" to differentiate between multiple services. In this step, the transport layer assigns source and destination port numbers to each segment, facilitating communication between the correct applications. In TCP, the source port is chosen randomly for each connection, while the destination port is predefined (e.g., port 80 for HTTP). This assignment allows the receiving system to know which application or service should handle the data once it reaches the destination, ensuring correct delivery and service operation.

Multiplexing

Multiplexing is the core process of combining multiple data streams from different applications into a single communication channel for efficient transmission. The transport layer uses the assigned port numbers to distinguish between different data streams and ensure that they are transmitted over the same network connection. Each application's data is identified by its unique source and destination port number. This allows multiple applications on the same device to share the same network resource, such as a network interface or physical connection. The multiplexing process ensures that multiple streams of data can coexist and be delivered to the correct application or service at the receiving end without interference. Essentially, multiplexing enables efficient use of network resources, minimizing the need for separate connections for each application while maintaining data integrity and separation.

Transmission

Once the data has been multiplexed and assigned to appropriate port numbers, it is transmitted over the network. In this phase, the transport layer at the sender's end packages the data into segments and sends them through the network. The segments travel across various network devices and protocols, potentially over multiple routes, until they reach the destination. Upon arrival, the transport layer at the receiving system uses the destination port number to demultiplex the incoming data and route it to the appropriate application. This ensures that data from different applications is correctly processed, with each segment being delivered to its corresponding service. Transmission is a vital stage in data communication, as it directly influences the speed and reliability of data transfer across networks, and it ensures that data integrity is maintained through mechanisms like error detection and retransmission in protocols like TCP.

Connection Management

Connection management refers to the process of establishing, maintaining, and terminating communication sessions (connections) between two or more endpoints in a network. In the context of the Transport Layer of the OSI model, connection management plays a crucial role in facilitating reliable data transmission between hosts, ensuring that connections are properly established, maintained during communication, and terminated when no longer needed. There are two primary types of connection management:

Connection-Oriented Communication

Connection-oriented communication is a communication model where a reliable, dedicated connection is established and maintained throughout the communication session. This connection is set up before any data transmission begins and remains active for the duration of the session. The primary feature of connection-oriented communication is that it ensures data integrity, sequence, and reliability. Acknowledgements are used to confirm successful delivery of data, and if any errors occur during transmission, mechanisms such as retransmissions are implemented to ensure that the communication is completed accurately. The connection-oriented model is commonly used in applications that require guaranteed data delivery, such as web browsing and file transfers. Transmission Control Protocol (TCP) is the most widely used connection-oriented protocol. It is responsible for segmenting the data into smaller packets, managing flow control, and ensuring error-free delivery through retransmission and acknowledgment mechanisms. This approach prioritizes accuracy over speed and efficiency.

Connectionless communication

Connectionless communication is a communication model where messages are sent independently of each other, with no dedicated or persistent connection established between the sender and the receiver. In this model, each data packet is treated as a standalone unit, without any guarantee of successful delivery, sequence, or error correction. The sender simply transmits the data, and the receiver processes it without establishing any long-term communication session. This model is generally faster and more efficient since it eliminates the overhead of maintaining a dedicated connection and the need for retransmissions. However, it sacrifices reliability, which makes it suitable for applications where speed is more critical than data accuracy, such as live streaming or online gaming. User Datagram Protocol (UDP) is the most commonly used connectionless protocol. It is lightweight, does not require acknowledgment, and does not guarantee the delivery or ordering of data, making it ideal for real-time applications that can tolerate occasional data loss.

Connection-Oriented Communication (TCP)

In a connection-oriented communication, such as TCP, a connection must be established between the sender and receiver before data can be transmitted. This ensures that data is reliably delivered, in order, and without duplication. The Key Phases of Connection Management in TCP:

Connection Establishment (Three-Way Handshake)

When two devices need to communicate using TCP, they must first establish a reliable connection. This is done through a process called the three-way handshake. The three-way handshake ensures that both the sender and receiver are ready to exchange data.

Steps in the Three-Way Handshake:

SYN (Synchronize)

The first step in the TCP three-way handshake involves the client initiating the connection. The client sends a SYN (synchronize) packet to the server, indicating that it wishes to establish a connection. The SYN packet contains an Initial Sequence Number (ISN), which is used to keep track of the data sent during the connection. This packet signifies the beginning of the communication process. After sending the SYN packet, the client enters the SYN_SENT state, waiting for a response from the server. The SYN request serves as the foundation for the rest of the handshake, ensuring both parties are synchronized before any data exchange begins.

SYN-ACK (Synchronize-Acknowledge)

In response to the client's SYN packet, the server sends a SYN-ACK packet. This packet acknowledges the receipt of the client's SYN by incrementing the client's ISN by 1. In addition, the server provides its own ISN to begin its part of the communication. The SYN-ACK packet serves as the server's way of saying, "I received your request, and I am ready to proceed." Upon sending the SYN-ACK packet, the server transitions to the SYN_RECEIVED state, indicating that it is prepared to complete the handshake. This stage confirms that both sides have acknowledged each other's requests, and they are ready to finalize the connection.

ACK (Acknowledge)

The final step of the three-way handshake is when the client sends an ACK packet back to the server. This ACK packet acknowledges the server's SYN-ACK by incrementing the server's ISN by 1. The ACK packet serves as confirmation that the client received the server's response and is now fully synchronized. Upon receiving the ACK packet, both the client and the server transition to the ESTABLISHED state. At this point, the TCP connection is established, and data transmission can begin. This final acknowledgment ensures that both parties are synchronized and ready to exchange information securely and reliably.

Data Transfer

Data transfer in TCP (Transmission Control Protocol) refers to the process by which data is exchanged between the sender and receiver over a reliable connection. Once the connection is established through a handshake, data is segmented and transmitted across the network. Segmentation breaks down large data packets into smaller manageable units, known as segments, for more efficient transmission. TCP ensures that these segments are transferred reliably by managing their order, retransmitting lost or corrupted segments, and ensuring flow control between sender and receiver. Flow control is particularly important to regulate the amount of data sent at once, avoiding receiver overflow. This is managed through a sliding window mechanism, which dynamically adjusts the size of the window based on network conditions. Additionally, error detection is performed using checksums, and the receiver acknowledges each segment to confirm successful receipt. If an acknowledgment is not received within a set time, retransmission is triggered to ensure data integrity.

Segmentation

In TCP, segmentation plays a crucial role in ensuring efficient and reliable data transmission. Large data is split into smaller, more manageable chunks called segments. This segmentation reduces the chances of data loss and makes it easier for the network to handle smaller packets of information. By breaking the data into smaller pieces, TCP reduces the probability of congestion on the network and ensures that each segment can be routed independently, optimizing the use of available bandwidth. Each segment is transmitted separately, and it includes a sequence number that helps the receiver reassemble the segments in the correct order. Additionally, segmentation allows for error handling, as each segment can be independently checked for integrity, making retransmission of corrupted or lost data more manageable. The receiver also sends acknowledgments for each segment, informing the sender of the successful reception and ensuring smooth data transfer.

Flow Control

Flow control in TCP ensures that the sender does not overwhelm the receiver with too much data at once. The receiver may not be capable of processing large amounts of data quickly, so it is crucial to manage the rate of transmission to avoid buffer overflow and data loss. TCP uses a sliding window mechanism to manage this flow. The sliding window specifies the amount of data that can be sent before needing an acknowledgment from the receiver. As the receiver processes data and sends acknowledgments, the window slides forward, allowing the sender to send more data. This dynamic approach helps maintain an optimal data transfer rate, ensuring that both sender and receiver can operate efficiently without overloading the receiver's buffer. Flow control is essential for maintaining the stability and performance of the network, especially in environments where network conditions fluctuate or where the receiver's processing power is limited.

Error Detection

Error detection in TCP is a vital mechanism to ensure data integrity during transmission. As data is transferred across the network, various issues such as noise, packet corruption, or loss may occur. To handle this, TCP uses checksums to verify the integrity of each segment of data. A checksum is a calculated value derived from the content of the data. The sender calculates the checksum before transmission and includes it with the segment. Upon receipt, the receiver recalculates the checksum based on the received data and compares it to the checksum sent by the sender. If there is a mismatch, it indicates that the data has been corrupted during transmission. In such cases, the receiver requests the sender to retransmit the affected segment. This mechanism ensures that data errors are detected and corrected, providing reliable data delivery over the network.

Acknowledgments

Acknowledgments are a critical part of the reliable data transfer process in TCP. For each segment of data sent by the sender, the receiver sends an acknowledgment (ACK) back to the sender to confirm successful receipt. This acknowledgment informs the sender that the segment has arrived correctly and can be processed. If the sender does not receive an acknowledgment within a certain time frame, it assumes the segment has been lost or corrupted and triggers a retransmission. This mechanism is essential for ensuring the reliable delivery of data, as it enables both the sender and receiver to track the status of each segment. The use of acknowledgments helps avoid unnecessary retransmissions of data that has been successfully received, optimizing network efficiency. This feedback loop is vital for maintaining the integrity of the data transfer and for managing the flow of information across the network.

Sequence Numbers

In TCP, sequence numbers are essential for the proper assembly and management of data. Each segment of data transmitted by the sender is assigned a unique sequence number. This number helps the receiver correctly reassemble the segments in the correct order, as segments may take different paths through the network and arrive out of sequence. The sequence number also plays a key role in ensuring data reliability, as it allows both the sender and receiver to track which data has been successfully received and which segments need retransmission. Sequence numbers also help the sender and receiver identify any lost or duplicate segments. This numbering system is fundamental in TCP's reliability mechanisms, ensuring that the data is received intact and in the correct order, regardless of the network's unpredictable nature. By utilizing sequence numbers, TCP guarantees that even large data transfers are accurately reassembled.

Connection Termination (Four-Way Handshake)

Connection termination in TCP is achieved through a four-way handshake process, which ensures a proper closure of the communication channel between the client and the server. This prevents any resource leakage and ensures all data is transmitted before closing the connection. The first step involves the side that wishes to terminate the connection sending a FIN (Finish) packet. This signals to the other party that the sender has no more data to transmit. The sender then enters the FIN_WAIT_1 state, waiting for an acknowledgment from the receiver.

FIN (Finish)

The FIN packet is sent by the client or server that wishes to end the connection. This indicates that the sender has completed all data transmission and intends to close the connection. Once the recipient receives the FIN packet, it acknowledges the request by sending back an ACK (Acknowledge) packet, confirming the receipt of the termination request. After this, the sender transitions to the FIN_WAIT_1 state, awaiting further actions to complete the connection termination.

ACK (Acknowledge)

After receiving the FIN packet, the other side acknowledges the termination request by sending back an ACK packet. This confirms that the sender's FIN packet has been received. The recipient of the initial FIN packet moves to the CLOSE_WAIT state, which means it is waiting for its own opportunity to send its own termination request. After sending the ACK, the recipient is still capable of receiving data, but it will not transmit any more data. This acknowledgment is critical to ensure both sides agree on the termination process before finalizing the closure.

FIN (Finish)

The second FIN packet is sent by the recipient after it has acknowledged the initial FIN packet. This indicates that the recipient has also finished transmitting its data and is now ready to terminate the connection from its side. Once the recipient sends this second FIN packet, it transitions to the FIN_WAIT_2 state, awaiting acknowledgment of the termination. This is an essential step in the four-way handshake, as it ensures both parties agree on the closure of the connection and that no data is lost during the transition to termination.

ACK (Acknowledge)

The final step in the four-way handshake involves the original side acknowledging the second FIN packet sent by the recipient. This acknowledgment is made by sending an ACK packet, confirming that both parties are aware of the connection's termination. At this point, both sides enter the CLOSED state, indicating that the connection is fully closed, and the resources are freed. The connection termination process is now complete, with both sides ensuring that all data was transmitted successfully before closing the connection. This procedure ensures that all communication is properly concluded.

Connection States in TCP

During the connection management process, the connection goes through different states, including:

1. LISTEN: Server is waiting for a connection request.

2. SYN_SENT: Client is waiting for an acknowledgment after sending the SYN request.
3. SYN_RECEIVED: Server has received the SYN request and sent a SYN-ACK in return.
4. ESTABLISHED: Connection is established, and data transfer can begin.
5. FIN_WAIT_1, FIN_WAIT_2: Phases during the termination process.
6. CLOSE_WAIT: The receiver has received a FIN, waiting for the application to close the connection.
7. CLOSED: The connection has been fully closed.

Connectionless Communication (UDP)

In connectionless communication, such as User Datagram Protocol (UDP), there is no need for a formal connection setup between the sender and receiver. Data is transmitted in the form of individual packets called datagrams, which are sent independently. UDP does not guarantee the successful delivery of these packets, nor does it provide error checking or recovery mechanisms. If a packet is lost in transit, UDP does not attempt to retransmit it. This lack of guarantee makes UDP a "best-effort" protocol. Additionally, there is no need for a handshake process to establish a connection before data transfer, which eliminates any delays associated with connection initiation. While this can make UDP less reliable than protocols like TCP, its simplicity and reduced overhead make it suitable for applications where speed is more important than guaranteed delivery, such as real-time applications like video streaming, online gaming, and VoIP.

Key Characteristics of UDP

One of the defining characteristics of UDP is that it does not require connection establishment between the communicating parties. Unlike connection-oriented protocols like TCP, which initiate a handshake before sending data, UDP sends packets directly without establishing any formal connection. This lack of connection setup leads to a reduction in overhead, making UDP a lightweight protocol for data transmission. UDP's reliability is minimal; it does not guarantee that the data will reach its destination, nor does it ensure that the packets arrive in the correct order. If any datagrams are lost during transmission, UDP does not handle retransmission, which contrasts with protocols like TCP, where lost packets are retransmitted. This feature of UDP, while offering lower reliability, is advantageous for real-time applications where receiving data quickly, even if it is occasionally lost, is more critical than ensuring every packet reaches its destination.

No Flow Control or Congestion Control

UDP does not implement flow control or congestion control mechanisms, which are typically used by connection-oriented protocols like TCP. Flow control is a technique used to manage the rate at which data is sent to ensure that the receiver's buffer does not overflow. Without flow control, UDP sends data at a constant rate, which can lead to issues if the receiver cannot process the data quickly enough. Similarly, UDP does not respond to network congestion. While protocols like TCP reduce their sending rate when congestion is detected in the network, UDP will continue to transmit at the same rate, regardless of the network's current state. This lack of congestion control means that UDP can be more efficient in networks with low traffic but may suffer from packet loss or delays in congested networks. As a result, UDP is more suited for applications where timely delivery is essential, and occasional data loss is acceptable, such as streaming services or VoIP.

Low Latency

One of the primary advantages of UDP is its low latency. Since UDP does not require the overhead of establishing and maintaining a connection or performing error checking and correction, it tends to have faster transmission times compared to connection-oriented protocols like TCP. There is no waiting time for handshakes or acknowledgments, so data can be transmitted almost immediately. This makes UDP an ideal choice for real-time applications, such as online gaming, live video streaming, and voice over IP (VoIP), where timely data delivery is critical. Even though there is no guarantee of delivery, the priority for these applications is to minimize the delay, and UDP's design enables this. The absence of error correction processes also means that there is no need for additional round trips for confirming the receipt of data, further reducing latency and making UDP an effective protocol for applications where real-time communication is essential.

Usage of User Datagram Protocol

UDP, or User Datagram Protocol, is a connectionless protocol that plays a vital role in several network applications due to its low overhead and speed. Since it does not require establishing a connection before sending data, it is ideal for real-time applications like audio and video streaming. These applications, such as online video conferences, live broadcasts, and gaming, prioritize speed over reliability, as a slight loss of data may not significantly affect the user experience. The protocol's minimalistic approach ensures low latency, which is crucial for interactive communication and real-time media delivery. UDP is also suitable for scenarios where the continuous flow of data is more critical than ensuring every packet is delivered without loss. This allows real-time services to operate efficiently even under network congestion, delivering smoother experiences for users in applications like VoIP (Voice over IP) and online gaming.

Real-time Applications

UDP is widely used in real-time applications where time-sensitive delivery is more critical than data integrity. For example, audio and video streaming services rely on UDP for its low latency. When streaming content, if a packet is lost, it is usually more important to keep the stream flowing rather than retransmitting the lost data. Similarly, in online gaming and VoIP (Voice over IP) communications, even a slight delay can lead to poor user experience. Since UDP lacks the overhead of connection establishment and error correction mechanisms like TCP, it offers faster transmission speeds, making it ideal for these time-sensitive applications. These real-time applications are tolerant of minor packet loss as long as the overall performance remains uninterrupted. This enables smooth, uninterrupted experiences in real-time communication, such as live video conferencing or online gaming, where the continuity of service is paramount.

DNS Queries

DNS (Domain Name System) queries are an essential part of network communication, allowing domain names to be resolved into IP addresses. These queries are typically performed over UDP rather than TCP due to UDP's inherent speed and efficiency. DNS lookups are usually short, requiring only a request and a response, making the connectionless nature of UDP highly suitable for this purpose. With UDP, there is no need to establish a connection or perform handshakes, which saves time and resources. Furthermore, DNS systems are designed to handle packet loss, meaning that the failure of a single query does not disrupt the overall functioning of the system. If a packet is lost, the DNS client can simply retry the request. This tolerance for loss and the protocol's ability to quickly send and receive data make UDP the preferred choice for DNS queries, contributing to faster domain resolution and more efficient internet browsing.

Broadcasting

UDP is commonly used in broadcasting, where data needs to be transmitted from one sender to multiple receivers without the need for establishing a direct connection with each recipient. Broadcasting allows for efficient communication in scenarios like media streaming, network discovery, or multicast video feeds. Unlike TCP, which requires a connection-oriented approach and results in more overhead, UDP allows data to be sent in a one-to-many fashion, optimizing network resources. This is particularly useful for applications such as multicast video broadcasting, where the same data stream needs to be delivered to multiple users at once. Additionally, since UDP doesn't maintain connection states or guarantee delivery, it minimizes the need for system resources, which is crucial in large-scale broadcasting scenarios. Broadcasting with UDP helps ensure that all recipients receive the data at the same time, making it an ideal choice for applications requiring simultaneous communication across a broad audience.

Connectionless Communication (UDP)

In connectionless communication (e.g., UDP), no formal connection setup or termination is required. Each packet (called a datagram) is sent independently, and there is no guarantee of delivery, order, or error checking. The Key Characteristics of UDP:

No Connection Establishment

UDP (User Datagram Protocol) is a connectionless protocol, meaning that it does not require any preliminary handshake or setup before data transmission. In contrast to protocols like TCP (Transmission Control Protocol), which must establish a connection between the sender and receiver before any data is exchanged, UDP sends data immediately as individual packets, known as datagrams. This characteristic reduces the overhead associated with establishing and maintaining connections. It allows for faster transmission of data, which is especially useful in scenarios where real-time performance is crucial, such as in video streaming or online gaming. However, the lack of connection establishment also means that there is no built-in mechanism to verify if the recipient is ready to receive the data or if the data has been properly received. While this can increase efficiency, it also introduces challenges in ensuring reliable communication.

Unreliable

One of the defining characteristics of UDP is that it is an unreliable protocol. Unlike TCP, which ensures that data is reliably delivered by requiring acknowledgments and retransmissions in case of packet loss, UDP does not provide any guarantees for successful data delivery. When using UDP, there is no confirmation that the data has arrived at its destination, and the protocol does not check if packets are missing or corrupted. Furthermore, it does not ensure that packets are delivered in the order they were sent. If packets are lost or arrive out of order, UDP does not attempt to recover them, leaving the responsibility of handling such issues to higher layers in the application. This unreliability makes UDP suitable for applications where timely delivery is more important than complete accuracy, such as real-time voice communication or video streaming, where occasional packet loss can be tolerated.

No Flow Control or Congestion Control

UDP does not implement any form of flow control or congestion control. Flow control in protocols like TCP ensures that the sender does not overwhelm the receiver with too much data at once. Similarly, congestion control in TCP helps manage network congestion by adjusting the data rate to avoid overloading the network. UDP, however, sends data without any mechanisms to regulate the pace of transmission, and it does not react to network congestion. This means that UDP can flood the network with packets, which could potentially lead to packet loss, network congestion, or performance degradation, especially in environments with limited bandwidth or high traffic volumes. While this lack of control allows UDP to operate with low overhead and minimal latency, it can be a disadvantage in situations where maintaining network stability is crucial. As a result, it is typically used in applications where speed is prioritized over network stability, such as DNS lookups or live media streaming.

Low Latency

UDP is often preferred for applications that require low-latency communication due to its lack of connection establishment and error recovery mechanisms. Since UDP does not require a connection handshake, data can be transmitted immediately after being sent, minimizing delays. In contrast, connection-oriented protocols like TCP introduce additional latency due to the need to establish a connection, perform error checking, and manage retransmissions. This makes UDP ideal for real-time applications where quick transmission is essential, such as voice over IP (VoIP), online gaming, and video conferencing. The absence of features like acknowledgment, flow control, or retransmission further reduces latency, ensuring that the application can operate with minimal delay. However, the trade-off is that UDP sacrifices reliability and consistency, as lost packets or errors in transmission are not handled by the protocol. Despite these drawbacks, the low-latency characteristics of UDP make it highly valuable in time-sensitive scenarios.

Connection Management in Hybrid Protocols

Some protocols, such as SCTP (Stream Control Transmission Protocol), combine the characteristics of both TCP and UDP. SCTP is a message-oriented, reliable, connection-oriented protocol designed for scenarios that require multiple streams of data to be delivered reliably. The Key Features of SCTP:

Multi-homing Support

Stream Control Transmission Protocol (SCTP) is designed to provide multi-homing support, which means it allows a single connection (or association) to utilize multiple IP addresses. This capability enhances network resilience, as SCTP can maintain communication even if one of the network paths becomes unavailable. For example, if a device has multiple network interfaces (such as Ethernet and Wi-Fi), SCTP can use them simultaneously, switching between them as needed without dropping the connection. This makes SCTP more robust compared to other transport protocols like TCP and UDP, which typically rely on a single IP address per connection. The ability to handle multiple paths also optimizes resource usage and reduces the likelihood of network disruptions. Multi-homing support is particularly valuable in environments where network reliability is critical, such as in telecommunications and real-time data transfer applications, ensuring that connections are less susceptible to failures.

Multi-streaming

SCTP supports multi-streaming, which allows multiple data streams to be sent within a single association, improving efficiency and eliminating head-of-line blocking. In traditional transport protocols like TCP, if one packet in a stream is delayed or lost, all subsequent packets in that stream are held up until the lost packet is retransmitted. However, SCTP bypasses this limitation by allowing independent delivery of data across multiple streams. This means that if a packet in one stream experiences delay, packets in other streams can continue to be delivered without waiting, improving overall throughput and reducing latency. Multi-streaming is particularly beneficial for applications requiring high-performance data transmission, such as video conferencing or voice over IP (VoIP), where different types of data (e.g., video and audio) can be handled separately. It ensures that delays in one stream don't impact the entire communication, leading to a more efficient data transfer process.

Reliable and Ordered Delivery

SCTP, like TCP, guarantees the reliable and ordered delivery of data, ensuring that data transmitted between endpoints reaches its destination accurately and in the correct sequence. This is crucial for applications that require the integrity of data, such as file transfers, database synchronization, and communication in real-time systems. SCTP provides reliability through mechanisms like acknowledgment of received data and retransmission of lost packets. Additionally, it maintains data order within each stream, ensuring that packets are delivered in the same sequence they were sent. This makes SCTP a suitable protocol for scenarios where message ordering and data integrity are important. However, unlike TCP, SCTP offers the flexibility of multi-streaming, which allows different streams of data to be handled independently. This feature ensures that SCTP delivers the best of both worlds: reliable, ordered delivery of data without the performance bottleneck of head-of-line blocking found in traditional protocols. SCTP can be used for scenarios where TCP's features are needed, but additional capabilities like multi-streaming and multi-homing are required, such as in telecommunication networks and signaling protocols.

Flow Control and Retransmission

Flow control and retransmission are key concepts in ensuring reliable data communication, particularly in connection-oriented protocols like TCP. They play a crucial role in managing how data is transmitted across the network and in dealing with issues related to packet loss or network congestion in Figure 5.5.

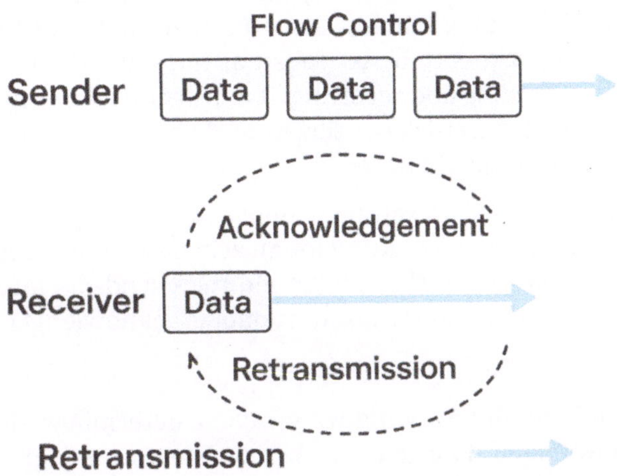

Figure 5.5: Mechanism of Flow Control and Retransmission.

Flow Control

Flow control is a mechanism that prevents the sender from overwhelming the receiver with data. It ensures that the rate at which data is transmitted does not exceed the receiver's ability to process and store the data. Without flow control, the sender could send data too quickly, leading to buffer overflow at the receiver, causing data loss and inefficiency. The Key Features of Flow Control:

Receiver's Buffer Capacity

Receiver's buffer capacity plays a critical role in flow control in network communication. The buffer is essentially temporary storage that holds incoming data before it is processed by the receiver. The sender must be aware of the available space in this buffer to avoid overwhelming the receiver. If the buffer is full, the receiver can't accept more data, leading to potential data loss or delays. Flow control mechanisms, like those in TCP, ensure that the sender transmits data at a pace the receiver can handle, preventing congestion. By continually monitoring the buffer's capacity, the sender adjusts its data transmission rate. If the buffer has space, the sender continues sending data. However, once it reaches its capacity, it will temporarily halt until the receiver processes enough data to free up space, thus maintaining a steady flow without overloading the receiver.

Sliding Window Protocol

The sliding window protocol is a fundamental mechanism in flow control for TCP, allowing efficient data transmission without overwhelming the receiver. It involves a dynamic window that defines how much data can be sent before receiving an acknowledgment. The sender is permitted to send data within this window, and once the receiver acknowledges part of it, the window slides forward, allowing more data to be sent. This process ensures that the sender doesn't transmit more data than the receiver can handle, and it maintains an orderly flow of information. The sliding window also optimizes network throughput by enabling multiple data packets to be in transit at the same time, thus reducing the wait time between sending and receiving. It adjusts dynamically based on the network's conditions, offering efficient utilization of bandwidth while minimizing the risk of congestion or packet loss.

Example: Imagine a sender with a sliding window size of 3 segments, meaning it can send up to 3 segments before waiting for an acknowledgment. If the receiver acknowledges the first segment, the sender can then send the fourth segment. This process continues, sliding the window as data is acknowledged.

Window Size

The window size in the sliding window protocol determines the maximum amount of unacknowledged data that can be in transit at any given time. It is a crucial factor in managing flow control between sender and receiver. The window size can be adjusted dynamically based on the receiver's buffer capacity and network conditions. A larger window size allows the sender to send more data before waiting for an acknowledgment, which increases the throughput of the connection. However, this can lead to congestion if the receiver's buffer is not large enough to handle the influx of data. Conversely, a smaller window size reduces the risk of overloading the receiver but may lead to underutilization of the available bandwidth, as less data is sent at once. Thus, the window size needs to be carefully managed to optimize the flow of data without causing delays or packet loss.

Retransmission

Retransmission is a mechanism used in connection-oriented protocols like TCP to ensure reliable data delivery. It addresses the issue of packet loss, ensuring that lost or corrupted packets are retransmitted. In TCP, retransmission typically happens when the sender does not receive an acknowledgment for data that was sent. This mechanism ensures that all data eventually reaches the receiver in the correct order, even in the presence of network issues like packet loss, corruption, or timeouts. The Key Aspects of Retransmission:

Timeout-Based Retransmission

In TCP, timeout-based retransmission is a critical mechanism used to detect packet loss and ensure reliable data transfer. The sender sets a timer upon sending a segment and waits for an acknowledgment (ACK) from the receiver. If the ACK is not received within a specific time frame, known as the timeout period, the sender assumes the packet has been lost. It then retransmits the segment. The timeout period is dynamically calculated based on the round-trip time (RTT), which measures the time it takes for a packet to travel from the sender to the receiver and back. The timeout value is adjusted using algorithms that take into account the variation in RTT, ensuring that the retransmission process is efficient without triggering unnecessary retransmissions. This mechanism helps maintain data integrity and ensures that lost packets are quickly retransmitted to maintain connection reliability.

Duplicate Acknowledgments (Fast Retransmit)

TCP employs the use of duplicate acknowledgments to detect packet loss and trigger fast retransmission, thus reducing the time spent waiting for timeouts. When a sender receives multiple duplicate ACKs for the same segment, it interprets this as an indication that a segment has been lost. Typically, if three duplicate ACKs are received, the sender immediately retransmits the missing segment without waiting for the timeout. This process, known as fast retransmit, helps reduce the delay caused by timeout-based retransmission and enhances overall data delivery efficiency. By using duplicate ACKs to quickly detect missing packets, TCP can maintain higher throughput and minimize the impact of packet loss. This approach is particularly effective in cases where only one segment is lost in a stream of data, enabling the sender to quickly recover and ensure continued reliable transmission without waiting for long timeout periods.

Selective Acknowledgment (SACK)

Selective Acknowledgment (SACK) is an enhancement in TCP that improves retransmission efficiency when multiple packets are lost or delayed. Without SACK, a receiver acknowledges only the next expected segment, leading to inefficiencies when multiple segments are missing. SACK allows the receiver to specify exactly which packets have been received, even if they are out of order. This means that the receiver can acknowledge non-sequential segments, allowing the sender to retransmit only the missing packets instead of all the packets after the last acknowledged segment. By reducing unnecessary retransmissions, SACK optimizes network performance, particularly in scenarios involving high packet loss or congestion. This mechanism ensures that the retransmission process is more targeted, saving both bandwidth and time, and helping to maintain a stable and efficient connection, especially in networks with fluctuating conditions or high latency.

Cumulative Acknowledgments

TCP uses cumulative acknowledgments to simplify the process of confirming the receipt of data. When the receiver sends an ACK for a segment, it implicitly acknowledges all previous segments, even those that have not been explicitly acknowledged. For example, if a receiver sends an ACK with sequence number X, it signifies that all segments with sequence numbers up to X-1 have been successfully received. This method reduces the number of ACKs needed and simplifies the acknowledgment process, but it can be less efficient when multiple segments are lost. If a segment is lost, the receiver may have to wait until the missing segment is retransmitted before it can send an acknowledgment for subsequent segments. While cumulative acknowledgment improves overall efficiency in most cases, its effectiveness decreases in environments with high packet loss, where more advanced mechanisms like SACK may be required to ensure efficient retransmissions.

Steps in Retransmission Process

Data Transmission

In the process of data transmission, the sender initiates communication by transmitting a data packet to the receiver. Once the packet is sent, the sender waits for an acknowledgment (ACK) from the receiver. This acknowledgment confirms that the receiver has successfully received the packet, ensuring reliable communication. The sender typically uses a sliding window protocol in which multiple packets may be sent before receiving an acknowledgment, depending on the window size. The sender keeps track of which packets have been acknowledged and which ones are still pending acknowledgment. The transmission process involves various layers of error detection and correction mechanisms to ensure that the data remains intact during the journey. This waiting period for acknowledgment serves as a key part of the reliable delivery of data, where the sender must pause further actions until it is certain the data has been received properly.

Timeout or Duplicate Acknowledgments

Timeouts or duplicate acknowledgments play a crucial role in ensuring data reliability during transmission. When a sender transmits data, it waits for an acknowledgment from the receiver. If the sender does not receive the acknowledgment within a predefined time (known as the timeout period), it assumes the packet might have been lost or corrupted during transmission. In such a case, the sender triggers a retransmission of the unacknowledged packet. On the other hand, if the sender receives multiple duplicate acknowledgments for the same data packet, it suggests that the receiver has not received the next packet, likely due to packet loss. In response to this, the sender triggers a retransmission of the lost packet. Both mechanisms timeout and duplicate acknowledgments are vital for ensuring that all data is reliably transmitted and received in a TCP connection, avoiding any data loss.

Retransmission

Retransmission is a critical component of ensuring reliable data transmission in TCP (Transmission Control Protocol). When a sender fails to receive an acknowledgment for a transmitted packet within the timeout period or when it detects duplicate acknowledgments, it assumes that the data packet has been lost in transit. As a result, the sender will retransmit the lost or unacknowledged data packet. Retransmission ensures that the receiver eventually gets all the necessary data, even in the presence of packet loss. TCP uses mechanisms like sequence numbers to ensure that packets are retransmitted in the correct order. Furthermore, the sender typically reduces the transmission rate temporarily after a retransmission to avoid overwhelming the network. The retransmission process continues until the receiver acknowledges the lost packet or all data packets are successfully transmitted. This ensures the reliability of communication in networks with unpredictable conditions.

Acknowledgment

Acknowledgment is a fundamental part of the reliable data transmission process in TCP. Once the sender transmits a packet of data, it expects to receive an acknowledgment (ACK) from the receiver, confirming that the packet has been successfully received. If the packet is not acknowledged within a specified timeout, it is retransmitted. Once the receiver acknowledges the retransmitted data, the sender can move the window forward, allowing it to send additional packets. This acknowledgment process ensures that data is reliably transmitted in a sequence and that no packet is left unreceived. The receiver also uses acknowledgment numbers to indicate the next expected byte of data, which helps the sender track which packets have been successfully received. Once all data packets have been acknowledged, the sender can consider the data transfer complete. Acknowledgments thus form the cornerstone of data integrity and flow control in TCP.

Retransmission and Congestion Control

Retransmissions in TCP can indicate packet loss, which may be a result of network congestion. Congestion occurs when the network's data transmission capacity is overwhelmed, leading to dropped packets and delays. In response to packet loss, TCP employs congestion control algorithms such as Slow Start, Congestion Avoidance, and Fast Recovery. Slow Start initially starts the transmission at a low rate and increases it exponentially until a threshold is reached, after which it transitions to a linear increase. Congestion Avoidance reduces the transmission rate when packet loss is detected to alleviate congestion. Fast Recovery quickly retransmits lost packets without returning to the slow start phase, speeding up recovery from packet loss. These algorithms dynamically adjust the sender's transmission rate, balancing the need to send data quickly with the need to avoid further congestion, thus optimizing network performance and ensuring more reliable data delivery during high-traffic periods.

Flow Control and Retransmission in Action (Example)

Let's consider a scenario where a client and server are communicating over a TCP connection:

Step 1: Initial Data Transmission: The client sends data packets (segments) to the server using the sliding window protocol. The client waits for acknowledgment from the server. Let's say the window size is 4, so the client can send 4 packets before needing an acknowledgment.

Step 2: Flow Control Mechanism: The server processes the data and sends an acknowledgment for the received packets. If the server's buffer starts filling up, it reduces the window size, signaling to the client that it can send fewer packets.

Step 3: Packet Loss: Suppose the third packet sent by the client is lost in transit. The server sends duplicate acknowledgments for the fourth packet, indicating that it did not receive the third packet.

Step 4: Retransmission: The client, upon receiving three duplicate acknowledgments, triggers the fast retransmit and resends the third packet. Once the server receives the third packet, it acknowledges it, and the transmission continues.

Step 5: Data Acknowledgment: As the client receives the acknowledgment for the retransmitted packet, the sliding window slides forward, and the next packet is sent.

Window Management

Window management in the context of Transport Layer protocols, particularly TCP (Transmission Control Protocol), is a crucial concept for flow control and efficient data transmission between a sender and receiver. It refers to the technique of controlling how much data can be sent at a time before needing an acknowledgment and how data is buffered during transmission. Window management ensures that the network connection remains efficient, preventing congestion and packet loss while adapting to the varying capabilities of the sender and receiver.Window management is primarily implemented through the sliding window mechanism, which governs how many packets can be transmitted without waiting for acknowledgment.

Sliding Window Mechanism

The sliding window mechanism is a key concept in TCP that enables efficient flow control and congestion control between sender and receiver. It allows the sender to transmit multiple segments (data packets) without waiting for individual acknowledgments for each one. By allowing a set number of unacknowledged packets to be in transit, the sliding window mechanism improves the overall throughput of the network. The "window" refers to the range of sequence numbers the sender is allowed to send without receiving an acknowledgment. As packets are acknowledged by the receiver, the window moves or "slides" forward, enabling the sender to transmit additional data. This sliding process ensures that the sender does not overwhelm the receiver and maintains a steady flow of data. The window size can vary dynamically based on network conditions, such as congestion, allowing TCP to adapt to the changing state of the connection and optimize transmission efficiency.

Components of the Sliding Window

Window Size

The window size is a fundamental component of the sliding window mechanism in TCP. It dictates how many packets the sender can transmit before waiting for an acknowledgment. This size is dynamic, meaning it adjusts based on real-time network conditions. Factors like receiver buffer space, congestion control, and available bandwidth influence the window size. For example, during periods of low congestion and large buffer availability, the window size may increase to enhance throughput. Conversely, when network congestion is high, the window size may shrink to avoid overwhelming the receiver or the network. The dynamic nature of window sizing allows the sliding window to adapt to varying network conditions, optimizing data transmission efficiency and reducing packet loss. This flexibility plays a critical role in ensuring reliable and efficient data transfer across different network environments.

Sequence Numbers

Sequence numbers are essential to the sliding window protocol, ensuring that data packets are transmitted and received in the correct order. Every packet sent within a TCP connection is assigned a unique sequence number, which serves as an identifier for the data it contains. These numbers help both the sender and receiver keep track of the flow of data, guaranteeing that packets are not lost or duplicated. If a packet arrives out of order, the receiver can request the missing packet by referring to the sequence number. This ordering mechanism is particularly crucial in cases where multiple packets are transmitted in parallel or when network delays cause packets to arrive at the receiver out of sequence. Sequence numbers provide a means of maintaining the integrity of data transmission, facilitating accurate reassembly at the receiver's end.

Acknowledgments

Acknowledgments (ACKs) are a core feature of the sliding window protocol, enabling reliable communication between the sender and receiver. When a receiver successfully receives a packet, it sends an acknowledgment message back to the sender, indicating the sequence number of the next expected packet. This ensures that the sender knows which packets have been received and which need to be retransmitted. Acknowledgments also serve as a mechanism for controlling the flow of data: once a packet is acknowledged, the sender can slide the window forward, allowing the transmission of new packets. This feedback loop helps maintain data integrity, as any packet that is lost or corrupted can be quickly identified and retransmitted. The use of acknowledgments, in combination with the sliding window, ensures reliable data transfer and prevents issues such as data loss and excessive retransmission.

Buffering

Buffering is a key component in both the sender and receiver sides of the sliding window mechanism. Both sides maintain buffers to temporarily hold data during transmission. On the sender's side, the buffer holds packets that are ready to be sent, ensuring that data is queued for transmission until the window allows for their dispatch. On the receiver's side, the buffer stores incoming packets until they can be processed or acknowledged. The buffer size at both ends impacts the efficiency of data flow and the overall performance of the connection. If the buffer is too small, it may lead to dropped packets due to overflow, while excessively large buffers can cause delays in processing. The buffers ensure that data is handled smoothly, enabling the sender to transmit continuously without waiting for immediate acknowledgment and allowing the receiver to process data without interruption.

Types of Windows in Sliding Window Protocol

Sender's Window

The sender's window in the Sliding Window Protocol defines the range of sequence numbers that the sender can transmit before receiving acknowledgment from the receiver. It determines how many packets or frames can be sent in succession without waiting for an acknowledgment for each one. The window size plays a crucial role in controlling the flow of data; it ensures efficient use of the network bandwidth while avoiding congestion. The sender's window is dynamic, expanding or contracting depending on network conditions and receiver feedback. As the sender receives acknowledgments for the transmitted data, the window slides forward, allowing the sender to transmit more data. This process reduces latency and maximizes throughput. However, a window that is too large could result in packet loss or buffer overflow, while a small window size might underutilize the available bandwidth, resulting in inefficient transmission.

Receiver's Window

The receiver's window in the Sliding Window Protocol represents the amount of buffer space available at the receiver's end to store incoming data. It serves as a control mechanism to prevent the receiver from being overwhelmed by a large volume of data that it cannot handle. The receiver's window size is crucial for flow control, as it allows the receiver to regulate the rate at which the sender transmits data. When the receiver's buffer is nearing full capacity, it advertises a smaller window size, signaling the sender to slow down or stop transmission temporarily. Conversely, when the receiver has more buffer space available, it can advertise a larger window size, allowing the sender to send more data. This dynamic feedback mechanism helps maintain a balance between data transmission and reception, ensuring efficient and reliable communication in the network. The step-by-step process:

Sliding Window Works

The sliding window operates based on both the sequence numbers of packets and the window size. The sender and receiver use the window to control how much data is in transit at any time.

Initial Transmission: The sender sends the first set of packets (determined by the window size) to the receiver without waiting for acknowledgment. The receiver processes the packets and sends an acknowledgment (ACK) for the first segment received.

Sliding of Window: As the receiver acknowledges packets, the sender slides its window forward to send new packets. For example, if the window size is 3, the sender can send 3 segments before waiting for any acknowledgment. Once the first segment is acknowledged, the window "slides" forward, and the sender can send the next packet.

Dynamic Adjustment: The window size can change dynamically based on network conditions or the receiver's buffer availability. If the receiver is processing data slowly or if there's network congestion, the window size may shrink to avoid overwhelming the receiver. The receiver may advertise a smaller window size if its buffer is nearly full. Conversely, if the receiver can handle more data, it may advertise a larger window.

Acknowledgment of Packets: The receiver sends acknowledgments (ACKs) to indicate which packets have been successfully received. In TCP, these acknowledgments are typically cumulative, meaning an acknowledgment for packet n also implicitly acknowledges all previous packets.

Timeout and Retransmission: If a packet is lost or corrupted (detected via lack of acknowledgment within a timeout period or through duplicate ACKs), the sender will retransmit the missing packet. After the retransmission, the window will adjust to account for the retransmitted data.

Window Size and Its Dynamic Changes

The window size is a dynamic value that adjusts based on two primary factors:

Receiver's Advertised Window Size

In TCP, the receiver's advertised window size plays a critical role in controlling the flow of data. This value is communicated by the receiver to the sender within the TCP header, specifying the available buffer space for incoming data. The receiver dynamically adjusts the window size based on its current buffer capacity. When the buffer is nearing full capacity, the receiver advertises a smaller window size to signal to the sender that fewer data can be transmitted without risking buffer overflow. Conversely, when the buffer has more space available, the receiver increases the window size, allowing the sender to send more data. This mechanism helps prevent data loss due to overflows and ensures that the sender does not overwhelm the receiver's capacity. The receiver's advertised window size, therefore, facilitates an efficient and balanced flow of data, adapting to the receiver's real-time buffer conditions.

Congestion Control

Congestion control is an essential feature in TCP to prevent network overload and ensure stable data transmission. It involves the sender adjusting its transmission rate based on the current state of the network, especially in scenarios where network congestion may occur. TCP utilizes several congestion control algorithms to manage data flow effectively. The Slow Start phase begins with a small congestion window and increases exponentially until a threshold is reached, indicating potential congestion. Once congestion is detected, Congestion Avoidance ensures gradual increases in the congestion window to avoid further network strain. Fast Recovery is employed after a packet loss, allowing the sender to quickly resume data transmission by reducing the congestion window and then increasing it cautiously. These algorithms work together to regulate the flow of data, helping avoid congestion and maintain efficient network performance under varying conditions. This dynamic adjustment is crucial for optimizing data transfer without overwhelming the network.

Flow Control vs Congestion Control

The Table 5.4 provides a comparison between Flow Control and Congestion Control, two essential mechanisms in network communication. Flow Control is managed by the receiver, ensuring that the sender does not overwhelm the receiver's buffer by regulating the amount of data sent based on the advertised window size. Its primary goal is to prevent buffer overflow at the receiver's end.

In contrast, Congestion Control is the sender's responsibility, aimed at preventing network congestion by adjusting the transmission rate based on factors like packet loss, round-trip time (RTT), and congestion signals. While flow control focuses on the receiver's ability to handle incoming data, congestion control addresses the overall health of the network, maintaining an optimal data flow to avoid network congestion. Together, these mechanisms ensure smooth and efficient data transmission across networks.

Table 5.4: Comparison between the Flow Control vs Congestion Control.

Aspect	Flow Control	Congestion Control
Control Mechanism	Managed by the receiver.	Managed by the sender.
Purpose	Prevents the receiver's buffer from overflowing.	Prevents network congestion by controlling the sender's rate.
Responsibility	Receiver controls the window size to inform the sender.	Sender adjusts the transmission rate based on network feedback.
Scope	Ensures that the receiver can process data at the rate it is received.	Ensures the network does not become overwhelmed with too much data.
Parameters	Advertised window size, receiver buffer size.	Round-trip time (RTT), packet loss, congestion signals.
Impact on Transmission	Controls the flow of data between sender and receiver based on the receiver's available buffer.	Controls how fast the sender transmits data based on network conditions.
Example Algorithms	Sliding window protocol.	TCP algorithms like Slow Start, Congestion Avoidance, and Fast Recovery.

TCP Window Management Algorithms

TCP window management algorithms are essential for controlling data flow and ensuring network efficiency. One key algorithm is Slow Start, which helps avoid congestion during the initial stages of a connection. During Slow Start, the sender begins with a small window size and increases it exponentially with each acknowledgment received. This exponential increase continues until the window reaches a threshold (ssthresh), signaling the switch to the next phase, Congestion Avoidance. The goal is to quickly fill the available bandwidth without overwhelming the network. The Figure 5.6 on TCP Window Management

Algorithms illustrates the key stages involved in TCP congestion control. It begins with the "Slow Start" phase, where the window size increases exponentially until a threshold is reached. After this, the algorithm enters "Congestion Avoidance," where the window size grows linearly to prevent congestion. If packet loss occurs (indicated by timeouts), the system transitions back to "Slow Start." In the event of detecting three duplicate ACKs, the "Fast Retransmit" mechanism is triggered, enabling the retransmission of lost packets without waiting for a timeout, followed by "Fast Recovery," which avoids reducing the window size drastically. These stages ensure efficient and reliable data transmission in TCP connections.

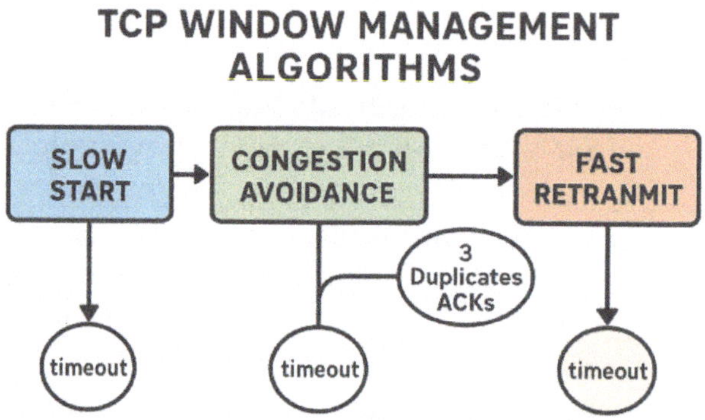

Figure 5.6: TCP Window Management Algorithms.

Slow Start

Slow Start is a critical algorithm in TCP's congestion control mechanism. It is employed at the start of a connection or when congestion is detected. The algorithm begins with a small congestion window, often one or two segments, and increases this window exponentially with each acknowledgment it receives. This exponential growth helps the sender probe the network's capacity quickly without overwhelming it. Once the congestion window reaches a threshold value, typically defined as ssthresh, the algorithm transitions to the Congestion Avoidance phase, where the window's growth becomes more controlled.

Congestion Avoidance

Congestion Avoidance follows the Slow Start phase in TCP's window management algorithm. Once the congestion window reaches the threshold (ssthresh), TCP enters Congestion Avoidance mode. In this phase, the window no longer increases exponentially but instead increases linearly, by one segment per round-trip time (RTT). The goal of this phase is to prevent congestion by ensuring that the sender does not send too many packets at once. This gradual increase in the congestion window allows the network to adjust and ensures that the sender does not overwhelm the available bandwidth. If congestion is detected again, TCP may enter the Slow Start phase once more.

Fast Retransmit & Fast Recovery

Fast Retransmit and Fast Recovery are two algorithms in TCP that help recover from packet loss without causing significant delays. Fast Retransmit is triggered when the sender receives three duplicate acknowledgments for a segment, indicating that a packet has likely been lost. In this case, the sender retransmits the missing packet immediately, avoiding the need for a timeout. Following the retransmission, TCP enters Fast Recovery, where it reduces the congestion window slightly but does not revert to the Slow Start phase. Instead, it continues sending data at a reduced rate, allowing the connection to recover efficiently without drastically reducing the window size. This combination of Fast Retransmit and Fast Recovery helps maintain throughput while recovering from packet loss.

Example of Sliding Window in Action

Let's assume:

Window Size = 3 segments.

Sender sends segments: A, B, C, D.

1. Receiver sends ACKs: ACK(A), ACK(B), ACK(C), and so on.
2. Initial State: Sender sends A, B, and C (within the window size of 3). The receiver sends back ACK(A), ACK(B), and ACK(C) as each segment is received.
3. First Acknowledgment: Once ACK(A) is received, the sender moves the window forward and sends D. The sender now waits for the acknowledgment of B and C and sends D as the new segment in the window.
4. Further Acknowledgments: As the receiver acknowledges B and C, the sender moves the window forward and can send the next set of segments.
5. Timeout: If any segment is lost (e.g., C), the sender waits for duplicate acknowledgments (e.g., ACK(B)) and retransmits C.

TCP Congestion Control

TCP (Transmission Control Protocol) uses congestion control mechanisms to manage the flow of data across the network to prevent congestion, which can lead to packet loss, delays, and reduced network performance. The key objectives of TCP congestion control are to avoid overwhelming network routers and ensure fair bandwidth allocation to all active connections. TCP employs several algorithms to control congestion:

Slow Start

Slow Start is the initial phase of TCP's congestion control mechanism, where the sender starts with a minimal congestion window (cwnd), typically one or two segments. This conservative approach is designed to gradually probe the network's available bandwidth without overwhelming it. The congestion window size increases exponentially with each acknowledgment the sender receives, doubling the window size every round-trip time (RTT). This exponential growth continues until the congestion window reaches a threshold called the slow-start threshold (ssthresh). At this point, TCP transitions to the Congestion Avoidance phase, where it uses a more conservative growth strategy. The slow start phase is crucial in preventing the sudden transmission of large amounts of data, which could cause network congestion and packet loss. It provides a controlled, step-by-step approach to gauge the network's capacity, ensuring stable and efficient transmission of data.

Congestion Avoidance

Congestion Avoidance is the phase that follows the Slow Start in TCP's congestion control mechanism. Once the slow-start threshold (ssthresh) is surpassed, TCP switches to a more conservative approach to avoid overwhelming the network. In this phase, TCP gradually increases the congestion window (cwnd) size, but rather than growing exponentially as in Slow Start, the window size increases linearly. This slower, more controlled increase helps prevent the network from becoming overloaded with data packets, which could lead to packet loss and delays. The primary goal of Congestion Avoidance is to find a balance between efficient data transmission and network stability. By adjusting the data transmission rate more cautiously, TCP ensures that the network resources are used fairly across all active connections while preventing congestion. This phase helps maintain network performance by preventing a rapid increase in the data flow that could cause packet loss or delays.

Fast Retransmit

Fast Retransmit is a mechanism in TCP designed to recover lost packets quickly without waiting for the usual timeout. In normal circumstances, when a packet is lost, the sender would typically wait for a timeout to occur before retransmitting the lost packet. However, Fast Retransmit accelerates this process. When the sender receives three duplicate acknowledgments for the same packet, it assumes that the packet was lost and immediately retransmits it, bypassing the timeout delay. This is particularly useful in scenarios where network congestion causes packet loss, and waiting for a timeout could lead to unnecessary delays. By quickly detecting packet loss and retransmitting the lost data, Fast Retransmit helps maintain smooth and efficient data flow, reducing the time required for error recovery. It is an essential part of TCP's strategy to maintain reliable and efficient communication across networks, especially in environments with frequent packet loss.

Fast Recovery

Fast Recovery is a TCP congestion control mechanism that allows the sender to continue transmitting data after a packet loss is detected, without reverting to the Slow Start phase. Typically, after Fast Retransmit detects a lost packet, TCP reduces the size of the congestion window (cwnd) to control the flow and avoid further congestion. Instead of starting over from scratch, Fast Recovery allows the congestion window to gradually increase, helping to maintain data transmission without unnecessarily stalling. This mechanism ensures that the sender can continue transmitting packets even as it adjusts the window size to cope with congestion. After the loss event, TCP avoids a full restart of the connection, which would result in delays and reduced throughput. By using Fast Recovery, TCP minimizes the impact of packet loss and congestion on the overall data transfer process, enhancing network efficiency and maintaining a steady flow of data even in the presence of congestion.

TCP Reno, TCP Vegas, and TCP Cubic

Different versions of TCP implement slight variations of the basic congestion control principles to enhance performance. This Table 5.5 summarizes the differences in congestion control, efficiency, and network suitability for the three TCP versions.

Table 5.5: Difference between the TCP Reno, TCP Vegas, and TCP Cubic.

Aspect	TCP Reno	TCP Vegas	TCP Cubic
Congestion Control Mechanism	AIMD (Additive Increase Multiplicative Decrease)	TCP Vegas uses a more advanced version of AIMD, combining it with RTT-based congestion avoidance.	TCP Cubic uses a cubic function for the increase of the congestion window, which is less aggressive than AIMD.
Window Size Growth	Exponential during slow start, linear during congestion avoidance	Uses both slow start and congestion avoidance based on round-trip time (RTT). Increases window size when RTT is stable, decreases during congestion.	Cubic function allows a faster increase of the congestion window compared to Reno but with a smoother approach.
Packet Loss Detection	Based on packet loss (timeout or triple duplicate ACKs)	Based on RTT measurement (if RTT increases, congestion is inferred)	Based on packet loss or timeout; adjusts the window size slower than Reno to prevent overreaction to loss.

Aspect	TCP Reno	TCP Vegas	TCP Cubic
Efficiency	High packet loss under congestion can lead to inefficient bandwidth usage	More efficient under light congestion but struggles in highly variable RTT conditions	More efficient in high-speed networks due to smoother congestion window adjustment.
Behavior Under Congestion	Slow to recover after a loss, especially when large window sizes are involved	Tries to avoid congestion by monitoring RTT, reducing window size before packet loss occurs	Reduces congestion window more gradually, thus improving performance in networks with high bandwidth and latency.
RTT Sensitivity	Less sensitive to RTT variations	Highly sensitive to RTT variations, adjusts window based on the measured RTT	Moderate sensitivity to RTT but prioritizes throughput.
Suitability for Networks	Best suited for networks with moderate or low loss rates	More effective in environments with stable RTTs but can be inefficient in networks with fluctuating RTTs.	Works best in high-speed, high-latency networks due to its smoother window scaling.
Implementation Complexity	Simple and widely deployed	More complex due to RTT-based adjustments	More complex, relies on cubic growth function and additional RTT management.

TCP Reno

TCP Reno is a widely used version of the Transmission Control Protocol (TCP) designed to improve the reliability and efficiency of data transmission over networks. It utilizes several methods to handle congestion: slow start, congestion avoidance, fast retransmit, and fast recovery. The slow start phase begins with a small congestion window and increases exponentially until it reaches a threshold. Once this threshold is surpassed, congestion avoidance mode takes over, increasing the window size linearly. In case of packet loss, TCP Reno uses fast retransmit to quickly resend the lost packet, followed by fast recovery to avoid entering the slow start phase again. These mechanisms help manage network congestion dynamically, improving throughput while maintaining network stability.

TCP Vegas

TCP Vegas improves upon traditional congestion control methods by introducing a proactive approach to managing network congestion. Unlike other TCP variants, which react to congestion after packet loss, TCP Vegas attempts to detect and prevent congestion before it causes packet loss. It does so by measuring round-trip time (RTT) and adjusting the congestion window based on the observed RTT. If the RTT exceeds a predefined threshold, indicating potential congestion, the window size is reduced to prevent further issues. This early congestion detection allows TCP Vegas to operate more efficiently, reducing the chances of packet loss and providing better performance in networks with varying levels of traffic. The proactive approach enhances throughput and reduces delays, making it suitable for applications requiring lower latency.

TCP Cubic

TCP Cubic is an enhanced version of the Transmission Control Protocol that was developed to optimize performance in high bandwidth-delay product (BDP) networks, such as long-distance and high-speed networks. It modifies the congestion window's growth behavior by using a cubic function rather than a linear or exponential one. In TCP Cubic, the window size increases rapidly at first and then slows down as it approaches the network's bandwidth limit. This allows for more efficient bandwidth utilization and faster recovery after packet loss, especially in networks with large delays. The cubic growth function helps improve the overall throughput and reduces the time needed for the window to reach its optimal size. TCP Cubic is particularly beneficial for modern networks with large bandwidth and long round-trip times, ensuring efficient data transmission over long distances and reducing the risk of congestion-related issues.

Quality of Service (QoS)

Quality of Service (QoS) refers to the techniques and mechanisms implemented in a network to manage traffic and ensure that the network can meet the specific needs of different applications. It involves ensuring appropriate allocation of network resources like bandwidth, delay, and packet loss for various types of traffic such as voice, video, and data. In a network environment with diverse traffic types, QoS plays a vital role in maintaining optimal performance for time-sensitive applications, like VoIP or video streaming, by giving them higher priority over less time-sensitive data. The goal is to ensure that network performance aligns with the requirements of different applications while maintaining fairness, avoiding congestion, and minimizing packet loss. Effective QoS allows the network to accommodate varying traffic loads without sacrificing performance for critical services, helping maintain a seamless user experience even in high-demand environments. The Key aspects of QoS include:

Traffic Classification

Traffic classification is the process of categorizing network traffic into different types based on specific criteria such as packet headers, application type, or network protocols. In QoS, this classification is crucial as it helps determine which traffic should receive higher or lower priority. The classification can be done based on various parameters such as source or destination IP addresses, port numbers, and the type of application being used (e.g., VoIP, web browsing, or video streaming). Once traffic is classified, different types of data packets are treated according to their importance, which allows network devices like routers and switches to apply specific QoS policies. For example, voice traffic might be given higher priority than data traffic to ensure that voice calls are clear and not delayed. The process ensures that critical applications get the necessary bandwidth and latency levels, contributing to efficient resource allocation across the network.

Traffic Policing

Traffic policing is a QoS technique that monitors the rate of network traffic and enforces traffic flow limits. Its primary function is to ensure that the network does not become overwhelmed by excessive traffic and that the service level agreements (SLAs) for network performance are maintained. Traffic policers evaluate the incoming data stream and compare it to predefined rate limits. If traffic exceeds these limits, it can be penalized in various ways, including being delayed, dropped, or marked for lower priority. This process helps prevent network congestion by managing burst traffic and ensuring that the network does not become overloaded, which can lead to packet loss and performance degradation. For example, if a user sends more traffic than their allocated bandwidth, the excess traffic may be dropped or reclassified with a lower priority, ensuring that the network resources are fairly distributed and high-priority traffic is not negatively impacted.

Traffic Shaping

Traffic shaping is a QoS technique designed to smooth out bursts of network traffic to prevent congestion. It works by delaying excess traffic to fit a specified rate, ensuring that traffic flows smoothly and does not overwhelm the network. This is particularly important for applications that require consistent bandwidth and low latency, such as voice or video calls, where sudden bursts of data can degrade performance. The shaping process uses buffers to collect excess packets during peak demand and then releases them at a steady rate, ensuring that the network's throughput remains stable. By managing traffic in this way, traffic shaping can avoid situations where packets are dropped due to congestion. It also helps prevent network devices from becoming overloaded, thus ensuring that all applications can operate at their optimal performance levels. In short, traffic shaping optimizes network efficiency and minimizes disruptions caused by traffic spikes.

Queue Management

Queue management is a crucial aspect of QoS, as it involves controlling how network traffic is buffered and processed within network devices like routers and switches. Different types of traffic, based on priority or classification, are placed in distinct queues to ensure that high-priority traffic is processed before lower-priority traffic. For example, time-sensitive traffic such as VoIP and video streaming might be placed in a high-priority queue, while bulk data transfers (such as file downloads) might be placed in a lower-priority queue. During periods of network congestion, lower-priority traffic may be delayed or dropped to make room for higher-priority data, ensuring that critical applications maintain the required level of performance. Effective queue management helps to ensure that the network resources are utilized optimally, preventing performance degradation in real-time applications and maintaining fairness in overall traffic handling. It is an essential component of maintaining consistent network performance across varying conditions.

Scheduling Algorithms

To prioritize certain types of traffic over others in case of congestion.

Common Algorithms

FIFO (First-In-First-Out)

FIFO is one of the simplest and most widely used packet scheduling techniques in networking. In this method, packets are processed in the exact order they arrive at the network device, without regard to the type or priority of the data. The first packet that enters the queue is the first one to be transmitted. This approach is straightforward and easy to implement but does not offer any mechanism to differentiate traffic types or prioritize critical data. While this simplicity can be advantageous in low-traffic environments, FIFO may lead to inefficient handling of network resources in scenarios with mixed traffic or real-time requirements, where higher priority packets should ideally be processed faster. FIFO can also result in delays for time-sensitive packets if the queue contains low-priority data. Thus, while reliable, FIFO is often inadequate for complex or high-demand networking situations.

Priority Queueing (PQ)

Priority Queueing (PQ) is a packet scheduling method that categorizes traffic into multiple queues, with each queue assigned a specific priority level. When a packet arrives, it is placed into the queue that corresponds to its priority, which is typically determined by packet type, application requirements, or predefined rules. High-priority packets are processed first, ensuring that critical data, such as real-time voice or video, is delivered with minimal delay. Lower-priority queues are processed afterward, ensuring that important traffic is always given precedence. However, PQ can lead to issues such as starvation, where lower-priority packets are consistently delayed if high-priority traffic continues to dominate the queue. While PQ is beneficial for managing critical traffic, its inability to fairly distribute bandwidth among lower-priority packets means that it is best suited for networks where high-priority data outweighs the need for fairness.

Weighted Fair Queueing (WFQ)

Weighted Fair Queueing (WFQ) is an advanced packet scheduling technique designed to provide more fairness in how network resources are allocated. In WFQ, packets are assigned to different queues based on weights, where the weight determines the proportion of the available bandwidth each queue receives. High-weight queues are allowed to send more packets in a given time frame, while lower-weight queues are granted less bandwidth. This ensures that each type of traffic gets a fair share of the network resources, balancing the needs of different applications. WFQ also respects the priority of traffic by processing higher-weight queues more frequently. This method is particularly effective in managing mixed traffic environments, where both real-time and background traffic coexist. It helps avoid congestion and ensures that no single flow monopolizes the available bandwidth. However, WFQ's complexity can introduce computational overhead and require more sophisticated network management.

Class-Based Weighted Fair Queueing (CBWFQ)

Class-Based Weighted Fair Queueing (CBWFQ) is a refinement of WFQ that allows for more granular traffic prioritization based on predefined classes. In CBWFQ, traffic is divided into several classes, each with its own weight and bandwidth allocation. These classes could correspond to specific applications, such as VoIP, video, or standard data traffic, and the weight assigned to each class determines its share of the available bandwidth. Like WFQ, CBWFQ ensures that higher-weight classes are processed with higher priority, but it provides more flexibility by allowing network administrators to define classes based on specific traffic patterns. This allows for better control over traffic, particularly in environments where different types of applications have varying performance needs. CBWFQ is ideal for scenarios where multiple types of traffic need to be treated differently, ensuring that critical applications receive the required resources while maintaining fairness across all other traffic classes.

Differentiated Services (DiffServ)

Differentiated Services (DiffServ) is a network architecture designed to provide scalable Quality of Service (QoS) solutions by marking packets with DiffServ Code Points (DSCP). The DSCP values indicate the priority level and the type of service a packet requires. This method allows routers and network devices to interpret the DSCP value to apply appropriate forwarding behavior without the need for complex configurations or per-flow state tracking. High-priority traffic, such as Voice over IP (VoIP) or real-time video, can be given precedence with minimal delay by being classified and forwarded based on the DSCP value. Conversely, lower-priority traffic like bulk data transfers can be delayed or handled at a lower priority to prevent network congestion. DiffServ offers a more scalable alternative to traditional QoS models, enabling traffic differentiation while minimizing the overhead required for managing individual traffic flows.

Integrated Services (IntServ)

Integrated Services (IntServ) is a QoS model that aims to provide end-to-end guarantees for applications that require strict bandwidth and delay constraints, such as video conferencing or voice calls. IntServ achieves this by using a resource reservation protocol, such as RSVP (Resource Reservation Protocol), which allows applications to request a guaranteed level of service before transmitting data. The RSVP protocol enables end-to-end resource reservation, ensuring that the necessary bandwidth and delay requirements are met across the network for each individual flow. This guarantees that high-priority traffic receives the resources it needs, regardless of network congestion or other traffic. While IntServ provides precise control and guarantees for critical applications, it can be less scalable than DiffServ due to the overhead of maintaining state information for each flow across network devices. IntServ is typically used in networks where precise QoS management is essential, particularly in environments with delay-sensitive applications.

Conclusion

The Transport Layer is an essential component in the OSI model, serving as the intermediary between the application and network layers to ensure reliable communication between processes across different devices. Its core functions include process-to-process delivery, which guarantees that data reaches the correct application on the destination device. The Transport Layer employs protocols like TCP and UDP to manage data transmission, offering mechanisms for error correction, flow control, and retransmission. Multiplexing, another critical function, allows multiple applications to share a single communication channel efficiently, while connection management ensures that connections are established, maintained, and properly terminated. The Transport Layer also plays a pivotal role in managing flow control and windowing, enabling smooth data transmission even under varying network conditions. Through TCP congestion control, the network can dynamically adjust to traffic conditions, preventing bottlenecks and packet loss. Additionally, the Quality of Service (QoS) functionality of the Transport Layer prioritizes critical data, such as VoIP or video streaming, to ensure minimal delay and higher reliability. Overall, the Transport Layer is vital for optimizing data flow, maintaining connection stability, and ensuring efficient communication, making it indispensable for the smooth operation of modern networks.

Exercise Questions

- What is the primary function of the Transport Layer in the OSI model?
- Name the two main transport layer protocols.
- How does multiplexing work in the Transport Layer?
- What is the purpose of flow control in the Transport Layer?
- Explain the concept of window management in TCP.
- How does TCP handle data retransmission?
- Describe the difference between TCP and UDP.
- What is the significance of congestion control in TCP?
- How does Quality of Service (QoS) affect network traffic?
- What is the role of connection management in the Transport Layer?

CHAPTER

6

APPLICATION LAYER

The Application Layer is the topmost layer of the OSI (Open Systems Interconnection) model and plays a crucial role in the communication between different applications over a network. This layer is responsible for enabling end-user processes to interact with each other through the network. The Application Layer essentially facilitates the functions of various network applications and provides services like email, file transfer, web browsing, and remote login. It defines how applications on different systems communicate by providing standard protocols, data formats, and application services. Thus, this layer acts as an interface between the underlying network infrastructure and the applications that users directly interact with, making it indispensable in modern networking. At the heart of the Application Layer are its protocols, which are specialized rules and standards that enable applications to function correctly in a networked environment. Some common protocols include HTTP (HyperText Transfer Protocol), SMTP (Simple Mail Transfer Protocol), FTP (File Transfer Protocol), and DNS (Domain Name System). These protocols define how data is exchanged, ensuring that communication between applications is standardized, reliable, and secure. HTTP, for instance, is used for web browsing, allowing users to retrieve web pages by sending requests to web servers and receiving responses in return. Similarly, SMTP is used for sending emails, ensuring that messages reach their intended recipients over the internet. Another important aspect of the Application Layer is its role in enabling the efficient use of network resources by managing data transmission between different applications. This layer is responsible for transforming data from the application into a format that can be transmitted across the network. It does so by utilizing the transport layer protocols such as TCP (Transmission Control Protocol) or UDP (User Datagram Protocol). The Application Layer encapsulates data in a way that is appropriate for the specific application being used, while the transport layer ensures that the data is delivered reliably and in the correct order. This separation of responsibilities allows for greater flexibility and scalability in network communication. Furthermore, the Application Layer is not just about the exchange of data but also encompasses a variety of services that make the user experience more efficient and secure. For example, secure communication protocols like HTTPS (HyperText Transfer Protocol Secure) encrypt data between web browsers and servers to protect user privacy. Authentication services are also part of the Application Layer, ensuring that users are properly verified before accessing sensitive information or services. Similarly, email services may include anti-spam measures to filter out unwanted messages, and file-sharing applications often provide checksums to verify the integrity of transferred files. These features are essential for maintaining the overall security and usability of networked applications. The Application Layer is also integral in supporting various types of networked services that go beyond traditional computing environments. In modern times, cloud-based applications and services have become a cornerstone of business operations and personal productivity. The Application Layer supports cloud-based solutions by ensuring compatibility with the underlying network protocols and offering flexible, scalable applications that can function across different devices, operating systems, and network configurations. As businesses and individuals increasingly rely on cloud computing for everything from data storage to software-as-a-service (SaaS), the Application Layer continues to evolve to meet the demands of the digital age.

Finally, the Application Layer's ability to integrate with various network technologies and devices enhances its importance in the context of the Internet of Things (IoT). IoT devices rely on the Application Layer to connect to the internet and exchange data with other devices and systems. For example, smart home devices use Application Layer protocols to communicate with mobile apps or web servers, enabling users to control their home environment remotely. The interoperability of devices from different manufacturers is facilitated by the Application Layer, which defines common protocols that ensure smooth communication. As the IoT ecosystem grows, the Application Layer will continue to play a pivotal role in enabling seamless interaction between a diverse range of devices, networks, and services. The Application Layer is central to enabling communication and interaction between users, applications, and networks. Its protocols, services, and integration capabilities make it a fundamental component of modern networking. Whether for web browsing, email, cloud computing, or IoT devices, the Application Layer ensures that network communication is standardized, efficient, secure, and user-friendly. As technology continues to advance, the role of the Application Layer will only become more significant, adapting to meet the ever-evolving needs of digital communication.

Domain Name System

The Domain Name System (DNS) is a fundamental component of the internet infrastructure that is responsible for translating human-readable domain names (like www.example.com) into machine-readable IP addresses (such as 192.168.1.1) in Figure 6.1. This system is necessary because, while humans find it easier to remember names, computers communicate using numerical

IP addresses. DNS makes it possible for users to access websites and other resources on the internet using easy-to-remember names instead of complex numeric addresses.

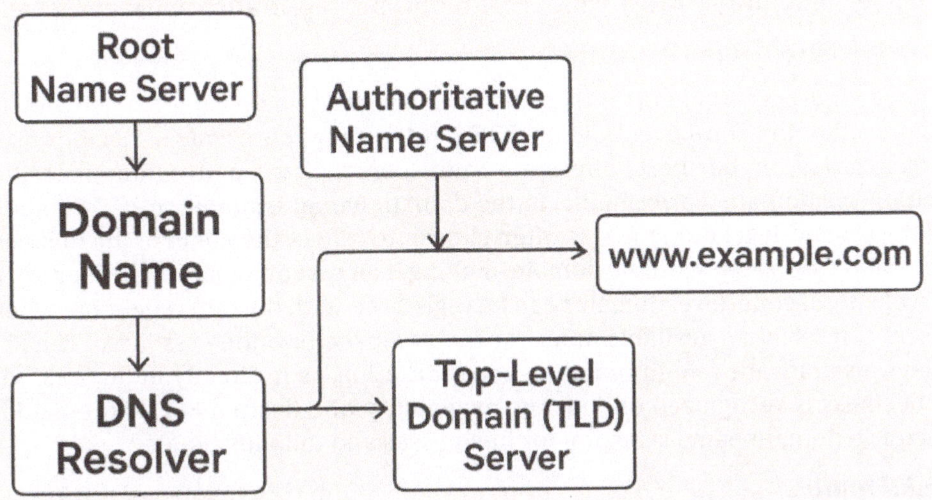

Figure 6.1: Process of Domain Name System.

Key Components of DNS

Domain Names

Domain names are hierarchical, alphanumeric strings that serve as user-friendly addresses for websites and resources on the internet. They provide an easily recognizable way for users to access websites instead of typing out numerical IP addresses. The hierarchy of domain names follows a specific structure, organized from right to left, where each section of the domain name serves a particular purpose. At the far right is the Top-Level Domain (TLD), followed by the Second-Level Domain (SLD), and then potentially further divided into subdomains. The design of domain names is crucial for ease of access and navigation, allowing users to find and interact with online services with ease. The organization of domain names is maintained by the Domain Name System (DNS), which maps the human-readable addresses to IP addresses, ensuring accurate routing of data across the internet.

Top-Level Domain (TLD)

The Top-Level Domain (TLD) is the rightmost segment of a domain name, such as .com, .org, .edu, or .net. TLDs are critical in organizing the internet's domain name system (DNS) into manageable categories and help define the domain's purpose or geographical origin. For instance, .com is primarily used by commercial entities, while .org is typically assigned to non-profit organizations. TLDs can be further categorized into two main groups: generic top-level domains (gTLDs), like .com or .net, and country code top-level domains (ccTLDs), such as .uk or .jp, which are assigned to specific countries. In addition to the well-known TLDs, new gTLDs are regularly introduced, providing a broader range of options for website owners to select from. The TLD system is maintained by the Internet Assigned Numbers Authority (IANA), which ensures proper registration and management.

Second-Level Domain (SLD)

The Second-Level Domain (SLD) is the portion of the domain name located directly to the left of the Top-Level Domain (TLD). It typically represents a specific entity, organization, or business, offering a more personalized and unique identifier within the domain. For example, in the domain name "example.com," "example" is the second-level domain. It is often chosen to reflect the name of the business or brand associated with the domain, making it an essential part of the identity of a website. Second-level domains can be registered with domain registrars, where users can select an available name for their website or online resource. The SLD plays a significant role in branding and marketing, as it directly influences how a business is recognized online. The availability of a desired SLD is often a key factor in domain name selection for businesses and individuals.

Subdomains

Subdomains are extensions or divisions within a domain name, offering further categorization and organization for different sections or services within a website. Positioned to the left of the second-level domain, subdomains help create more specific addresses for various parts of a website, such as "www" or "blog" in "www.example.com" or "blog.example.com." They allow for better management of content and services by dividing a website into manageable units. Subdomains can be created to represent different departments, sections, or even entirely separate entities within the main domain. For instance, a business may use a subdomain for its online store (store.example.com) and another for its blog (blog.example.com). Subdomains are versatile tools for organizing content and services, allowing a single domain to serve multiple purposes or provide easier navigation for users. Additionally, subdomains can be used to target different regions or languages by offering country-specific content.

DNS Servers

DNS servers are crucial components of the Domain Name System (DNS), designed to store DNS records and process requests for domain name resolution. The DNS infrastructure allows users to access websites using human-readable domain names, which are converted into machine-readable IP addresses. The DNS servers play a key role in maintaining the DNS hierarchy, ensuring that the correct IP address is retrieved in response to a user's query. These servers are responsible for various operations, ranging from caching queries to querying other servers when necessary. The proper functioning of DNS servers ensures smooth navigation on the internet, minimizing delays and enabling reliable access to websites and online services. With a robust structure comprising various server types, DNS servers are essential for translating domain names into IP addresses and facilitating the seamless operation of the internet.

DNS Resolver (Recursive Resolver)

A DNS Resolver, also known as a recursive resolver, is a server that handles user queries and plays a vital role in the DNS lookup process. When a user enters a domain name in their browser, the resolver is the first server that receives the query. If the resolver has previously cached the IP address corresponding to the domain name, it can return the result directly, thus speeding up the process. If the information is not available in its cache, the resolver will query other DNS servers, beginning with the root name servers, and proceed through the hierarchy to find the authoritative DNS server for that domain. After retrieving the required IP address, the resolver sends it back to the user's device. The recursive resolver ensures efficient and accurate domain name resolution, reducing query times and enhancing the overall browsing experience by caching results and minimizing the need for redundant lookups.

Root Name Servers

Root name servers are the highest level in the DNS hierarchy and serve as the foundation for domain name resolution. There are 13 root server clusters, strategically located across the globe, which are managed by various organizations. These servers are responsible for handling queries related to top-level domains (TLDs) such as .com, .org, and .net. When a DNS resolver queries the root servers, it receives information about which authoritative name servers manage the specific TLD being queried. The root servers do not store domain-specific information themselves but instead guide the resolver to the appropriate authoritative servers for further resolution. As the starting point for DNS queries, root name servers are crucial to the proper functioning of the entire DNS system, ensuring that users can access the correct websites by directing queries toward the correct TLD servers, facilitating a smooth and organized domain name resolution process across the internet.

Authoritative Name Servers

Authoritative name servers are specialized DNS servers that store and provide DNS records for a specific domain. These servers are the final authority when it comes to answering queries about domain names. When a DNS resolver queries an authoritative name server, it retrieves the actual IP address for the domain name in question. Authoritative name servers are configured to store various types of DNS records, including A (Address) records, MX (Mail Exchange) records, and CNAME (Canonical Name) records. These records define how traffic should be routed to the domain, ensuring that users are directed to the correct web servers and email servers. Since authoritative name servers hold the definitive DNS information for a domain, they are crucial for the accurate resolution of domain names into IP addresses. Proper management and security of authoritative name servers are vital for ensuring the reliability and integrity of domain name resolution.

DNS Records

DNS servers store different types of records that map domain names to various resources. Some common DNS record types include:

A Record (Address Record)

The A Record (Address Record) is one of the most fundamental and frequently used DNS record types. It maps a domain name to an IPv4 address, allowing users to access websites using human-readable domain names, such as "example.com." Without an A record, a domain name would be unresolvable by DNS servers and would not point to any IP address. This record is essential for the standard operation of websites on the internet. For instance, when someone types "example.com" in a browser, the A Record directs their browser to the corresponding IP address of the web server hosting the site. The A Record can also be used for pointing subdomains to specific IP addresses. Each A Record contains an IPv4 address, typically written in a dot-decimal format, such as "192.0.2.1." This makes it possible for users to interact with web services through domain names rather than needing to remember numerical IP addresses.

AAAA Record

An AAAA record, or IPv6 Address Record, is similar to an A Record but instead maps a domain name to an IPv6 address rather than an IPv4 address. The main difference lies in the format of the IP address; an IPv6 address is significantly longer and written in hexadecimal form, allowing for more unique addresses compared to the older IPv4 format. IPv6 was developed to solve the shortage of available IPv4 addresses due to the increasing number of devices connected to the internet. The AAAA record is especially important as the internet transitions towards IPv6 for the future of global connectivity. While IPv4 addresses use a 32-bit format (e.g., 192.0.2.1), IPv6 addresses use a 128-bit format (e.g., 2001:0db8:85a3:0000:0000:8a2e:0370:7334). These records allow DNS servers to resolve domain names to IPv6 addresses, making them crucial for the functionality of modern internet services. Without AAAA records, websites with only IPv6 addresses would be inaccessible to users relying on DNS.

MX Record (Mail Exchange)

MX Records (Mail Exchange Records) are a vital component in the DNS system, directing email traffic to the correct mail servers for a domain. An MX record specifies which mail server is responsible for receiving emails sent to a domain. It ensures that emails sent to an address like "user@example.com" reach the correct destination server. Each MX record has two key elements: the mail server's hostname and a priority value, which determines the order in which mail servers are tried when sending emails. The priority allows for failover systems, where secondary mail servers are used if the primary one is unavailable. A domain can have multiple MX records with different priorities to ensure email delivery even in the event of server failure. These records are essential for the functioning of email systems and make sure that messages reach the intended recipients reliably and without interruption.

CNAME Record (Canonical Name)

A CNAME (Canonical Name) record is a type of DNS record used to create an alias for an existing domain name. This allows multiple domain names to point to the same resource, such as a website or server. The CNAME record maps one domain to another, with the second domain being the canonical (or primary) domain. For example, if you have a website accessible through "www.example.com," you can set a CNAME record so that "blog.example.com" or any other subdomain also points to "www.example.com." This simplifies DNS management, especially when dealing with multiple subdomains that should direct to the same server. The main benefit of using a CNAME record is that it allows for easier updates to the primary server address. If the canonical domain's IP address changes, you only need to update the A or AAAA record for the primary domain, rather than for every alias.

NS Record (Name Server)

NS Records (Name Server Records) are used to specify the authoritative name servers for a domain. These servers are responsible for answering queries about the domain's DNS records and ensuring that users can resolve domain names to their corresponding IP addresses. When a DNS query is made for a domain, the resolver checks the NS record to determine which server holds the authoritative data for that domain. NS records are critical for domain delegation, as they tell the DNS system where to find the authoritative data for a particular domain or subdomain. Domains are typically assigned to specific name servers provided by the domain registrar or hosting service. Additionally, NS records can also be used to point subdomains to different name servers, offering flexibility in managing DNS records for large or complex websites. These records ensure that the internet's infrastructure remains accurate and reliable for domain name resolution.

PTR Record (Pointer Record)

A PTR (Pointer Record) is used in reverse DNS lookups, mapping an IP address back to a domain name. Unlike the standard DNS query, which resolves domain names to IP addresses, a reverse DNS query uses PTR records to determine the domain associated with a given IP address. This process is essential for various applications, such as spam prevention, network troubleshooting, and security protocols. For example, when an email server receives a message, it might perform a reverse lookup to check if the sending IP address matches the claimed domain in the email headers. If the PTR record for the sending IP address is missing or doesn't match, the email may be flagged as suspicious. PTR records are particularly important in security and identity verification on the internet, as they provide a way to validate the origin of network traffic. These records are typically maintained by the organization that owns the IP address.

DNS Query Process

The process by which DNS resolves domain names involve multiple steps:

Step 1: The user types a domain name (e.g., www.example.com) in their browser.

Step 2: The local DNS resolver checks its cache for the corresponding IP address.

Step 3: If the IP address is not in the cache, the resolver sends a query to the root name servers.

Step 4: The root name servers respond with a referral to the authoritative name servers for the TLD (.com in this case).

Step 5: The resolver queries the authoritative name servers for the specific domain (example.com), which responds with the IP address.

Step 6: The resolver returns the IP address to the user's browser, which then connects to the web server at that IP address to load the website.

DNS Caching

DNS caching is an important mechanism used to enhance performance and reduce the load on DNS servers. By temporarily storing DNS query results, this system helps avoid unnecessary repetitive lookups for frequently accessed domain names. The cached data can be used to respond quickly to subsequent requests, thus improving the speed of accessing websites or online resources. This caching process reduces the time it takes to resolve domain names by bypassing the need to query authoritative DNS servers each time a request is made, ultimately resulting in faster browsing experiences for users.

DNS Resolver Cache

A DNS resolver cache is a temporary storage system located in the DNS resolver that holds the results of previously resolved queries. This cache stores the resolved IP addresses for domain names, allowing the DNS resolver to respond to future requests for the same domains without having to contact external DNS servers. By holding this data in memory, the resolver cache helps minimize latency, reduce network traffic, and improve the overall efficiency of the DNS resolution process. However, entries in the resolver cache have a time limit based on the TTL of the DNS records they store.

Browser Cache

Most modern web browsers also implement DNS caching to improve user experience by reducing the need for repeated domain lookups. This browser-level cache stores DNS information for websites that users have recently visited, allowing the browser to resolve domain names more quickly when revisiting these sites. Since this cache is stored locally within the browser, it minimizes the need for external DNS queries, improving browsing speed. Each browser maintains its own cache, and users can clear or disable this cache through their browser settings if necessary. Caching at the browser level helps speed up web navigation by reusing DNS results from previous visits.

TTL (Time to Live)

Time to Live (TTL) is a critical attribute of DNS records that dictates how long a particular DNS record is valid and can be cached by resolvers or browsers. The TTL value is set by the authoritative DNS server when the record is created and specifies the duration (usually in seconds) before the record should be discarded or refreshed. Once the TTL expires, the cached DNS record is no longer considered valid, and a new query must be made to retrieve the most up-to-date information. TTL values can vary depending on the type of record and the needs of the domain, with shorter TTLs ensuring fresher data but potentially resulting in more frequent queries to the DNS server.

DNS Security

Since DNS is an essential part of internet communication, it is a target for attacks in Figure 6.2. Some common DNS-related security issues include:

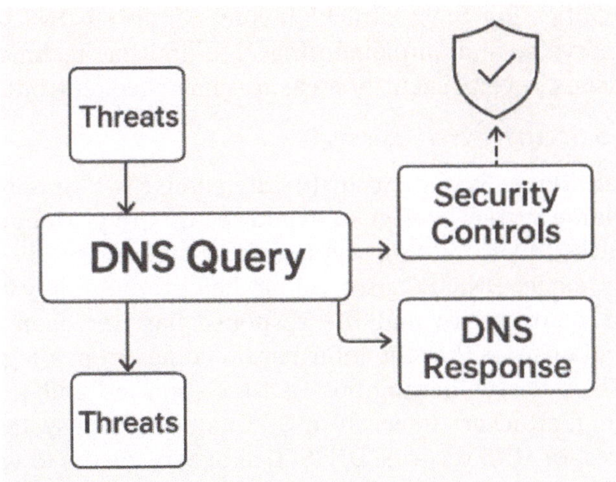

Figure 6.2:Working of DNS security system.

DNS Spoofing (Cache Poisoning)

DNS spoofing, also known as cache poisoning, is a cyber-attack that manipulates the Domain Name System (DNS) by injecting false or malicious data into a DNS resolver's cache. This causes the DNS resolver to return incorrect IP addresses, redirecting users to malicious websites instead of their intended destinations. Attackers achieve this by sending fake DNS responses that appear legitimate, thus tricking the DNS server into storing the malicious information. Once cached, these incorrect DNS entries can affect all users querying the compromised DNS server, potentially exposing them to phishing attacks, malware infections, or fraud. DNS spoofing is particularly dangerous because it is difficult to detect and often goes unnoticed until significant damage has been done. The prevention of DNS spoofing typically involves securing DNS servers through encryption (DNSSEC), monitoring for irregularities, and regularly clearing DNS caches to mitigate the impact of cached malicious data.

DNS Amplification Attacks

A DNS amplification attack is a type of Distributed Denial-of-Service (DDoS) attack where attackers exploit publicly accessible DNS servers to overwhelm a target with a massive volume of traffic. The attacker sends a small query to a vulnerable DNS server with a spoofed IP address of the target. The DNS server responds by sending a much larger response to the target, amplifying the attack's size. This method allows attackers to generate high-bandwidth traffic with relatively low resource usage on their part, making the attack both effective and difficult to trace back to the origin. The target is overwhelmed by the massive influx of DNS responses, causing service outages or network congestion. DNS amplification attacks leverage the reflective nature of DNS servers, and they can cause significant damage to both targeted organizations and the broader internet infrastructure. Mitigating these attacks involves filtering DNS traffic, blocking unauthorized servers, and implementing rate-limiting techniquesTo protect against these issues, several security measures have been introduced:

DNSSEC (DNS Security Extensions)

DNSSEC (Domain Name System Security Extensions) is a suite of extensions to DNS (Domain Name System) designed to add security to prevent certain types of attacks. It achieves this by adding cryptographic signatures to DNS data. When a DNS query is made, DNSSEC uses public key cryptography to authenticate responses. This helps verify that the response has not been altered during transmission and ensures that the information comes from a legitimate source. DNSSEC addresses the vulnerabilities of DNS spoofing and cache poisoning, which occur when attackers inject false DNS data into the system. By enabling digital signatures for DNS records, DNSSEC allows resolvers to validate that the received data is indeed the authoritative response from the correct source. This security measure is essential for safeguarding the integrity of DNS queries and preventing cybercriminals from redirecting users to malicious websites.

DNS over HTTPS (DoH)

DNS over HTTPS (DoH) is a protocol that enhances the security and privacy of DNS queries by encrypting them using HTTPS. Traditionally, DNS queries are transmitted in plaintext, which means they are vulnerable to interception, eavesdropping, and tampering by malicious actors. DoH addresses these concerns by sending DNS queries over a secure, encrypted HTTPS connection, ensuring that the communication is confidential and cannot be easily altered by third parties. This prevents attackers from manipulating DNS queries, a technique often used in DNS spoofing and man-in-the-middle attacks. DoH also enhances user privacy by hiding DNS traffic from potential surveilling entities like ISPs or government agencies. By leveraging the HTTPS protocol, DoH makes DNS traffic indistinguishable from regular HTTPS traffic, making it harder for attackers to detect and intercept DNS queries. This is an important step towards securing user data and preserving online privacy

Importance of DNS

User-Friendly Web Access

The Domain Name System (DNS) plays a crucial role in simplifying web access for users. Instead of requiring individuals to remember complex numerical IP addresses to access websites, DNS allows users to interact with easily recognizable and memorable domain names. For example, instead of typing an IP address like 192.168.1.1, users can simply enter "www.example.com." This conversion of user-friendly domain names to machine-readable IP addresses is handled seamlessly by DNS servers, which translates these names into the correct addresses. This eliminates the need for users to memorize long strings of numbers, improving overall user experience and accessibility to websites. Furthermore, DNS enhances web navigation by providing an efficient and fast routing system, which significantly contributes to the ease of accessing websites from various devices without the complexity of managing IP addresses manually.

Load Balancing

DNS is an essential tool for enhancing website performance by enabling load balancing across multiple servers. When a website experiences high traffic, DNS can distribute incoming requests to various servers, preventing any single server from being overloaded. This process ensures that no one server becomes a bottleneck, allowing for more efficient use of server resources and maintaining a smooth user experience. Load balancing through DNS is often implemented by directing traffic based on factors such as server health, geographical location of users, or server capacity. This strategy not only improves the performance of websites but also optimizes server utilization, making it more cost-effective for website owners. In high-traffic scenarios, this can lead to faster response times, reduced server downtime, and an overall more reliable experience for end-users, especially for global websites with users spread across different regions.

Redundancy

DNS provides critical redundancy capabilities that enhance the reliability and availability of websites by ensuring continuous access even if the primary server fails. This is achieved through failover mechanisms, which direct user traffic to secondary or backup servers when the main server becomes unreachable. By configuring DNS with multiple server addresses, it can automatically reroute requests to the available servers, minimizing downtime and improving service continuity. Redundancy through DNS is vital for businesses and websites that cannot afford significant periods of inaccessibility, such as e-commerce platforms or news outlets. It ensures that users always have access to the content, regardless of server failures, and enhances the robustness of web infrastructure. This failover capability is an essential part of high-availability systems, providing seamless user experience even during server maintenance or unforeseen failures. It also reduces the risk of lost revenue and customer dissatisfaction due to downtime.

Common DNS Issues

DNS Resolution Failures

DNS (Domain Name System) resolution failures occur when a DNS server becomes unavailable or cannot properly resolve domain names to their corresponding IP addresses. This issue may arise due to various factors such as server outages, network misconfigurations, or connectivity issues. When a user attempts to visit a website, the browser sends a request to a DNS server to translate the human-readable domain name (e.g., www.example.com) into an IP address that the computer can understand. If the DNS server is down or unreachable, the resolution process fails, resulting in an error message like "DNS server not found" or "Server DNS address could not be found." Such failures disrupt access to websites, and users are unable to load pages or connect to the desired services. DNS resolution failures are often temporary but can significantly impact internet usage, particularly if the DNS server is down for extended periods.

DNS Propagation Delays

DNS propagation delays occur when DNS records are updated, such as changes to a website's IP address, and those updates take time to spread throughout the global DNS network. When a DNS record is modified, the change is first made at the authoritative DNS server. However, this update must propagate through various intermediate DNS servers across the internet, a process that can take anywhere from a few minutes to 48 hours. During this propagation period, some users may still be directed to the old IP address, causing temporary access issues or inconsistencies. The delay happens because DNS servers cache the resolved records to reduce query times, and this cached information needs to expire before the new records can be retrieved. This propagation delay can result in users experiencing downtime, website unavailability, or misdirection to outdated server locations until the entire network has updated.

World Wide Web and Hyper Text Transfer Protocol

The World Wide Web (WWW) and Hypertext Transfer Protocol (HTTP) are foundational elements of the modern internet, enabling the exchange of information and communication across diverse systems and platforms. Below is a detailed explanation of both:

World Wide Web (WWW)

The World Wide Web is a global system of interconnected resources, such as websites, applications, and documents, accessible via the internet. It enables users to interact with various types of media, text, and services, providing a dynamic environment for communication, information retrieval, and entertainment. The Web was developed in 1989 by Sir Tim Berners-Lee at CERN, primarily to facilitate document sharing and collaboration.

How It Works:

When a user enters a URL into a browser, the browser sends a request to a web server to retrieve the associated web page. The server processes the request and returns the requested resource, which is rendered on the browser for the user to view.The World Wide Web is different from the internet itself. The internet is the global network infrastructure, whereas the web is a service that uses this infrastructure to deliver content.

Key Components of the WWW

Web Pages

A web page is a document displayed on the World Wide Web, typically created using HTML (HyperText Markup Language). HTML provides the structure for the page, allowing the inclusion of various multimedia elements such as text, images, videos, and interactive content. Web pages are often designed to be responsive, adapting to different screen sizes and devices. They can include styles via CSS (Cascading Style Sheets) and functionality with JavaScript, making them dynamic and user-interactive. These pages are stored on web servers and accessed by users through web browsers. Every web page has a unique URL (Uniform Resource Locator) which serves as its address, making it possible for users to find and view content. Web pages form the foundation of the internet, providing access to information, services, and communication platforms.

Web Browsers

A web browser is an essential software application that enables users to access and navigate the World Wide Web. Browsers interpret and display the content of web pages, which is written using technologies like HTML, CSS, and JavaScript. Popular web browsers include Google Chrome, Mozilla Firefox, Safari, and Microsoft Edge. Browsers allow users to enter URLs in the address bar, retrieve content from web servers, and display the web pages in a readable format. They also provide additional functionalities like bookmarks, extensions, and privacy controls. Web browsers are capable of processing dynamic content, supporting features like cookies, JavaScript interactions, and multimedia displays. Furthermore, browsers ensure security through protocols like HTTPS, encrypting the data transmitted between the user and the web server, and offering tools like private browsing and blocking malicious sites for a safer web experience.

Web Servers

A web server is a system that stores and serves web pages to users when requested through a web browser. Web servers are responsible for processing incoming HTTP/HTTPS requests, retrieving the appropriate content from their databases or files, and sending it back to the requesting browser. These servers are integral to the function of the World Wide Web, acting as intermediaries between the client (browser) and the web page's resources. Web servers utilize protocols such as HTTP (Hypertext Transfer Protocol) or HTTPS (its secure version) to ensure the proper transfer of data. In addition to static content, web servers can also handle dynamic content, responding to more complex requests by interacting with databases or running scripts. The performance and reliability of web servers directly impact user experience, with load balancing, caching, and redundancy being key aspects of modern server infrastructure to ensure speed and uptime.

URLs (Uniform Resource Locators)

A URL, or Uniform Resource Locator, is a web address that identifies and locates resources on the World Wide Web. It serves as the reference point for browsers to fetch specific content, whether it be a web page, image, or video. A URL consists of several components: the protocol (e.g., HTTP or HTTPS), the domain name (e.g., www.example.com), and the path to the resource (e.g., /about). The protocol indicates how the browser should communicate with the server, with HTTPS providing a secure, encrypted connection. The domain name is a human-readable address that maps to an IP address, making it easier to access the content. The path specifies the location of the resource within the website. URLs can also include query strings and fragments, allowing for more specific targeting of web content and dynamic page generation based on user input.

Hypertext Transfer Protocol (HTTP)

Hypertext Transfer Protocol (HTTP) is the communication protocol that governs how data is exchanged between a client (usually a web browser) and a server hosting a web resource. HTTP is an application layer protocol in the OSI model, which means it is responsible for data exchange at the highest layer, facilitating the retrieval and display of web pages.

HTTP Request and Response Cycle

When a user interacts with a web page, HTTP enables the browser and server to communicate. This process is divided into two main steps: the request and response.

HTTP Request

When a browser (the client) wants to fetch a web page, it sends an HTTP request to the web server. This request includes:

1. Method: Indicates the action to be performed (e.g., GET, POST, PUT, DELETE).

2. URL: Specifies the location of the resource on the server.
3. Headers: Additional metadata like browser type, accepted response formats, or cookies.
4. Body: In the case of methods like POST or PUT, the body contains data sent to the server (e.g., form data).

HTTP Response

The server processes the request and sends back an HTTP response, which includes:

1. Status Code: Indicates the result of the request (e.g., 200 for success, 404 for "not found").
2. Headers: Contains information about the server and response (e.g., content type, caching policies).
3. Body: Contains the requested resource (e.g., an HTML page, image, or JSON data).

HTTP Methods

Common HTTP methods include:

GET

The GET method is one of the most commonly used HTTP methods. It is designed to retrieve data from a server. When a client sends a GET request, it asks the server to return a specific resource, such as a webpage, image, or other data. GET requests are typically used to fetch information without making any modifications to the data on the server. They are considered safe and idempotent, meaning they do not cause any side effects on the server or its data. The data is usually included in the URL as parameters, and the server responds with the requested information. A key characteristic of GET requests is that they can be cached by browsers and search engines to improve performance for frequently requested resources. Additionally, GET requests are limited by the URL length, making them unsuitable for transferring large amounts of data.

POST

The POST method is used to send data to the server to be processed. It is commonly used for form submissions, such as logging in, registering a user, or submitting comments on a webpage. Unlike GET, POST requests send data within the body of the request, making it suitable for transmitting large amounts of data, including file uploads. The server processes the data and may create or update resources based on the information provided. POST requests are not idempotent, meaning repeated requests with the same data can lead to different results. For example, submitting a form multiple times can create multiple entries in a database. POST is also used in RESTful APIs for creating resources, as it triggers the server to perform specific actions based on the request data. Given its ability to modify the server's state, POST requests should always be treated securely, especially when transmitting sensitive data.

PUT

The PUT method is used to update or create a resource on the server. It typically replaces an existing resource with the data provided in the request. When a client sends a PUT request, it provides a complete replacement of the resource's current state. This method is often used to modify a resource's attributes, for example, updating a user's profile information or changing an article's content. PUT requests are idempotent, meaning that making the same PUT request multiple times will result in the same server state without causing additional changes. A PUT request should include all the necessary data for the resource being updated, as it typically replaces the entire resource, not just specific fields. This distinguishes PUT from the PATCH method, which is used for partial updates. Due to its ability to overwrite data, PUT requests should be used carefully to avoid unintended loss of information.

DELETE

The DELETE method is used to remove a specified resource from the server. When a client sends a DELETE request, it asks the server to delete the resource identified by the provided URL. This could involve deleting a file, a database record, or any other resource on the server. DELETE requests are idempotent, meaning that calling the same DELETE request multiple times will have the same effect—once the resource is deleted, it remains absent. However, unlike GET and POST, DELETE requests are generally not cacheable, and they can potentially cause data loss, so they must be used with caution. The server's response to a DELETE request typically indicates whether the resource was successfully deleted or if any errors occurred. In RESTful API design, DELETE requests are commonly used to delete objects or data from a system, making it an essential operation in CRUD (Create, Read, Update, Delete) functionality.

PATCH

The PATCH method is used to make partial updates to a resource on the server. Unlike PUT, which replaces an entire resource, PATCH only modifies the specific fields that need to be updated, leaving other fields unchanged. This makes PATCH an efficient method for updating large resources where only small portions need alteration. For example, if a user wants to update only their email address, a PATCH request can be sent to modify just that attribute, without affecting the other details like name or address. PATCH requests are not necessarily idempotent, meaning that sending the same PATCH request multiple times might result in different outcomes, depending on the state of the resource. This method is commonly used in RESTful APIs for partial resource updates, particularly when efficiency is required, and the resource's full state is not needed. The body of a PATCH request typically contains the fields to be updated and their new values.

HTTP Status Codes

HTTP status codes inform the client about the result of the request:

1xx (Informational)

HTTP status codes in the 1xx range indicate that the server has received the request and is processing it, but no final response is available yet. These codes are used to provide the client with feedback on the ongoing request. For example, a 100 Continue status code tells the client to proceed with sending the request body after the initial headers have been received, while the server processes the request. These codes are usually temporary and are rarely seen by users directly since they primarily facilitate communication between the server and client during the request/response process. Although useful for handling certain scenarios, such as large file uploads, 1xx responses generally do not provide any significant feedback regarding the success or failure of the final result. These status codes are mainly for informational purposes in the request lifecycle.

2xx (Success)

The 2xx HTTP status codes represent successful responses from the server. These codes indicate that the request was received, understood, and successfully processed. The most common status code in this category is 200 OK, which means the server has successfully processed the request and returned the requested resource or response. Other examples include 201 Created, which is used when a resource has been successfully created, often in the context of API requests (such as creating a new user). The 2xx category confirms that the client's request has been handled properly without any errors, making these codes essential for the proper functioning of web applications and APIs. The 2xx codes provide confirmation that no issues occurred during the communication between client and server, and they are crucial for confirming successful data retrieval, submission, or modification requests.

3xx (Redirection)

HTTP status codes in the 3xx range indicate that the client's request has resulted in a redirection. This means that the requested resource has either been moved to a new location or requires further actions to complete the request. A common example is the 301 Moved Permanently status, which tells the client that the requested resource has been permanently moved to a new URL, and future requests should use the new URL. Another example is the 302 Found code, which signals a temporary redirect, meaning the resource is temporarily located elsewhere but should be accessed using the original URL for future requests. These codes are often seen in URL forwarding, search engine optimization, or website maintenance scenarios. Redirections help ensure that users are routed to the appropriate locations, but they can also introduce challenges like slower load times or increased server load due to multiple redirects.

4xx (Client Error)

HTTP status codes in the 4xx range indicate that the client has made an error in their request. These errors typically occur when the request is malformed or when the client does not have permission to access the requested resource. A well-known 4xx status is 404 Not Found, which is returned when the server cannot find the requested resource on the server. This error is commonly encountered by users when a webpage or file has been removed or the URL was typed incorrectly. Another common 4xx code is 403 Forbidden, which indicates that the server understood the request but is refusing to fulfill it due to insufficient permissions. These codes are essential in alerting the user or application to issues that require their attention, such as incorrect URLs, missing resources, or authentication problems. They provide important diagnostic information for both developers and users.

5xx (Server Error)

The 5xx HTTP status codes indicate that the server has encountered an error or is otherwise incapable of performing the requested operation. These errors are server-side issues, meaning the client's request was valid, but something went wrong on the server's end. One of the most common 5xx codes is 500 Internal Server Error, which is a general-purpose error message indicating that something unexpected occurred on the server, preventing it from fulfilling the request. Other examples include 502 Bad Gateway, which is returned when one server acting as a gateway or proxy receives an invalid response from an upstream server, and 503 Service Unavailable, which indicates that the server is temporarily unable to handle the request, usually due to overload or maintenance. 5xx codes signal that the client's request cannot be processed due to an issue beyond their control, and these often require attention from the server administrator or hosting provider to resolve.

HTTP Versions and Security

HTTP/1.1 and Security

HTTP/1.1, the most widely used version of the HyperText Transfer Protocol until recently, brought several important advancements over its predecessor, HTTP/1.0. A significant feature introduced with HTTP/1.1 is persistent connections. This allows multiple requests to be sent over a single TCP connection, reducing the overhead of establishing new connections for each request. It also added chunked transfer encoding, which helped in streaming data dynamically. However, HTTP/1.1 has inherent limitations in terms of speed and security. While it supports secure connections via HTTPS (by using SSL/TLS), the protocol does not address modern challenges like reducing latency or improving multiplexing, making it less efficient compared to newer versions. Additionally, HTTP/1.1's reliance on TCP can contribute to delays, especially on mobile networks where packet loss and latency are more pronounced, thus limiting its overall performance in certain scenarios.

HTTP/2 and Security

HTTP/2, introduced as a major improvement over HTTP/1.1, focuses primarily on enhancing performance and reducing latency. One of the standout features of HTTP/2 is multiplexing, which allows multiple requests and responses to be sent over a single connection simultaneously, instead of waiting for one request to finish before sending the next. This significantly reduces the delay associated with network round-trips. HTTP/2 also incorporates header compression, which decreases the size of data transmitted between the client and server, further improving performance. While HTTP/2 improves upon HTTP/1.1, it still operates on top of TCP, meaning that it does not completely overcome issues like head-of-line blocking. However, HTTP/2 does offer enhanced security through mandatory encryption (HTTPS). This ensures that all data transmitted between the client and server is encrypted, reducing the potential for eavesdropping and man-in-the-middle attacks, thus providing better security over HTTP/1.1.

HTTP/3 and Security

HTTP/3 represents the next evolutionary step in the Hypertext Transfer Protocol family, building on the QUIC (Quick UDP Internet Connections) protocol developed by Google. Unlike HTTP/2, which relies on TCP for connections, HTTP/3 uses UDP (User Datagram Protocol), which allows for faster and more reliable communication, particularly in environments with higher latency or packet loss. By eliminating the overhead associated with TCP's connection setup and congestion control, HTTP/3 offers improved performance, especially for mobile and remote access. In terms of security, HTTP/3 inherently integrates Transport Layer Security (TLS) 1.3, ensuring that data encryption is always enabled by default, thus providing better protection against attacks like eavesdropping and tampering. The protocol's design also helps reduce connection establishment times, leading to quicker page loads and more responsive applications. While HTTP/3 is still in the process of widespread adoption, it offers a promising future for more secure and faster web browsing, addressing many limitations of earlier HTTP versions.

Secure HTTP (HTTPS)

HTTPS (HyperText Transfer Protocol Secure) is a secure version of HTTP, where the communication is encrypted using SSL/TLS (Secure Sockets Layer/ Transport Layer Security) protocols. HTTPS ensures that data sent between the client and server is encrypted, protecting sensitive information like login credentials, financial details, and personal data from unauthorized access.HTTPS uses an SSL/TLS handshake to establish a secure connection before any data is exchanged.Websites with HTTPS have a padlock symbol in the browser address bar, signifying that the connection is encrypted.

Electronic Mail

Electronic Mail (email) is one of the most widely used services on the Internet, allowing users to send, receive, and store messages in Figure 6.3. Email refers to the exchange of digital messages between people or systems over a network. It is a method of communication that involves the transmission of text, files, images, and multimedia between users.Here's a breakdown of its key components and functions:

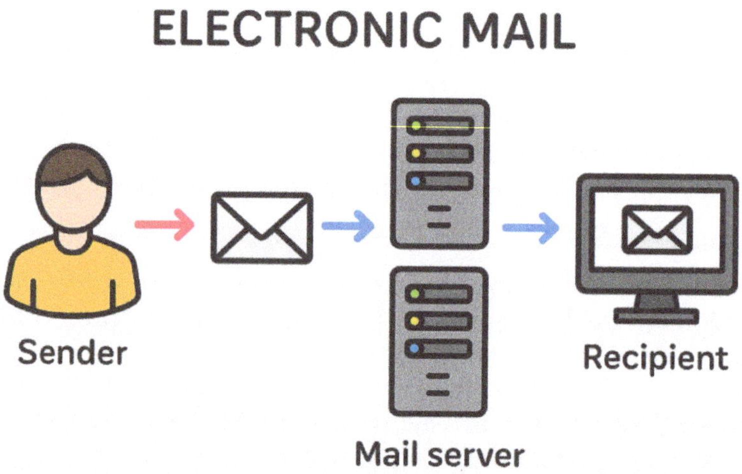

Figure 6.3: Step by step process of electronic mail.

Email Components

Email Client

An email client is a software application or program used to manage and interact with email accounts. It allows users to send, receive, organize, and store email messages. Some common email clients include Microsoft Outlook, Gmail, and Apple Mail. These clients may be installed on a device or accessed via a web interface. They offer features like folders for organizing emails, spam filtering, search functionality, and integration with calendars and contacts. Additionally, email clients support various protocols, such as POP, IMAP, and SMTP, enabling efficient email handling. Through an email client, users can also manage attachments, set up automatic replies, and manage multiple email accounts in one interface. Whether for personal or business communication, the email client is the central tool that ensures smooth interaction with mail servers, allowing users to manage their messages easily.

Mail Server

A mail server is a system that stores and routes email messages between senders and recipients. It functions as a digital post office, handling the transmission and reception of emails. A mail server is typically composed of two major components: the incoming mail server and the outgoing mail server. The incoming server often uses protocols like Post Office Protocol (POP) or Internet Message Access Protocol (IMAP) to retrieve emails from the server and deliver them to the user's email client. The outgoing mail server, using the Simple Mail Transfer Protocol (SMTP), is responsible for sending emails from the client to the destination server. Mail servers work together to ensure proper email delivery, maintain storage of messages, and provide secure authentication and encryption. Depending on the server's configuration, it may also have capabilities for spam filtering, message prioritization, and backup storage.

Email Address

An email address is a unique identifier used to route electronic mail messages to the correct recipient. It consists of two main parts: the local part (the username) and the domain part, separated by the "@" symbol. The local part represents the specific user or mailbox, while the domain part identifies the mail server hosting the recipient's email account. For example, in the email address username@ domain.com, "username" is the local part, and "domain.com" is the domain part. This format ensures that emails are delivered accurately to the right user within a particular domain or service provider. Email addresses also facilitate organization by allowing users to create aliases, manage forwarding addresses, or set up separate accounts for personal and professional communication. Furthermore, email addresses are integral to web forms, login credentials, and many online services, serving as an essential digital identity for communication.

Process

Sending Email

Sending an email involves composing a message in an email client, such as Microsoft Outlook, Gmail, or Apple Mail. The email client allows the sender to write the content of the message, include attachments, and specify the recipient's email address. Once the sender hits the "send" button, the email client communicates with the Simple Mail Transfer Protocol (SMTP) server, which is responsible for transmitting the message to the recipient's email server. SMTP ensures the message is properly formatted and delivered across the internet, passing through various servers until it reaches its destination. The server checks if the recipient's email address is valid, and if so, it temporarily stores the message until the recipient retrieves it. SMTP handles only the sending aspect, while the receiving and storing of emails are managed by different protocols, such as POP or IMAP, which are essential for email retrieval.

Receiving Email

When an email is received, it is temporarily stored on the recipient's email server. This server acts as a repository, holding incoming emails until the recipient accesses them. There are two main protocols used to retrieve emails from the server: Post Office Protocol (POP) and Internet Message Access Protocol (IMAP). POP allows the recipient to download emails from the server to their local email client. Once downloaded, the email is typically removed from the server, although some configurations allow for retention on the server. On the other hand, IMAP syncs the emails between the server and the email client, allowing the recipient to access their email from multiple devices while keeping the messages on the server. IMAP is typically preferred for users who need to access their email from different locations or devices, as it maintains the synchronization of the inbox across platforms.

Protocols

Email protocols are essential for the sending, receiving, and managing of emails across networks. The Simple Mail Transfer Protocol (SMTP) is used for sending emails from the sender's email client to the recipient's email server. SMTP operates as a push protocol, ensuring the message is transmitted across the internet and is delivered to the recipient's server. For receiving emails, two common protocols are used: Post Office Protocol (POP) and Internet Message Access Protocol (IMAP). POP is a download protocol that retrieves emails from the server and stores them locally on the recipient's device, removing them from the server in most configurations. IMAP, however, is a sync protocol that keeps emails on the server, allowing recipients to access and manage their messages from multiple devices while maintaining consistency. Each protocol serves a specific purpose, with SMTP focused on sending, and POP and IMAP focused on email retrieval and management.

File Transfer Protocol (FTP)

File Transfer Protocol (FTP) is a standard network protocol used to transfer files between a client and a server over a computer network. FTP allows for the retrieval, uploading, and manipulation of files across different systems. FTP is used to transfer files between computers over a TCP/IP-based network (like the Internet). It enables users to upload or download files from a server, making it integral to website management, data sharing, and backup solutions.

Components

FTP Client

An FTP client is a software application that enables users to connect to an FTP server and manage files on remote servers. It allows users to upload, download, delete, rename, and manage directories and files. FTP clients are designed to simplify file management by providing a graphical interface for users to interact with the server. Examples of popular FTP clients include FileZilla, Cyberduck, and WinSCP. These applications support features like drag-and-drop functionality, secure FTP (SFTP) connections, and the ability to transfer multiple files simultaneously. FTP clients can connect to any FTP server, as long as the correct login credentials (username and password) are provided. They play a crucial role in both personal and business file management, particularly in environments where large files or frequent file exchanges occur, offering an intuitive way to interact with remote file systems.

FTP Server

An FTP server is a specialized system that stores and manages files, allowing remote users to access and transfer data using the FTP protocol. It hosts files that can be retrieved, uploaded, or modified by clients connected to the server. The FTP server can be configured to restrict access based on user permissions, offering various levels of control over what users can or cannot do with the files. Commonly used FTP servers include vsftpd, ProFTPD, and FileZilla Server. These servers use the FTP protocol to communicate with FTP clients, ensuring that the correct data and files are transferred securely. FTP servers can be used for a wide range of applications, such as sharing large files between organizations, maintaining backups of important data, or distributing software packages. Security configurations such as firewalls, encryption, and access control policies are important aspects of managing an FTP server.

Protocol

The FTP protocol operates over two separate channels: the command channel and the data channel. The command channel, usually on port 21, is used for transmitting control commands such as login requests, file retrieval instructions, and file directory listings. These commands facilitate the interaction between the FTP client and server, ensuring proper communication. On the other hand, the data channel handles the actual transfer of files between the client and the server. This channel can operate in two modes: active mode or passive mode. In active mode, the client opens a data port for the server to connect and send the data. In passive mode, the server opens the port, and the client connects to it. This separation of control and data channels allows FTP to efficiently manage and prioritize data transfers while maintaining control over the communication process.

Process

Connection

The FTP client establishes a connection with the FTP server through a login process. The user provides a username and password to authenticate the session, which can either be an anonymous or authenticated login. In the case of anonymous access, the username is typically "anonymous" and the user is asked to provide an email address as a password, although this is often optional. Once the client successfully logs in, it gains access to the server's file system, where it can perform various operations. These include browsing directories, uploading or downloading files, and managing the server's files. The connection between the client and server relies on the FTP protocol, which operates over

TCP/IP, ensuring reliable communication. The login process may also involve the negotiation of secure connections, particularly when using FTP over SSL/TLS (FTPS) to ensure data privacy during file transfers.

File Transfer

Once the FTP client has successfully logged in and established a connection with the FTP server, the file transfer process begins. Users can browse the server's directories, much like navigating through a local file system. They can choose to upload or download files to and from the server, depending on the required task. File management operations such as renaming, moving, and deleting files are also possible, provided the user has the necessary permissions. Uploading involves sending files from the local system to the remote server, while downloading transfers files in the opposite direction. During this process, the FTP protocol ensures reliable and orderly data exchange, using mechanisms like checksums to verify the integrity of the transferred data. The efficiency of file transfer can be influenced by factors such as network speed, server capacity, and the number of concurrent connections allowed.

Data Mode

FTP supports two modes of data transfer:

Active Mode and Passive Mode

These modes dictate how the data connection between the client and server is established during file transfers. In Active Mode, the server opens a port and listens for incoming data connections from the client. The client, after establishing the control connection, sends a PORT command to the server with the IP address and port number where it is ready to receive data. The server then connects to the client on that port, and the file transfer begins. However, Active Mode can encounter issues when the client is behind a firewall or NAT (Network Address Translation) device, as the server may not be able to initiate the connection. In contrast, Passive Mode addresses this issue.

Passive Mode

The client initiates the data connection by sending a PASV command. The server then opens a random port and informs the client about it, allowing the client to establish the data connection. This mode is particularly useful for clients behind firewalls, as it eliminates the need for the server to connect to the client, allowing both parties to establish connections independently. Passive Mode is often preferred in modern FTP usage, particularly in environments with strict firewall configurations.

Remote Login

Remote login allows a user to access and interact with a computer system from a distant location using network protocols. This is particularly useful for system administration, troubleshooting, and working remotely. Remote login refers to the practice of accessing a remote computer or server from a different location, usually over a network or the internet.

Key Protocols

Telnet

Telnet is one of the earliest protocols developed for remote login, allowing users to access and manage computers over a network via a text-based interface. Initially, it provided a simple and effective way to interact with remote systems. However, Telnet operates without encryption, meaning that data transmitted between the client and server is sent in plain text. This lack of encryption makes it vulnerable to various security risks, including eavesdropping and man-in-the-middle attacks. As a result, sensitive information, such as passwords and commands, can be intercepted by malicious actors. Despite its historical significance, Telnet has been largely replaced by more secure alternatives in modern computing environments, especially in scenarios that require handling confidential or sensitive data. Its usage today is generally limited to legacy systems or specific use cases where security concerns are minimal.

SSH (Secure Shell)

SSH, or Secure Shell, is a widely used network protocol designed to provide secure communication between systems over an unsecured network. It was introduced as a replacement for Telnet, addressing the significant security flaws inherent in its predecessor. Unlike Telnet, SSH encrypts all communication between the client and server, ensuring that sensitive data such as passwords, commands, and system information are transmitted securely. SSH uses asymmetric cryptography to establish a secure connection, followed by symmetric encryption for data transmission. It also includes mechanisms for authentication, such as public key authentication, which further enhances its security. SSH is extensively used for remote login to servers, secure file transfers (via SCP or SFTP), and executing remote commands. Due to its robust security features, SSH has become the standard for remote administration in modern IT infrastructure and is commonly deployed in various operating systems, including Linux, macOS, and Windows.

Process:

Initiate Login

The first step in initiating a remote login is for the user to open a terminal or an SSH client on their local machine. SSH (Secure Shell) is the most commonly used protocol for remote logins, providing encrypted communication between the local and remote machines. The user enters the IP address or hostname of the remote machine they wish to access. This serves as a way to uniquely identify the remote system on the network. The client attempts to establish a connection to the server using this information. In some cases, the user may also specify a particular port number, although the default for SSH is port 22. After initiating the connection, the system on the remote machine responds to the request, awaiting authentication from the user. If the system is reachable and the IP/hostname is correct, the connection proceeds to the next step: authentication.

Authentication

Once the connection to the remote machine is initiated, the next step is authentication. Authentication ensures that only authorized users can access the remote system. In most cases, the user is prompted to enter a password, which is compared against the stored password on the remote machine. If the password matches, access is granted. Alternatively, users may utilize cryptographic key pairs for SSH, which provide an extra layer of security. In this case, a public key is stored on the remote machine, and the user signs in with a private key stored securely on their local machine. This form of authentication is more secure than passwords alone, as it is difficult for attackers to guess or brute-force the private key. Once the user is successfully authenticated, they gain access to the remote system's command line and can start interacting with it.

Session

After authentication, the user is granted access to the remote system and enters an interactive session. During this session, the user has full command-line control over the remote machine, allowing them to execute commands, manage files, install software, or configure system settings. The environment of the remote machine may be slightly different from the local machine, depending on the operating system and configuration of the system being accessed. The session typically operates within the bounds of a terminal interface, but the user can perform virtually any task they would be able to do locally. File management commands such as ls, cp, and mv can be used to navigate and manipulate files, while commands like apt-get or yum may be used for package management, depending on the system's package manager. The session remains active as long as the user continues to interact with it.

Session Termination

When the user is done with their remote session, they can close the session by logging out or disconnecting from the remote machine. This is typically done by typing the exit command or pressing the shortcut keys (e.g., Ctrl + D in many terminals), which safely terminates the active connection. When the session is terminated, the remote system will close the terminal or shell instance and release any associated resources, effectively ending the user's access to the system. In some cases, users might experience a timeout or disconnection due to network issues, but the session is still considered terminated when the remote system no longer allows the user to interact with it. Properly terminating the session is crucial for security purposes, as it prevents unauthorized access to the remote system once the user has finished their tasks.

Advantages

Access from anywhere

Remote login offers the flexibility for users to access their systems from virtually any location, provided there is a stable network connection. This capability allows professionals to work remotely, increasing productivity and enabling them to carry out tasks outside the confines of a traditional office setting. Whether traveling, at home, or working from a different city or country, users can securely access their workstations, servers, or cloud resources. This unrestricted access helps reduce delays, speed up decision-making, and maintain business continuity without the need to be physically present in the office. It also makes it easier for IT teams to provide support and resolve issues across different time zones. As long as there is an internet connection, users can stay connected to their systems and continue working seamlessly.

Secure and efficient management

Remote login, particularly when implemented via Secure Shell (SSH), provides a highly secure way to manage servers, network devices, and other IT infrastructure. SSH encrypts all traffic, including passwords, ensuring that sensitive data is protected from eavesdropping and unauthorized access. This secure channel is essential for managing systems remotely, especially when dealing with critical infrastructure or confidential data. With remote login, administrators can perform maintenance, troubleshooting, and system configuration tasks without being physically present, significantly improving operational efficiency. It allows for quick responses to emerging issues, reducing downtime and preventing potential security breaches. The ability to manage systems from any location also helps in the rapid identification and resolution of problems, ensuring smooth and uninterrupted service delivery, especially for businesses with a global presence.

Cost-effective

One of the primary advantages of remote login is its cost-effectiveness. By eliminating the need for physical access to distant machines, organizations can save substantial amounts of time and money. Travel expenses for on-site troubleshooting, server maintenance, or software updates can quickly add up, especially when dealing with multiple locations. With remote login, IT staff can access and manage systems across various sites without the need for costly travel or relocation. Additionally, businesses can make better use of their human resources, as remote login allows IT professionals to manage multiple systems simultaneously, reducing the need for on-site staff and improving workforce efficiency. Remote access also allows for greater scalability as organizations expand, as they can remotely manage growing infrastructure without the need to hire additional personnel for physical maintenance tasks

Network Management

Network management refers to the process of administering, managing, and maintaining computer networks to ensure their smooth operation in Figure 6.4. It includes tasks like monitoring network performance, ensuring network security, and troubleshooting problems that arise.

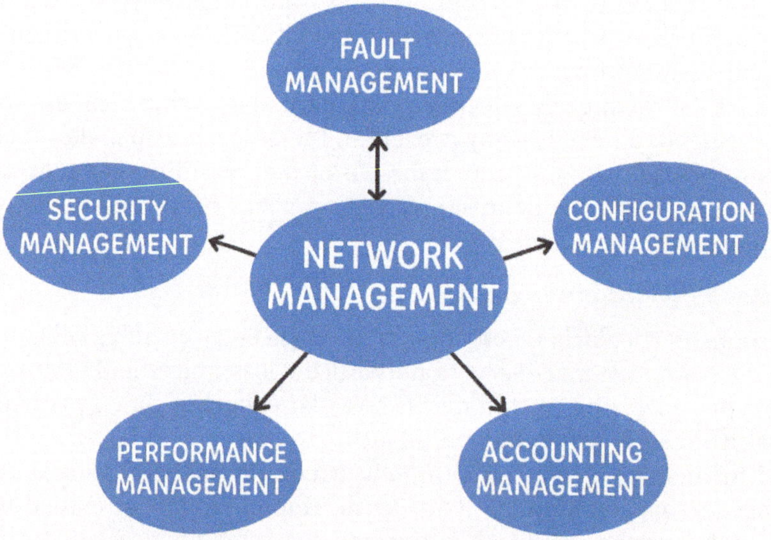

Figure 6.4: Types of network management.

Key Concepts in Network Management

Network Monitoring

Network monitoring is the continuous process of overseeing the operational status of a network. Its primary purpose is to ensure that the network performs optimally without interruptions. Network monitoring tools are equipped to detect issues such as latency, congestion, and connectivity failures. By proactively identifying and alerting administrators about potential bottlenecks, these tools help maintain a steady flow of data and prevent network downtimes. Commonly used tools, such as SNMP (Simple Network Management Protocol) and NetFlow, allow administrators to gather real-time data on network activities. This information is crucial for troubleshooting problems before they affect users, ensuring network reliability, and optimizing performance. Network monitoring can also track trends over time, helping to anticipate future resource needs or capacity upgrades. In essence, effective network monitoring allows for the smooth functioning of a network, minimizing the impact of potential disruptions on the overall system performance.

Configuration Management

Configuration management is a critical aspect of network management that focuses on maintaining and ensuring the correct configuration of network devices such as routers, switches, firewalls, and other essential infrastructure components. It involves systematically organizing, tracking, and modifying the settings of these devices to ensure they function optimally and meet network requirements. Configuration management tools are used to back up device configurations, apply updates, and automate changes to reduce human errors. These tools also allow administrators to enforce compliance with security policies and network standards. By ensuring proper configuration, the network is more resilient to faults, security breaches, and performance issues. Changes made to configurations can be audited to provide traceability, making it easier to troubleshoot and reverse modifications when necessary. The goal of configuration management is to maintain a stable and secure network environment while ensuring devices are always set up to handle the evolving network demands.

Fault Management

Fault management is the process of identifying, isolating, and rectifying problems within a network infrastructure. It is a proactive approach to minimize downtime and maintain network reliability. Fault management tools are designed to detect hardware or software failures, communication errors, and service disruptions in real time. Once a fault is detected, the system triggers an alert for network administrators, who can then troubleshoot and resolve the issue promptly. Fault management also includes logging incidents for future reference, allowing administrators to spot recurring issues or systemic problems. The process is essential for maintaining the overall health of a network and ensuring that users experience minimal disruptions. To support fault management, automated systems and diagnostic tools can pinpoint the root cause of a problem, whether it's related to network devices, configurations, or connections. In critical environments, fault management is crucial for keeping services running without significant interruptions, ensuring business continuity.

Performance Management

Performance management involves the ongoing monitoring and optimization of network performance to ensure efficient data transfer and service delivery. It focuses on key performance indicators (KPIs) like data throughput, latency, packet loss, and jitter, which are essential for assessing the health of a network. Administrators use performance management tools to identify network bottlenecks, slowdowns, or deviations from expected performance. For instance, high latency can significantly affect real-time applications like VoIP or video conferencing, while packet loss can result in data corruption or delivery failures. By continuously monitoring these factors, performance management helps administrators take corrective actions such as re-routing traffic, upgrading hardware, or optimizing protocols to improve efficiency. Furthermore, performance management enables the identification of trends and patterns over time, assisting in the long-term planning of network resources and the anticipation of future scalability needs. Ultimately, it ensures that the network meets performance standards required for end-user satisfaction.

Security Management

Security management is a crucial aspect of network management that aims to protect the network infrastructure from unauthorized access, attacks, and other security threats. It encompasses a wide range of practices, including the implementation of firewalls, intrusion detection systems (IDS), encryption protocols, and secure authentication methods. Security management tools monitor network traffic for suspicious activity and prevent unauthorized access by enforcing security policies. Firewalls act as barriers between trusted internal networks and untrusted external networks, filtering incoming and outgoing traffic based on predefined rules. Intrusion detection systems detect and respond to potential threats by analyzing traffic patterns and flagging any anomalous behavior. Additionally, network security management involves applying encryption methods to protect sensitive data during transmission, ensuring confidentiality and integrity. Regular security audits, vulnerability assessments, and the application of patches also play a significant role in securing the network and safeguarding against emerging threats.

Accounting Management

Accounting management in network management refers to tracking and monitoring network usage, resources, and services to ensure that policies are followed and appropriate charges are applied, particularly in service provider environments. This involves recording data on bandwidth consumption, access time, and the overall utilization of network resources. By accurately tracking usage, administrators can enforce network access policies, prevent abuse, and ensure compliance with service-level agreements (SLAs). In service providers' networks, accounting management helps determine how resources are consumed and ensures that customers are billed correctly based on their usage. For enterprise networks, accounting management can aid in managing internal costs by identifying areas where resource usage can be optimized. Detailed usage records can also assist in forecasting future network capacity requirements and identifying potential bottlenecks. In essence, accounting management plays a key role in controlling costs, ensuring fair resource allocation, and supporting financial accountability within network environments.

Protocols and Tools

SNMP (Simple Network Management Protocol)

SNMP is a widely adopted network protocol designed for managing and monitoring network devices, such as routers, switches, servers, and printers, in an IP network. It provides a framework for network administrators to monitor device performance, gather status information, and configure settings remotely. SNMP operates in a client-server model, where the network device acts as a server, and the management station is the client. SNMP supports three main versions: SNMPv1, SNMPv2c, and SNMPv3, with SNMPv3 providing enhanced security features. The protocol relies on a Management Information Base (MIB), which is a hierarchical structure defining the data available for network management. Through SNMP, administrators can detect problems in real-time, automate device configuration, and track network health. It is commonly used in large-scale networks for its simplicity, scalability, and efficiency in monitoring diverse networked devices and ensuring their optimal performance.

NetFlow

NetFlow is a network protocol developed by Cisco Systems, primarily used for collecting, analyzing, and monitoring network traffic data. It provides detailed insights into network traffic patterns, allowing network administrators to understand traffic flow, bandwidth utilization, and performance issues. NetFlow captures key attributes of network traffic, including source and destination IP addresses, ports, protocols, and packet counts, among others. This data can be processed to identify trends, detect anomalies, and optimize network performance. It also enables administrators to troubleshoot problems like congestion, packet loss, and inefficient routing. NetFlow data is often used for capacity planning, security monitoring, and accounting purposes. Since its introduction, NetFlow has been adopted widely by organizations to enhance network visibility and performance analysis. Today, similar protocols, such as sFlow and IPFIX, have emerged, but NetFlow remains one of the most robust and widely used tools for network traffic analysis.

Wireshark

Wireshark is an open-source network protocol analyzer widely used by network professionals, engineers, and cybersecurity experts for capturing and analyzing network traffic. It allows users to inspect the data packets transmitted across a network in real-time, providing deep visibility into network communication. Wireshark supports hundreds of network protocols, making it versatile in troubleshooting network issues, ensuring network security, and performing detailed network forensics. The tool can capture packets from various interfaces such as Ethernet, Wi-Fi, and Bluetooth. Wireshark provides an intuitive graphical interface for filtering, sorting, and analyzing captured packets based on specific criteria like IP address, port, protocol type, and packet length. It also allows users to view the content of the packets at various levels, from raw data to high-level protocol details. Wireshark is highly regarded for its accuracy, depth of analysis, and the ability to troubleshoot complex networking issues efficiently.

Data Compression

Data compression is the process of reducing the size of data files to save space or reduce transmission time. It can be applied to any data type, including text, images, audio, and video.

Types of Data Compression

Lossless Compression

Lossless compression is a technique where the original data can be perfectly reconstructed from the compressed data without any loss of information. This is crucial for applications where even a small loss of data can be detrimental, such as text files, executable files, and certain image formats like PNG. In this method, the compression algorithms preserve the integrity of the original content, ensuring that after decompression, the exact original data is restored. Lossless compression is commonly used in scenarios where fidelity to the original data is of utmost importance, such as archival storage and high-quality image formats. Since it doesn't discard any information, lossless compression algorithms are often less efficient than lossy compression algorithms, meaning the resulting file sizes tend to be larger. However, the trade-off is the assurance that no information is lost during compression or decompression.

Huffman Coding

Huffman Coding is a popular lossless compression algorithm that works by assigning variable-length codes to input characters based on their frequencies of occurrence. Characters that appear more frequently are assigned shorter codes, while characters that appear less frequently are assigned longer codes. This approach ensures that the compressed data is as small as possible, since it minimizes the number of bits required to represent the most common characters. Huffman Coding is widely used in data compression formats like ZIP files, JPEG image compression, and other applications that require efficient text encoding. The algorithm begins by creating a binary tree where each leaf node represents a character and its frequency, and the tree structure ensures that the most frequently used characters have the shortest paths. Huffman Coding is efficient and guarantees the optimality of the encoding scheme in terms of minimizing the file size.

Lempel-Ziv-Welch (LZW)

Lempel-Ziv-Welch (LZW) is a dictionary-based compression algorithm that is commonly used in image formats like GIF and TIFF. Unlike algorithms that rely on predefined tables, LZW creates a dictionary during compression to store sequences of data that appear repeatedly. As the input data is processed, LZW replaces repeating sequences with shorter codes that correspond to entries in the dictionary. This dynamic approach allows LZW to effectively compress data with a wide variety of patterns and structures, making it suitable for both text and image data. One of the key advantages of LZW is its ability to adapt to the specific data being compressed, which results in efficient compression ratios. LZW is lossless, meaning that no data is lost during compression, and the original data can be perfectly reconstructed upon decompression. It is widely used in formats like GIF for efficient image storage.

Deflate

Deflate is a lossless compression algorithm that combines both Huffman coding and the Lempel-Ziv algorithm to compress data efficiently. It is commonly used in formats like ZIP and GZIP for compressing files. The algorithm works by first applying a dictionary-based compression technique, similar to Lempel-Ziv, followed by a final pass of Huffman coding to further reduce the file size. This combination of techniques allows Deflate to achieve high compression ratios while maintaining the ability to recover the original data without loss. One of the reasons for Deflate's popularity is its balance between compression efficiency and speed, making it suitable for applications where both storage space and processing time are important factors. The algorithm is particularly effective at compressing data that contains repetitive patterns, such as text files or software executables, while being widely supported across a range of operating systems and software tools.

Lossy Compression

Lossy compression is a technique used to reduce file sizes by permanently discarding certain data, resulting in a reduction in quality. This method is most commonly employed in multimedia files such as images, audio, and video, where a slight reduction in quality is often deemed acceptable for the sake of smaller file sizes. The primary advantage of lossy compression is its ability to significantly reduce the amount of data, which is crucial for applications where storage or bandwidth is limited. However, the trade-off is that the original file cannot be fully recovered once compressed. Lossy compression works by analyzing the data to identify and remove information that is less noticeable or redundant, ensuring the essential content remains intact. While this approach may introduce artifacts or a decrease in clarity, the compression ratio achieved makes it highly effective in reducing file sizes for practical use in streaming, storage, and transmission.

JPEG

JPEG (Joint Photographic Experts Group) is one of the most commonly used lossy compression techniques, particularly for digital images. It works by discarding visual data that is considered less important or perceptible to the human eye, allowing for significant reductions in file size. The JPEG compression algorithm uses a process called discrete cosine transform (DCT) to convert spatial domain image data into frequency domain data, where it quantifies and eliminates the less significant frequency components. JPEG allows users to adjust the compression level, giving a trade-off between image quality and file size. With high compression rates, image quality can degrade noticeably, with potential for blocky artifacts and loss of detail, especially in areas with fine textures. However, for many applications, such as web images or digital photography, JPEG strikes an ideal balance between quality and file size, making it a standard format for photographic content.

MP3

MP3 (MPEG-1 Audio Layer 3) is a popular lossy compression format used for audio files. It achieves file size reduction by removing audio data that the human ear is less likely to perceive, such as very high or low frequencies that are inaudible or masked by other sounds. MP3 uses psychoacoustic models to analyze the audio signal and selectively remove or reduce data based on human hearing sensitivity. The result is a smaller file size while maintaining an acceptable level of audio quality. The compression level in MP3 files can be adjusted by setting a bitrate, which determines the level of compression and, consequently, the audio quality. Higher bitrates typically result in better sound quality, while lower bitrates lead to greater compression but reduced fidelity. MP3 is widely used for music, podcasts, and other audio content due to its efficient compression and widespread compatibility across devices and platforms.

H.264

H.264, also known as AVC (Advanced Video Coding), is a widely adopted lossy compression standard for video files. It is commonly used in video streaming, video conferencing, and video storage due to its efficient compression techniques, which offer high-quality video at relatively low bitrates. The H.264 compression algorithm works by analyzing video frames and eliminating redundancies both within a single frame (spatial redundancy) and between consecutive frames (temporal redundancy). This allows for significant data reduction while maintaining visual quality. H.264 also supports various compression levels, enabling it to be adaptable for different applications, from low-bitrate streaming to high-definition video storage. The codec balances video quality and compression by using advanced techniques like motion compensation and transform coding. While the lossy nature of H.264 may introduce some artifacts or slight quality degradation, it is widely regarded for its performance in delivering clear and smooth video content across various devices and networks.

Compression Techniques

Entropy Coding

Entropy coding is a form of data compression that assigns variable-length codes to input symbols based on their probabilities. The central idea behind entropy coding is that more frequent symbols are assigned shorter codes, while less frequent ones are assigned longer codes. This method exploits the statistical properties of the input data to minimize the average length of the codeword, which reduces the overall data size. One popular example of entropy coding is Huffman coding, where the algorithm builds a binary tree based on the frequency of symbols, with shorter paths representing more frequent symbols. Other variations of entropy coding include arithmetic coding, where a single floating-point number represents the entire data set. Entropy coding is particularly useful in lossless data compression scenarios, as it ensures that the original data can be reconstructed exactly from the compressed data.

Dictionary-based Compression

Dictionary-based compression is a technique in data compression where patterns or substrings within the input data are replaced by shorter, fixed-length codes. The algorithm maintains a dictionary of these patterns, which are dynamically built as it processes the data. One well-known example of this technique is Lempel-Ziv-Welch (LZW) compression. In LZW, substrings of data are added to the dictionary, and subsequent occurrences of those substrings are replaced by the dictionary's index. This reduces the data's size by replacing repetitive patterns with shorter representations. The dictionary is usually reset at certain intervals to ensure it does not grow too large. Dictionary-based methods are widely used in formats like GIF and TIFF for lossless image compression, as they efficiently handle repeating patterns in the data. This approach can be extended to other types of data such as text and files, achieving significant compression ratios.

Run-Length Encoding (RLE)

Run-Length Encoding (RLE) is a simple yet effective technique for data compression, especially when the data contains long sequences of repeated symbols. In RLE, a sequence of the same value (a "run") is replaced by a pair consisting of the symbol and the number of occurrences. This method is particularly efficient for compressing data like images or text where long stretches of identical characters occur. For example, the string "AAAAA" could be compressed to "5A", where '5' represents the number of 'A's in the run. RLE is commonly used in formats like BMP images and certain document types. While effective for compressing simple and repetitive data, RLE may not perform well for data with high variability, as it may even increase the size if the runs are very short or absent. Thus, it is most useful in contexts where data redundancy is high.

Cryptography-Basic Concepts

Cryptography is the practice of securing communication and data through encryption and decryption techniques, ensuring that only authorized parties can access the information in Figure 6.5.

Key Concepts in Cryptography

Encryption

Encryption is the process of converting readable data, known as plaintext, into an unreadable format, called ciphertext, using algorithms and encryption keys. This technique is employed to secure sensitive information from unauthorized access, ensuring confidentiality during transmission or storage. When data is encrypted, it becomes incomprehensible to anyone who does not possess the correct decryption key. The strength of encryption lies in the complexity of the encryption algorithms and the key length. In modern encryption systems, both software and hardware solutions are used to encrypt data effectively. Encryption plays a crucial role in a wide range of applications, from protecting personal communications in email and messaging systems to securing financial transactions and data storage in cloud services. It is an essential component in cybersecurity, providing confidentiality, integrity, and authenticity to data in transit or at rest.

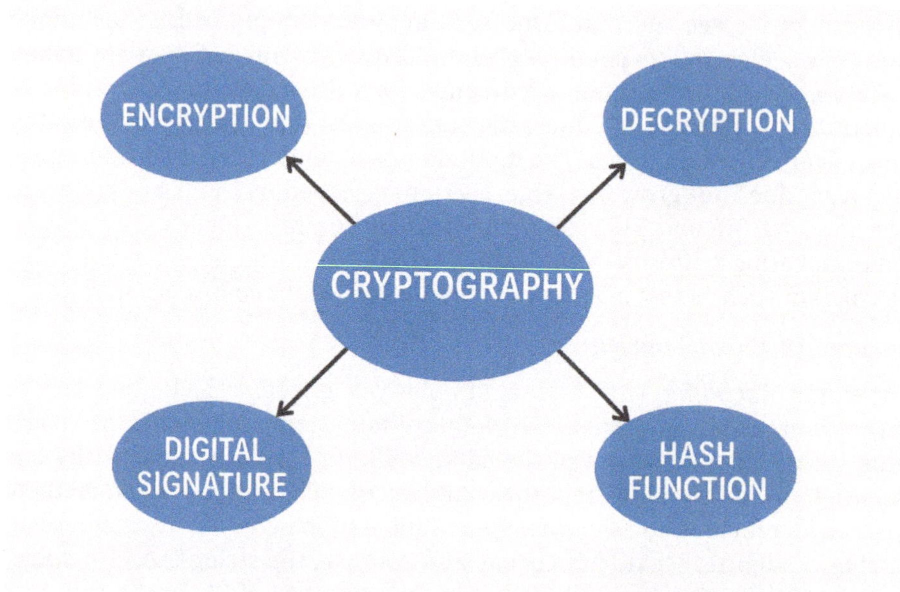

Figure 6.5: Types of Cryptography.

Symmetric Encryption

Symmetric encryption is a method in cryptography where the same key is used for both the encryption and decryption processes. This means that both the sender and the receiver share a secret key that allows them to encrypt and decrypt messages. The primary advantage of symmetric encryption lies in its speed and efficiency. Since the same key is used on both ends, the encryption and decryption process tend to be faster than asymmetric encryption. However, the challenge with symmetric encryption is the secure distribution of the key. If the key is intercepted or leaked, the encrypted data is no longer secure. Common examples of symmetric encryption algorithms include AES (Advanced Encryption Standard), which is widely used in various applications, including securing internet communications and data storage, and DES (Data Encryption Standard), though it is now considered obsolete due to its vulnerability to brute-force attacks.

Asymmetric Encryption

Asymmetric encryption, also known as public-key encryption, uses two different keys for encryption and decryption. One key, known as the public key, is used to encrypt the message, while the other key, the private key, is used to decrypt it. The public key can be freely distributed, while the private key is kept secret by the receiver. This method eliminates the need for the sender and receiver to share a secret key in advance, as is required in symmetric encryption. Asymmetric encryption provides enhanced security and is particularly useful in scenarios where secure communication needs to be established between parties who have never met before. RSA (Rivest-Shamir-Adleman) is one of the most widely known asymmetric encryption algorithms. Asymmetric encryption is the foundation of many security protocols, including SSL/TLS for securing websites, and is also used for digital signatures and secure email encryption.

Decryption

Decryption is the process of converting encrypted data back into its original, readable format, known as plaintext. It is the reverse operation of encryption and is performed using an appropriate decryption key. In symmetric encryption, the same key used for encryption is used to decrypt the data, while in asymmetric encryption, the private key corresponding to the public key used for encryption is employed for decryption. Decryption is a crucial aspect of any cryptographic system because, without it, the encrypted data remains inaccessible and unreadable. The goal of decryption is to ensure that only authorized parties can access and interpret the original data. The security of a decryption process depends on the strength of the encryption algorithm and the secrecy of the decryption key. Decryption is widely used in securing communication channels, such as email or instant messaging, and in protecting sensitive data.

Hash Functions

A cryptographic hash function is an algorithm that takes an input of any length and produces a fixed-size string of characters, which typically appears as a digest. This digest is unique to the input data, meaning even a small change in the input will produce a significantly different hash value. Hash functions are widely used for ensuring data integrity and verifying the authenticity of data. One of the most well-known cryptographic hash functions is SHA-256 (Secure Hash Algorithm), which produces a 256-bit hash value. Hash functions are fundamental in areas such as digital signatures, password storage, and blockchain technology. They are also used in checksums to detect errors in data transmission. Since hash functions are designed to be one-way functions, it is computationally infeasible to reverse the process and retrieve the original data from the hash, ensuring the security and privacy of the input.

Digital Signatures

A digital signature is a cryptographic mechanism that ensures the authenticity, integrity, and non-repudiation of digital messages or documents. It is generated using a private key to compute a unique signature for a specific piece of data. The digital signature can then be verified by anyone using the corresponding public key. The primary purpose of a digital signature is to provide assurance that the message was not altered in transit (integrity) and that it indeed comes from the claimed sender (authentication). Digital signatures are widely used in secure communications, e-commerce transactions, and software distribution. They are a critical component of public key infrastructure (PKI) and are commonly used with certificates to verify the identity of parties involved in digital communications. One key benefit of digital signatures is that they provide non-repudiation, meaning the sender cannot deny sending the message after signing it.

Cryptographic Algorithms

AES (Advanced Encryption Standard)

AES is a widely used symmetric key encryption algorithm designed to secure data through a process called encryption. It operates using the same key for both encryption and decryption, which makes it efficient but requires key management to ensure the security of communications. AES supports key lengths of 128, 192, and 256 bits, with the 256-bit version being the most secure. It is used across various applications, including securing online transactions, communications, and data storage. AES was adopted as the encryption standard by the U.S. National Institute of Standards and Technology (NIST) in 2001. Its strong security and relatively fast processing speeds make it the encryption method of choice for many systems. AES is also resistant to most cryptographic attacks, including brute-force, making it a cornerstone of modern cryptography and one of the most trusted algorithms in the field.

RSA (Rivest-Shamir-Adleman)

RSA is an asymmetric encryption algorithm that uses a pair of keys, one public and one private, to secure data transmission. Unlike symmetric encryption algorithms like AES, RSA's asymmetric nature allows for secure data exchange without requiring the sender and receiver to share a secret key beforehand. RSA operates by generating a public key that can be freely distributed, while the private key is kept secret. Data encrypted with the public key can only be decrypted by the corresponding private key, providing a secure mechanism for data protection. RSA is widely used for securing sensitive communications over the internet, such as during the establishment of secure HTTPS connections and digital signatures. However, RSA encryption can be computationally expensive, particularly with longer key lengths, which makes it less efficient for encrypting large volumes of data when compared to symmetric algorithms like AES.

ECC (Elliptic Curve Cryptography)

Elliptic Curve Cryptography (ECC) is a modern form of public key cryptography that is based on the mathematical structure of elliptic curves. Compared to RSA, ECC provides a higher level of security with smaller key sizes, making it more efficient for encryption, decryption, and digital signature processes. ECC has gained popularity due to its efficiency in terms of computational resources, particularly in environments with limited processing power, such as mobile devices and IoT devices. ECC algorithms, like ECDSA (Elliptic Curve Digital Signature Algorithm), offer a high degree of security while requiring shorter key lengths to achieve the same level of security as RSA with larger key sizes. This makes ECC especially attractive for use in modern encryption standards, including those used in secure communications, blockchain technologies, and mobile applications, where processing speed and resource efficiency are paramount.

SHA-256 (Secure Hash Algorithm 256-bit)

SHA-256 is a cryptographic hash function that produces a fixed-size 256-bit hash value from an input message of any length. It is part of the SHA-2 family of algorithms, developed by the National Security Agency (NSA) to replace the older and less secure SHA-1. SHA-256 is widely used for ensuring data integrity and verifying the authenticity of data in various security protocols. It is used in blockchain technologies, digital signatures, certificates, and password hashing. The function operates by applying a series of mathematical transformations to the input data, generating a unique output for each unique input, even if the input only slightly changes. Because of its collision resistance and strong security features, SHA-256 is considered one of the most reliable hash functions and is crucial in the protection of sensitive information across numerous cybersecurity systems. It is particularly essential for Bitcoin and other cryptocurrencies.

Key Management

Public Key Infrastructure (PKI)

Public Key Infrastructure (PKI) is a framework designed to manage public and private keys, along with the digital certificates that ensure secure communication over the internet. PKI enables the use of asymmetric encryption, where each participant has a pair of keys: a public key for encryption and a private key for decryption. The infrastructure ensures the confidentiality, integrity, and authenticity of digital transactions by providing a secure way of exchanging data. PKI involves key management, including key generation, distribution, and revocation. It relies on trusted authorities, such as Certificate Authorities (CAs), to validate the identity of entities, ensuring that communications between them are secure and legitimate. The digital certificates issued by the CA bind public keys to specific identities, verifying that the key belongs to the individual or entity it claims. PKI plays a crucial role in e-commerce, email security, VPNs, and more.

Certificate Authorities (CAs)

Certificate Authorities (CAs) are trusted entities within a Public Key Infrastructure (PKI) that play a vital role in ensuring the authenticity and integrity of digital communications. A CA is responsible for issuing digital certificates, which are used to authenticate the identity of an entity or individual in online transactions. These certificates serve as a form of identification and verification, containing the public key of the entity along with other metadata, such as the validity period and the CA's signature. The CA acts as a third-party authority, verifying the identity of the certificate holder before issuing a certificate. By doing so, CAs facilitate secure communication by ensuring that the public key associated with a certificate truly belongs to the claimed entity. They also manage certificate revocation and renewal processes. CAs are essential in establishing trust between communicating parties in secure online environments.

Security Protocols

SSL/TLS

SSL (Secure Sockets Layer) and TLS (Transport Layer Security) are cryptographic protocols designed to provide secure communication over a computer network. SSL was the predecessor to TLS, which is now the more commonly used protocol. Both protocols work by encrypting the data exchanged between a client and a server, ensuring that it cannot be intercepted or tampered with during transmission. They also authenticate the identities of both parties to ensure that the connection is legitimate. SSL/TLS protocols are widely used in web browsers to secure HTTP traffic (HTTPS), as well as in other applications like email and instant messaging. The process begins with a handshake in which both parties exchange keys and agree on encryption algorithms. Once the session is established, the data is transmitted securely with encryption, integrity checks, and mutual authentication, providing confidentiality and trust in online transactions and communications.

IPSec

IPSec (Internet Protocol Security) is a comprehensive framework used to secure Internet Protocol (IP) communications by encrypting and authenticating data packets. It operates at the network layer, which means it can protect all traffic across an IP network, including not just web traffic but also email, VoIP, and other types of data. IPSec is commonly used in virtual private networks (VPNs) to ensure secure remote access to corporate networks. It provides two main modes: Transport mode, which encrypts only the data portion of a packet, and Tunnel mode, which encrypts the entire packet, including the header, providing an additional layer of security. IPSec uses cryptographic algorithms to provide confidentiality, integrity, and authentication of data packets, ensuring that they cannot be altered or read by unauthorized entities. It can also be configured to offer perfect forward secrecy, ensuring that even if encryption keys are compromised, past communications remain secure.These three conceptsnetwork management, data compression, and cryptographyare foundational in the modern digital world. Network management ensures the efficient operation and security of networks, data compression optimizes the use of storage and bandwidth, and cryptography secures sensitive data, preventing unauthorized access or tampering.

Conclusion

The Application Layer plays a crucial role in the overall functioning of computer networks. It serves as the interface through which users interact with network services, facilitating a variety of essential protocols and services such as DNS (Domain Name System), HTTP (Hypertext Transfer Protocol), FTP (File Transfer Protocol), and email systems. These protocols enable the transmission of data over the network and ensure smooth communication between different devices and applications. Additionally, network management and security protocols, like cryptography, help in maintaining data integrity and preventing unauthorized access. Data compression is another vital feature of the Application Layer, helping in reducing the amount of data transmitted over the network, improving efficiency. Understanding these basic concepts equips professionals with the knowledge required to design, implement, and manage networks effectively.

Exercise Questions

- What is the role of the Application Layer in the OSI model?
- Explain the functionality of DNS (Domain Name System).
- How does the HTTP protocol work in web browsing?
- Define FTP and its use in transferring files between systems.
- What is the significance of electronic mail in networking?
- Discuss the role of remote login protocols in accessing network resources.
- Explain the concept of network management at the Application Layer.
- What is data compression and how does it enhance network performance?
- How does cryptography contribute to data security in networks?
- List and describe two application layer protocols used for secure communication.

Bibliography

- Aisyah, S. (2015). Computer networking company in business area. International Research Journal of Management, IT & Social Sciences, 2(7), 1. https://doi.org/10.21744/irjmis.v2i7.67
- Gudhka, D. (2024). Computer network. International Journal for Research in Applied Science and Engineering Technology, 12(1), 78–87. https://doi.org/10.22214/ijraset.2024.57862
- Jennings, D. M., Landweber, L. H., Fuchs, I. H., Farber, D. J., & Adrion, W. R. (1986). Computer networking for scientists. Science, 231(4741), 943–950. https://doi.org/10.1126/science.231.4741.943
- Kearsley, G. (1985). Networking computer-based instruction. Education and Computing, 1(2), 109–116. https://doi.org/10.1016/S0167-9287(85)93794-X
- Liu, Q. (2024). Hardware-free network internals exploration. International Journal of Innovative Teaching and Learning in Higher Education, 5(1), 1–16. https://doi.org/10.4018/ijitlhe.339002
- Maddux, C. D. (1989). Computer networking in education. Computers in the Schools, 6(1–2), 37–43. https://doi.org/10.1300/J025v06n01_04
- Matsukata, J. (1987). Computer networking for large computers in universities. ACM SIGCOMM Computer Communication Review, 17(5), 78–87. https://doi.org/10.1145/55483.55492
- Smed, J. (2008). Networking for computer games. International Journal of Computer Games Technology, 2008, 1. https://doi.org/10.1155/2008/928712
- Sussex, R., & White, P. (1996). Electronic networking. Annual Review of Applied Linguistics, 16, 200–225. https://doi.org/10.1017/S0267190500001513
- Farsad, B. (1988). Networking your computer lab: Benefits and pitfalls. Hospitality Education and Research Journal, 12(2), 482. https://doi.org/10.1177/109634808801200259
- Alsebae, A. (2014). Network coding for computer networking [Doctoral dissertation, University of Warwick]. http://wrap.warwick.ac.uk/72647/
- Kamppi, T. (2011). ICT system for courses in computer networking [Master's thesis, KTH Royal Institute of Technology]. http://urn.kb.se/

resolve?urn=urn:nbn:se:kth:diva-53605

- Lurain, S. (1990). Networking security: Risk assessment of information systems [Master's thesis, University of Dayton]. http://hdl.handle.net/1850/10587
- Wright, C. E. (1996). Information networking for distributed semiconductor technology development [Master's thesis, Massachusetts Institute of Technology]. http://hdl.handle.net/1721.1/40205
- Yang, T. (2019). Connected car networking [Doctoral dissertation, Case Western Reserve University]. http://rave.ohiolink.edu/etdc/view?acc_num=case1544728665967784
- Bush, S. F. (2012). Active networking. In Handbook of computer networks (pp. 985–1011). Wiley. https://doi.org/10.1002/9781118256107.ch64
- Dommel, H.-P. (2011). Multimedia networking. In Handbook of computer networks (pp. 246–263). Wiley. https://doi.org/10.1002/9781118256114.ch18
- Longley, D., & Shain, M. (1985). Personal computer networking. In Expanding and networking microcomputers (pp. 221–236). Palgrave Macmillan. https://doi.org/10.1007/978-1-349-07625-3_30
- Robertazzi, T. G. (2017). Space networking. In Introduction to computer networking (pp. 97–112). Springer. https://doi.org/10.1007/978-3-319-53103-8_9
- Surianarayanan, C., & Chelliah, P. R. (2019). Cloud networking. In Texts in computer science (pp. 97–132). Springer. https://doi.org/10.1007/978-3-030-13134-0_4
- Beckmann, E. C., Jauco, L. M., & Koo, S. G. M. (2014). Green networking: Developing sustainable computer networks. In 2014 IEEE International Conference on Systems, Man, and Cybernetics (pp. 697–702). IEEE. https://doi.org/10.1109/SMC.2014.6974520
- Bellido, L., Mateos, V., Villagra, V.A., Fernandez, D., & Walid, O. (2012). Remote access to computer networking laboratories. In 2012 9th International Conference on Remote Engineering and Virtual Instrumentation (pp. 1–6). IEEE. https://doi.org/10.1109/REV.2012.6293156
- Cotter, D. (1997). Ultrafast computer networking. In Optics in Computing (pp. 1–4). Optica Publishing Group. https://doi.org/10.1364/OC.1997.OFB.1
- Erlinger, M. (2006). Lab exercises for computer networking courses. In Proceedings of the 11th Annual SIGCSE Conference (pp. 1–5). ACM. https://doi.org/10.1145/1140124.1140210

- Jin, G., Zhang, H., Xu, Q., & Qian, J. (2009). Visualization instruction on computer networking courses. In 2009 International Conference on Scalable Computing and Communications (pp. 1–6). IEEE. https://doi.org/10.1109/EmbeddedCom-ScalCom.2009.90
- Mikroyannidis, A., Kear, K., Smith, A., Jones, A., Rosewell, J., Donelan, H., Wermelinger, M., Sanders, C., Third, A., & Connolly, T. (2018). The Open Networking Lab: Hands-on vocational learning in computer networking. In 2018 IEEE Frontiers in Education Conference (pp. 1–5). IEEE. https://doi.org/10.1109/FIE.2018.8658838
- Rickman, J., McDonald, M., McDonald, G., & Heeler, P. (2001). Enhancing the computer networking curriculum. In *Proceedings of the 6th Annual

Reference Books

- Kurose, J. F., & Ross, K. W. (2017). Computer networking: A top-down approach (7th ed.). Pearson.
- Tanenbaum, A. S., & Wetherall, D. J. (2011). Computer networks (5th ed.). Pearson.
- Stallings, W. (2013). Data and computer communications (10th ed.). Pearson.
- Peterson, L. L., & Davie, B. S. (2011). Computer networks: A systems approach (5th ed.). Morgan Kaufmann.
- Forouzan, B. A. (2007). Data communications and networking (4th ed.). McGraw-Hill.
- Comer, D. E. (2014). Computer networks and internets (6th ed.). Pearson.
- West, J., Dean, T., & Andrews, J. (2018). Network+ guide to networks (8th ed.). Cengage Learning.
- Bonaventure, O. (2011). Computer networking: Principles, protocols and practice. Saylor Foundation.
- Robertazzi, T. G. (2017). Introduction to computer networking. Springer.
- Shannon, S. (Ed.). (2006). Computer networking and networks. Nova Science Publishers.

9 789348 642417

Printed at Repro India Ltd.